Wagons to the
Willamette

Duane,
Enjoy the journey and
don't never take no cutoffs

Wagons to the Willamette

Captain Levi Scott and the
Southern Route to Oregon, 1844-1847

Levi Scott and James Layton Collins
Edited by Stafford J. Hazelett

Stafford 4/12/19

WSU PRESS

Washington State University
Pullman, Washington

WSU PRESS
WASHINGTON STATE UNIVERSITY

Washington State University Press
PO Box 645910
Pullman, Washington 99164-5910
Phone: 800-354-7360
Fax: 509-335-8568
Email: wsupress@wsu.edu
Website: wsupress.wsu.edu

Library of Congress Cataloging-in-Publication Data

Scott, Levi, 1797-1890.
  Wagons to the Willamette : Captain Levi Scott and the Southern Route to
Oregon, 1844-1847 / Levi Scott & James Layton Collins ; edited and with
additional notes by Stafford J. Hazelett.
     pages cm
  Includes bibliographical references and index.
  ISBN 978-0-87422-333-0 (alk. paper)
1. Scott, Levi, 1797-1890—Diaries. 2. Applegate Trail—History. 3. Applegate
Trail—History—Sources. 4. Oregon Territory—History. 5. Oregon Territory—
History—Sources. 6. Pioneers—Oregon—Biography. 7. Oregon—Biography.
I. Collins, James Layton, 1833-1916. II. Hazelett, Stafford J., editor. III. Title.
IV. Title: Captain Levi Scott and the Southern Route to Oregon, 1844-1847.
  F880.S368 2015
  979.5—dc23
                                                          2015016666

Contents

Illustrations and Maps

Introduction

THIS IS THE STORY OF LEVI SCOTT, a common man and quintessential American pioneer who lived peaceably in uncommon times. He pioneered his way across the continent from Illinois to the Pacific Northwest as the United States expanded west, arriving in Oregon in his mid-forties. He lived all over Oregon while taking part in the events that shaped its destiny. His plainly written recollections, composed in his final years, reveal a man with nothing to hide and nothing to gain, offering a clear record of what happened as he saw it.

Levi Scott. *Courtesy Oregon Historical Society*

Indulging Levi Scott's reminiscence as a trusted history of events is to place faith in memory. And as historian Richard White notes, "history is the enemy of memory. The two stalk each other across the fields of the past, claiming the same terrain... If historians wish to go into this dense and tangled terrain, they must accept memory as a guide. In this jungle of the past, only memory knows the trails. Historians have to follow cautiously."[1]

In the case of Levi Scott, the "dense and tangled terrain" can be confirmed in many instances by contemporary accounts from other observers and parallel histories. As we find confirmation in these alternate sources, our trust in the storyteller's memory is legitimized. Scott's memory is exceptional, as are the events in which he played a part. In those cases where his recollections wander, we have attempted to provide correctives.

Scott is little remembered today. He founded the town of Scottsburg, situated at the head of tide waters on the Umpqua River. Over the years his role in opening the Southern Route into Oregon has occasionally

---

1   Richard White, *Remembering Ahanagran: A History of Stories* (Seattle: University of Washington Press, 2003), 4.

been remembered and celebrated. But the scope of his long life with its many accomplishments remains virtually unknown. He grew to manhood in Illinois and migrated by wagon train to Oregon in 1844. There he contributed to early settlement and exploration, was a member of the territorial legislature from 1852 to 1854, served at the State Constitutional Convention in 1857, and was the first janitor and groundskeeper at the University of Oregon in the middle 1870s.

Late in life, with a ninety-one-page reminiscence in hand, he approached Judge James Layton Collins and asked for assistance in revising and expanding his reminiscence and possibly securing its publication. Collins and Scott had met in 1846 when Collins was but thirteen and traveling with his family to Oregon over the newly discovered but not yet opened southern route.

Collins had a distinguished legal career. Traveling to Oregon with his family, he settled in Polk County, went to California in 1853 for a time, and then served in the Yakima War in Washington Territory. He was admitted to the bar in 1859 and was appointed county judge of Polk County in 1869. His personal reminiscence, including an account of the 1846 overland migration, was published in 1927.[2]

Sometime between 1886 and 1888 the two men signed an undated contract regarding development of an expanded version of Scott's manuscript, promising Collins compensation for his work if publication was secured, after which the proceeds would be held in common.

As Collins revised and polished Scott's story he had abundant resources at hand to flesh out the spare account prepared by the octogenarian. In addition to Scott's written account, he retained notes of his conversations with Levi Scott and perhaps his son John, a good friend of Collins. Other pioneers of the mid-1840s were close at hand for interviews. Collins's junior partner a few years earlier had been Jesse A. Applegate, son of Lindsay Applegate. And when Collins started his law practice, he purchased the law library of James W. Nesmith, who, though he crossed the plains in 1843, was much associated with the events of 1844

---

2   Herbert O. Lang, *History of the Willamette Valley* (Portland, OR: G. H. Himes, 1885), 654. Collins's own reminiscence was published in 1927. Sarah Hunt Steeves, ed., *Book of Remembrance of Marion County, Oregon, Pioneers 1840–1860* (Portland, OR: The Berncliff Press, 1927).

Pages 47 and 44a of Scott's Reminiscence. *Courtesy Stafford Hazelett.*

to 1846. Collins's source materials included a copy of the Pringle diary, transcribed and typed by Collins years before its eventual publication.

Scott reviewed and approved Collins's draft, and both men hoped to see it in print during their lifetimes. It was not to happen. Scott died in 1890 at age 93 after reviewing the second draft, and Collins died before he felt he had completed the work.

As Collins progressed with his manuscript, news of the work was publicized. *The Polk County Itemizer* on September 1, 1888, revealed "Judge Collins, has almost ready for the press a fascinating volume relative to the life and adventures of Capt. Scott. It will contain much about frontier life that has never before been in print, and will find many eager readers from the Pacific coast to the Mississippi Valley."

It was not until 1955, however, that publication seemed a possibility. At that time the youngest of Judge Collins's sons, Dean, approached Harper & Brothers, and the publishers requested a transcribed copy of the manuscript for review. It took Dean another decade to have the manuscript typed. The original manuscript remained with Dean Collins among other family papers.

Rumor of the manuscript materials, and of their value, spread. The University of Oregon Library contacted Dean Collins about his papers, and the Scott manuscript, in 1963. Edward Kemp, acquisition librarian, wrote that the library "would be honored to preserve this material," but instead Dean retired from the *Oregon Journal* and relocated to Alaska, taking all the archival material with him.

Dean continued to pursue the manuscript's publication, but age was his enemy. In 1967 he arranged to have his sister-in-law, Velma Stowe of Portland, Oregon, type the manuscript and make copies. He still felt Harpers would be interested in publishing, writing to Velma, "I feel that Harpers will be glad to publish it and will give us a reasonable down payment. After the book is out full advance payment will be given and after that, annual royalty checks covering the percentage we get from book sales, which I expect will go on for several years." Velma was less sanguine, as the introduction Dean had written was far from satisfactory, exhibiting a forgetfulness of facts.

Velma typed and made duplicates of the Collins manuscript in 1967. A very few copies of the original manuscript were soon available to a few family members and historians. A descendant of Levi Scott, Vira Cordano, used it in writing a fictional biography entitled *Levi Scott: Oregon Trailblazer* (Portland: Binford & Mort, 1982).

In 1994 local activists in Polk County engaged Arlie Holt, a retired drama teacher from Oregon City High School, to assist their effort to promote the name "Southern Route to Oregon," instead of "Applegate Trail" as designated by Congress. In his research Holt found mention of the Collins account of Scott's life. Finding a copy of the typescript at the Douglas County Museum, he wondered how the story was handled in Scott's original reminiscence. He contacted Dean Collins's daughter, Margaret Ballard of Sitka, Alaska, who had cared for him in his last years. In 1994 she invited Holt to visit her home and examine the manuscripts. During that visit Holt discovered a wealth of materials bearing on the

Scott-Collins story, including the original manuscripts, letters, and other documents.

When Dean Collins relocated to Alaska, he took with him many trunks of not only his own lifetime accumulation of writings, but the masses of letters and documents related to his father and literally thousands of letters kept in the family. Stored randomly in shacks and sheds in Sitka, the materials were in a state of near deterioration. Holt's trip to Alaska, and his friendship with Margaret Ballard and her daughter Kathy, opened a floodgate of materials flowing from Sitka to Oregon over several years and ultimately to their retention in the archives at the Polk County Museum and at the University of Oregon Knight Library.

For more than a decade Arlie Holt sought interest in the publication of both the Collins account and the original Scott reminiscence. In partnership with Stafford Hazelett, he corresponded with Robert Clark, editor of *Overland Journal* (quarterly journal of the Oregon-California Trails Association). Eventually, after Clark had joined Washington State University Press as their editor-in-chief, the manuscript was contracted for publication.

The Southern Route to Oregon, aka the Applegate Trail, is part of the larger story of westward migration. In the mid-1840s a number of alternatives to the original Oregon migration route were explored, including the final portion down the Columbia River. Prior to 1846 emigrants were forced to abandon their wagons at The Dalles because the narrow Columbia Gorge prevented their passage. The use of rafts and portaging exposed the travelers to much danger and loss of life.

In 1845 the sufferings of the emigrants who followed Stephen Meek into the deserts of central Oregon in the hope of a shorter and easier journey filled the community with horror. In 1846 the community sent three exploring parties to search for an alternative route into the Willamette Valley somewhere south of Salem. A party led by Joseph Gervais, a retired Hudson's Bay Company trapper, searched east up the Santiam River into the Cascade Mountains. Levi Scott, with his son John and other Oregon pioneers, began exploring for a far southern alternative route into the Willamette Valley. On their second exploration they were joined by two of the Applegate brothers.

Scott tells of the community interest and commitment to find a southern alternative route and provides a nearly day-by-day recounting of the outbound expedition. His narrative fills in many events and stories of the personalities involved which are missing from other reminiscences of the Southern Route expedition. Scott recounts fascinating stories of Jesse and Lindsay Applegate, David Goff, Moses Harris, James Nesmith, Cornelius Gilliam, Jesse Quinn Thornton, Phil Kearny, and other legendary figures of early Oregon.

As a fast-paced tale of adventure and danger on the frontier based on the observations of a perceptive and friendly man, this original account has few peers. Scott's richly detailed stories of community and family life illuminate our understanding of communities and families in the middle to late 19th century. Scott's recollections of the emigration experiences of 1844 over the main Oregon Trail, opening the southern emigrant route into Oregon in 1846, and events surrounding the assault on the Whitman Mission add to our knowledge and understanding of the events and the people involved.

The opening accounts of Scott's life in Illinois and Iowa (chapters 1-4 of Collins's manuscript) and following the death of the Whitmans (chapters 16-20) have been summarized by the editor. The original Scott reminiscence of his 1844 Oregon migration through 1847, used by Collins as the source work for his expanded manuscript, is included here as an appendix. The complete manuscripts of both Collins and Scott can be accessed at the University of Oregon Knight Library Special Collections, where the full collection of archival materials related to the Scott reminiscence, received by Arlie Holt from the Collins family, were deposited.

ℭ

Levi Scott's Life to 1844

L EVI SCOTT GREW UP IN THE AMERICAN BOTTOM. The flood plain on the east bank of the Mississippi River contains world-famous mounds, such as those at Cahokia, built in pre-Columbian times. Those builders had long abandoned the region by the seventeenth century when the French established the first European settlements in today's Illinois. Americans began to arrive near the end of the American Revolution.

Into this isolated frontier landscape, Levi Scott was born to James and Rebecca Scott on February 8, 1797. Levi would spend his life on the frontier, pushing its limits ever westward. A descendant of Scottish immigrants, his father James was a native of Maryland and, according to his son, a veteran of Washington's army in the late years of the American Revolution. In 1785 James married Rebecca Sparks, and in the summer of the following year they moved west in hopes of bettering their condition, in company with Raphael Drury and his wife.

Floating down the Ohio on a crude raft with a canoe in tow, they ran on a snag and sank their raft with all their belongings, but without loss of life. With assistance they were able to reach their destination up the Mississippi. The next few years were spent improving their lands and building their lives, but James died in 1799 leaving a widow and five children, including two-year-old Levi.

Almost ninety years later, Levi Scott began to record his experiences. He had spent a lifetime "fighting my own way through the world, independently. This is a strong part of my disposition, even up to oald age." His reminiscence, and the enlarged and polished version prepared at Scott's request by friend Judge James Layton Collins, preserves a unique history of the frontier in the Jacksonian period, the overland era, of Oregon, and of the greater West.

Scott's record covers his entire life, not all of which is connected to events in the Pacific Northwest prior to 1850. This preliminary section offers a summation of the events of his life east of the Missouri River contained in chapters one to four of the Collins's text. A similar section follows chapters five through fifteen of the Collins manuscript, condensing the events of his life after 1847. These summaries utilize the information found in both the Collins and Scott manuscripts.[1]

Newly widowed in 1799, Levi's mother soon remarried, but her new husband either refused or was unable to support her children. Under direction of the court they were placed with other families—all except Levi's oldest sister Sarah, who at seventeen was able to care for herself.

Thus, at age six Levi was bound to James Garretson, a "strange man" as Levi recalled. At thirteen Levi grew frustrated with his living conditions and the beatings he sometimes suffered. Off he ran, though not far enough. After two weeks he was found and brought back, but within the next year Garretson agreed to release him to the court, who placed him with Jacob Trout, a tanner, at Levi's request.

For the next few months he labored in the tannery by day in return for board. He learned the business, but could not abide the odors. At night he and a friend hunted raccoons and possum, which they sold for cash. Levi's skills in the woods, and with a gun, were sharpened. As the months passed he found other work cutting and splitting cord wood, helping with harvest—anything that offered board and a bit of cash to survive.

He sought out a few more months of schooling, aided by his Uncle John who offered free room and board. He was fifteen before he ever saw an almanac or newspaper. Of history, his only source was the Bible.

His recollections of frontier life along the Mississippi in a countryside inaccessible to travelers except by water, provides a colorful and detailed description of the social culture of the American Bottom in the first two decades of the nineteenth century. Politics, relations with Indians and the original French settlers, daily life in sickness and in health—all these topics are touched upon. Generally from the "middle states," the American settlers were distrustful of anyone from New England, who they disdainfully referred to as "Yankees." They raised their crops, cared for a few livestock,

---

1   The full manuscripts of Levi Scott and James Layton Collins are housed at the Special Collections and University Archives, Knight Library, University of Oregon, Eugene.

met their clothing and shelter needs with what was available from their farms, fields, and the woodlands beyond. And they were as poor as church mice. As Scott described it, "now thare was no money in the country and but very little use for it, for thay had no traffic or trade and very little communication with any other country, consiquently they had to depend all together on what thay could rais or manafacter."

As he grew to manhood, Levi showed himself a decisive and thoughtful pioneer. He sampled the whiskey that was ubiquitous in every household for man, woman, and child, and found it wanting. At about 170 pounds, he was formidable in a fight. He recalled, "I feard no man atall tho I knew thare was a grate meny stouter than I was, fiteing was very common and I delighted in it, though I never raised a mus with no man without a just cuase or never fight a small man if I could posable git around it...but now at this day I look apon fighting as a dogs calling and no gentleman would go in to it if he could posably avoid it."

Slowly the region began to open to trade up the river from New Orleans. Calico and broad cloth began to replace homespun, and the home folk "begin to complane whenever thay had no coffee for breakfast."

And Levi Scott sought a wife. After moving about the country working for wages, and receiving a few more months of schooling, he "branch[ed] out a mongst the girls and at the age of twenty married." Eda Ennis was sixteen when she and Levi set up housekeeping, but as Levi recorded, he had "married a pore girle that had naughthing. none of those things that I didant want because I had no house to put them in nor no money to buy with."

His wife's sister provided a straw bed and bedding, three knives and forks, a spoon or two, and tin cup, and "with this outfit I went to housekeeping."

Over the next twenty years he and his family moved from one piece of land to another, buying property, improving the land, then selling out for cash. He settled for some ten years in Morgan County, Illinois, finally establishing himself on 120 acres. "If I had stayed heare, I could have made a good living and had a good home, but [I] become dissatisfied and sold out in the spring and went to Iowa in the fall of 1834."[2]

---

2   Government Land Office Records show a patent issued to Levi Scott for a claim in Morgan County, Illinois, on March 7, 1831, at the District Land Office in Edwardsville. glorecords.blm.gov/search.

Prior to his departure from Illinois, Scott volunteered for military service in the Black Hawk War. Three months of duty spread over the spring of 1831 and summer of 1832 fulfilled his commitment to protect the frontier of Morgan County.[3]

Iowa was the new land of opportunity in 1834. Levi was one of the early settlers who controlled the potential land claims immediately after the extinction of Indian title. Scott settled on a plot of land a few miles northwest of today's Burlington. He built a good log house, improved sixty or seventy acres of land, and felt comfortably fixed. His recollections detail the shenanigans of the squatters in protecting their claims against speculators during land auctions. The land disputes led to his acquaintance with Colonel W. W. Chapman, who would emigrate to Oregon in 1847 by way of the route Scott and others opened in 1846. Chapman was a founder of Portland, prominent politician, and launched the *Oregonian* newspaper.[4]

By 1840 Levi Scott was a prominent member of his Iowa community. He was elected to the territorial legislature, defeating Jeremiah Lamson who would later settle in Oregon.[5] When the territorial legislature authorized the organization of a militia, he was elected captain of his company, a title he would carry through life. He seemed settled. But at age forty-three tragic circumstances changed everything and his eyes turned to the Far West.

---

3   Levi Scott of Morgan County was enrolled as a private on April 30, 1832, in Capt. William Gillham's Company, First Regiment, Third Illinois Brigade under Brigadier General James D. Henry. Illinois Adjutant General's Office, *Record of the Services of Illinois Soldiers in the Black Hawk War, 1831-32, etc.* (Springfield, IL: Journal Company, 1902), 55. For a modern history of the Black Hawk War, *see* Patrick J. Jung, *The Black Hawk War of 1832* (Norman: University of Oklahoma Press, 2007).

4   Chapman has his own recollection of these times and events which corroborates Scott. Elwood Evans, Col. L. F. Mosher, et al.; *History of the Pacific Northwest: Oregon and Washington* (Portland, OR: North Pacific History Company, 1889), 254-69.

5   Jeremiah Lamson arrived in Oregon in 1847 by the traditional Oregon Trail. He served as a member of Oregon's House of Representatives in the terms of 1858, 1859, and 1866. Cecil L. Edwards, *Chronological List of Oregon's Legislatures* (Salem, OR: Legislative Administration Committee Services, 1993), 55, 58, 83.

The Collins Manuscript:

The Life and Adventures
of Captain Levi Scott

Chapters V–XV

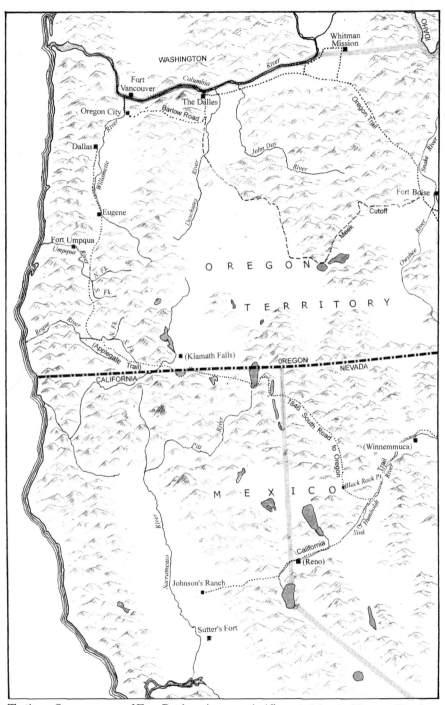

Trails to Oregon west of Fort Bridger (western half) 1846. *Map by Herman Zittel.*

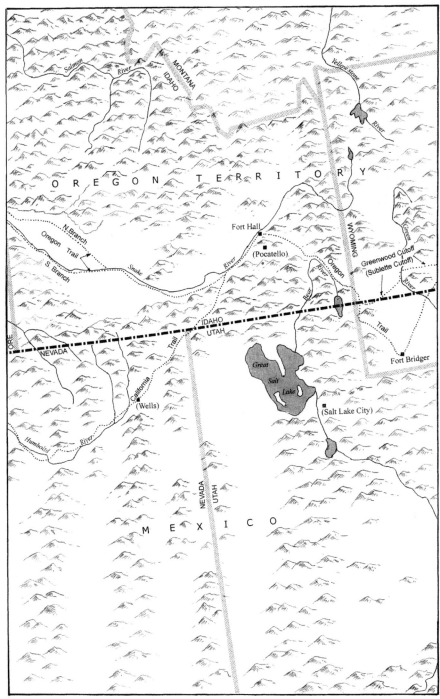

Trails to Oregon west of Fort Bridger (eastern half). *Map by Herman Zittel.*

∾

CHAPTER V

Tragedy and Departure
for Oregon, 1844

It was in the year 1840, I think that the Whigs nominated me for County Commissioner of Des Moines County, against the Hon. Jeremiah Lamson, who was the Democratic candidate. One of the questions that influenced the election to a very great extent, was the compound local question of fixing the county seat and building a court house. Perhaps it was because I happened to be on the popular side of this controversy more than any other reason that I was elected. My competitor was an estimable and popular gentleman and a good business man. He was a member of the Legislature of Oregon in the year 1866 I think it was. His son, Captain Roswell H. Lamson of the United States Navy, was a distinguished officer and actor in the Civil War. He accomplished the perilous feat of firing the powder ship at Fort Fisher, and performed services on the Nansemond River that secured for him a distinguished place in the history of the United States.

In 1842, I suffered the irretrievable misfortune to lose my wife. And we had lost six of our children before her death. This blow discouraged and broke me up. We had thirteen children altogether, five boys and eight girls. Three of our daughters have died since her death. Annie, our eldest child and Eliza, our youngest, are still living in Iowa. Our eldest son, William J. J. Scott, now lives near Eugene city, in Lane County, Oregon. He has a family of ten children, and is a thrifty farmer in good comfortable circumstances. Our second son, John M. Scott, lives in Malheur County, in the northeastern part of Oregon.[1] He is now a widower. He had nine children, eight of whom are now living. He is employed in stock raising on the Malheur River.

---

1   After Scott and Collins completed this draft, Scott moved to join John and his sons on their Malheur River property near the former town site of Beulah, north of Juntura, in Malheur County, Oregon.

After losing my wife, I struggled on not altogether aimlessly yet with no very definite or fixed purpose for about two years till the spring of 1844 and then concluded to go to Oregon to look at the country. I felt that a trip of this kind, with its new associations and vicissitudes, would have a tendency to withdraw my attention, to some extent, from my bereavements and misfortunes, and, might possibly be of benefit to me in several ways.

My son William was a young man; my daughters were comfortably provided for; and I resolved to take my youngest surviving son, John, who was a stout active boy of sixteen, with me.[2] A. F. Hedges, an intelligent, energetic young man agreed to go with me. And a young man, by the name of Charles Bennett, who had a wife but no children, wished to go with us, but was not able to furnish much of the outfit.[3] His wife was an industrious woman, and a good cook; and, as this was a very important and essential qualification for some of us to possess, we arranged that they should accompany us. Mrs. Bennett agreed to do the cooking, and Bennett to do his part of the general duties and services, with the rest of us.

Absolom F. Hedges afterwards settled just above the Falls of the Willamette River, where he took up a land claim and started the town of Canemah.[4]

Bennett settled at Salem, where he kept the "Bennett House," for several years before his death. He and Hedges were interested in the early introduction of steamboating on the Willamette River. They ran the first steamers on that river above the falls. Bennett was a Captain of volunteers

---

2   William reappeared in his father's life when he followed Jesse Applegate in 1846 from Fort Hall.

3   Charles Bennett traveled to California in 1847 and contracted with John Sutter and James Marshall to assist in building a sawmill. Bennett claimed to have found a gold nugget in the channel they dug and that he took it to Marshall who showed it to Sutter that world-changing day, January 24, 1848. Howard McKinley Corning, *Dictionary of Oregon History* (Portland, OR: Binford & Mort Publishing, 1965), 26. Erwin G. Gudde, *Bigler's Chronicle of the West* (Berkeley: University of California Press 1962).

4   *See* biographies of Absalom F. Hedges by Fred Lockley, "Impressions and Observations of the Journal Man [Absalom F. Hedges]," *Oregon Journal,* January 4, 1938, 10; Corning, *Dictionary of Oregon History,* 111; *Oregonian,* "The Late Captain A. F. Hedges," March 8, 1890, 6-7; Howard McKinley Corning, *Willamette Landings* (Portland, OR: Binford & Mort Publishing, 1947) 62-70. Hedges also served in the Territorial Legislature and was a delegate at the Oregon Constitutional Convention in 1857 with Scott.

in the war with the Yakima Indians in the years 1855 and 1856, and was killed in a battle fought by Lieutenant Colonel James K. Kelly against the Indians in the winter near Walla Walla in Washington Territory.

Hedges was Indian Agent for Oregon for sometime in the early history of Oregon. He married a daughter of William Barlow of Oregon City. His father-in-law was the discoverer of "Barlow's Pass," across the Cascade Mountains.[5]

I had a good wagon; we got four yoke of oxen for a team, and laid in a good supply of provisions. But we were late in starting and the roads were bad on account of an unusual quantity of rain. The high waters of this year so flooded the Missouri and Mississippi Rivers as to destroy many towns, lives, and property along their banks. So we traveled very slowly.

In passing through Missouri we purchased eight head of cows but when we arrived at the Missouri River we were unable to cross it for two days on account of high winds. Our cows strayed away and we lost all of them and were compelled to proceed without them. This was a great loss to us for we had intended to work the cows as part of our team, besides they would have been more valuable property than oxen after reaching Oregon—or to trade at the forts, and trading posts on the way.

After we had passed the city of Independence, Missouri, about six miles we fell in with a party of five men, all Germans, who had one wagon and were, like ourselves, behind time. We traveled together about a week when we overtook a small party from Indiana camped on the Waukierussia [Wakarusa] River who informed us that the main body of emigrants was but a little way ahead of us waiting for all to get together. We soon joined them at the general rendezvous near the crossing of the Kansas River where we found them already organized and ready to proceed on the journey.[6]

Supposing the way to be a difficult route to find, they had hired a man who, on account of his complexion, was known by the sobriquet of

---

5   Collins was muddled about the relationship. Hedges's father-in-law did indeed open "Barlow's Pass," but his name was Samuel. William Barlow was brother to Hedges's wife, Elizabeth Jane Barlow. Fred Lockley, "Impressions and Opinions of the Journal Man [Absalom Hedges and Barlow family]," *Oregon Journal*, January 4, 1938, 10, col. 5-6.

6   The best general source for the emigration of 1844 is Thomas A. Rumer, *The Wagon Trains of '44* (Spokane: The Arthur H. Clark Company, 1990).

"Black Harris," to act as a pilot for them in crossing the plains.[7] He had been to the Rocky Mountains with some of the trading companies and agreed to lead the emigrants to Oregon, for the sum of two dollars and fifty cents *per capita*.

There was another mountaineer here by the name of Adams who was trying to get employment on the same terms as interpreter and safeguard among the Indians. But he failed to get the contract and returned in a few days to Independence.

Harris had met the emigrants at Independence when he was very much involved in debt and by his representations, aided by the advice of his creditors, he succeeded in getting an advance of about five hundred dollars, and when we came up he had managed to get his pay from all who had fallen in before us. He turned out to be one of those self-conceited men who imagines himself to be just a little wiser than any one else and actually knows nothing that is of any value to any one. He knew next to nothing but he could keep up a constant flow of talk which he could make rather interesting to persons who did not have any knowledge of the facts or circumstances involved in the subject of his conversation. In a word, he was the most unmitigated liar I ever had the misfortune to meet with.[8]

7   Moses "Black" Harris was one of the most famous survivors of the fur trapping business. Many books have been written about him. He came to Oregon with the emigration of 1844 as pilot for the Ford wagon company. He participated in Dr. Elijah White's unsuccessful exploration in 1845 for an alternate route through the Cascades in the Santiam River drainage and the two explorations with Levi Scott beyond the Willamette Valley in 1846. Harris went forward along with Jesse Applegate toward Fort Hall to recruit emigrants to try the new route but departed from Applegate on the Humboldt River. Harris and David Goff traveled north cross-country to meet an old trapper friend, Medders Vanderpool, who was leading a company of emigrants, and persuaded them to try the new route. He remained in Oregon until spring 1847 when he left Oregon with Scott to recruit emigrants to try the Southern Route. Harris continued on to Missouri where he died in May 1849 while trying to gain employment as a guide to return to the golden fields of the far west. Corning, *Dictionary of Oregon History*, 107; Jerome Peltier, *Black Harris* (Spokane, WA: Ye Galleon Press, 1986). Harris was a white man whose skin had been blackened by exposure, according to Jesse A. Applegate, "Wearing Buckskin in the Forties," *Polk County Observer*, March 13, 1903, 1.

8   This last sentence is not in the original Scott manuscript, but reflects a common assessment. *See* Verne Bright, "Black Harris, Mountain Man, Teller of Tales," *Oregon Historical Quarterly* 52, no. 1 (March 1951): 1-20.

By the time we came up, some of those who had paid him the pilot-age fee and listened to his big stories till they had caught him—or rather, heard him entangle himself—in many glaring inconsistencies and con-tradictions and were thoroughly disgusted with him had come to the conclusion that he would be of no service at all. When we came up, some of them advised us to keep our money and not to pay Harris a cent, as they thought he would be of no use to us whatever. Others thought it would be of advantage to us to have his services and a few thought that he would be an indispensable auxiliary to us.

So we scarcely knew what to do about it. We were willing to pay if it were necessary and right to do so, but we were decidedly averse to being "bilked."

We and the Germans with whom we had first met after leaving Inde-pendence were entire strangers to each other before meeting on the road, but by this time we had become somewhat attached to each other, and agreed to stick together and render mutual assistance throughout this whole journey so far as necessary.

The Captain of the company, Nathaniel Ford, came to us to collect fees for the guide whom, he said, we could not possibly dispense with.[9] We told the Captain that we knew no more about this pilot than we did about the route we were to travel; that we doubted the necessity, or the utility, of a guide, but we were willing to pay him at the end of the jour-ney if his services proved to be of any value. We had about made up our minds not to pay him anything in advance. Still, we would like to travel with the company.

The Captain said it would be very unfair for us to travel with the com-pany and not pay our proportionate part of the fees to the pilot. However, we paid nothing. We thought it best to consider the matter a little while.

This company comprised about one half of the whole emigration to Oregon of this year, 1844. We had about one hundred and fifty wag-ons, while the other company, which was ahead of us, but was advanc-ing on another route, so that we did not exactly follow them on this part of the journey, consisted of about the same number of wagons, and

---

9   *See* biographies of Nathaniel Ford in Corning, *Dictionary of Oregon History*, 86; and
     John T. Ford, "Col. Nathaniel Ford," in Daughters of the American Revolution,
     Sarah Childress Polk Chapter No. 6, *Polk County Pioneer Sketches*, 2 vols. (Dallas,
     OR: Polk County Itemizer-Observer, 1927; reprint, Monmouth, OR: Polk County
     Historical Society, 1977) 1:43-45 (hereafter DAR, *Polk County Pioneer Sketches*).

was commanded by Captain Cornelius Gilliam, of Missouri, who had been an officer of volunteers in the Florida War, against the Seminole Indians.[10]

We had ferried our wagons and caused our stock to swim across the Kansas River without accident or any incident worth noticing and waited there till we thought all had come up who wished to join us.

On leaving the camp, on the north side of the Kansas, we fell in the rear of the line of wagons and traveled till about three o'clock in the afternoon when we reached a small stream called Knife Creek and camped before crossing it. There came on a heavy rain storm in the night which raised the stream so much that it was impassible for our wagons in the morning.

Several plans for crossing the creek were proposed and discussed but there seemed to be nothing definitely determined and there was no positive order from the Captain. No one seemed to know just what to do and, so, no one did anything.

I had made my wagon-bed in the shape of a small boat to meet just such emergencies and I proposed to take that and calk the seams in it and use it for a ferry-boat. Only one man besides our German friends fell in with the suggestion but the waters began to subside and he changed his mind. He said he would wait and ford the stream with the rest of the company. But we went on with our plans for crossing.

There were ten of us. The five Germans, Hedges, Bennett and myself—eight men—and my son John and Mrs. Bennett. We had twelve oxen, four cows, one mule, and three ponies.

We swam our stock across and, as soon as the boat was ready, began to ferry our wagons and goods over which occupied us till nearly night.

In the meantime, it commenced raining again and raised the water almost entirely over the little knoll of bare ground upon which we had landed till we were compelled to drive stakes into the ground and make a scaffold on which to put our goods to keep them out of the water.

We passed a dreadful night in this place with the angry waters roaring all round us and just covering the highest point of the ground on which we stood. But, fortunately for us, when the waters reached the top of our

10   *See* biographies of Cornelius Gilliam in Corning, *Dictionary of Oregon History*, 100; Fred Lockley, "Reminiscences of Mrs. Frank Collins, Nee Martha Elizabeth Gilliam," *Quarterly of the Oregon Historical Society* 17, no. 4 (Dec. 1916): 358-72.

mound, they had room to spread out over the bottom lands, otherwise we should have been swept away.

After having seen the rest of the party as comfortably fixed for the night as our wretched situation would admit of, I cast about to see if I could find any means to get a little rest and, if possible, some sleep. At length I found a large piece of bark which had been peeled from a tree or log. I wrapped my blanket around me and lay down in this and slept with the waters slowly rising about me till morning. When I arose, all streaming with water from my rude couch, it floated up like a boat.

We found that we had only a few feet of ground on which we could maintain a footing while we were surrounded by swimming water in every direction which was still very slowly, but very surely, rising about us. It was fully half a mile to land in the direction we wished to go, with the water from two to eight feet deep all the way, and it was as least a mile to a place where we could camp.

We took the running gear of my wagon across to dry land, yoked up a pair of oxen, and set one man to hauling our goods out to the place we selected for a camp, while the rest of us busied ourselves in boating them out to a landing place. And this gave us another day of hard work. So we got our camp pretty comfortably arranged by sundown.

All day the main crowd on the other shore were hooting, laughing, and jeering at us. But the joke turned on them, at last, for it was eight days before they got across that stream, and then they were compelled to make a raft and ferry over on it. But they went further up where they had better banks.

While we lay here waiting for the rest of the company to cross, I found a swarm of bees in an ash tree in a grove near our camp. We cut the tree but did not get more than half a gallon of honey. It was excellent quality, however, and we enjoyed it very much. It was the last honey we found.

I had always heard that the bee was a precursor of civilization, and had always preceded the settlements of the white people towards the west. But here we left the bee behind us and pushed on to the utmost boundary of the west, more than two thousand miles beyond the furthest outpost of the busy little worker.

When the main body of the company got everything in readiness they began crossing early in the morning, and by noon they had all their stock and some of their wagons over. It was evident that they would all be across before night.

In the afternoon, the pilot and four or five others came by our camp going in search of a good place to camp for the night. We were tired of lying in camp so we hitched up and followed them. They stopped at a good camping place and when we came up we asked, "Are you going to camp here?"

"Yes!" they answered.

We turned out our teams and pitched our camp. In about an hour, Captain Ford came riding by. "What," said he, "are you going to camp here?"

"Yes," we replied, "we have stopped for that purpose. We thought the whole company were going to camp here."

"No," said he, "we are not going to camp here; we will go on two or three miles further."

And he pressed on without saying anything more.

We understood this, at once, to be the cut direct, and intended as a rebuke to us for having refused to pay the pilot's fees and for having presumed to act on our own counsel in crossing the creek. So we talked the matter over that night and concluded to fall in with them the next morning, and travel with them, and abide by whatever rules they had established.

Early next morning we drove up to their camp before they were ready to start and stopped near where they were driving their wagons into line. Hedges was walking near their line when the Captain came riding along and said to the pilot, "Major, you had better convey those wagons off into the hills where they never can get out again." At the same time he pointed towards our wagons.

Hedges, who happened to be almost at his side when he spoke, responded with a quick, short energy, "You can't do it, sir! We are not so green as you may think!"

After passing a few hard words with the Captain, he came back and reported the conversation to us.

We started on without further delay, passed them, following the track of the emigration of the year before through the open prairie till noon, and we could see them coming on all the way behind us.

We found that so small a party as ours would not be safe traveling among the Indians. So, after we had consulted together, we took a vote on the question whether we should travel alone or fall in with them. Ten voted in favor of traveling with them and two of us against it. Mrs. Bennett was one of the minority. So, it was settled, we waited till they passed us and then fell in behind them.

We traveled on with them, complying with their rules and regulations, and everything went on peaceably and smoothly, except that the Captain was a little surly for a while. But this soon wore off and we found him a first rate man and we were, apparently, on an equal footing with the rest of the crowd.

The next stream of any importance we came to was the Blue River. Here we found that a party ahead of us had dug out a pair of large canoes and bound them together by pinning cross-timbers upon them so as to let the wheels of the wagons rest in the canoes, and in this way they had ferried over, and had left their rude ferry-boat for the use of any who might come after them. We found that the stream had been very high. It was now much lower, but was not yet fordable for our wagons, so we ferried them over and made our stock swim across.

I had never seen an antelope. But the next day after we crossed the Blue, I was out some two or three miles from the trail and saw one. I knew from its appearance and action, and from what I had heard of them, that it must be an antelope. It was out of gunshot from me and it would start off, suddenly and swiftly, as if it were terribly frightened, and intended to run clear away. Then it would take a circle and come back, and look, and then, with a sudden energy, it would dart away again. It did this three or four times.

I had heard that if the hunter would raise a flag and lie down under it, he could generally lure the antelope by this means within range of his rifle. So I tied my handkerchief to my ram-rod for a flag and lay down on the ground, but it did no good. The beautiful little animal refused to be swindled out of its life in this way and finally run off over the hills.

I saw several others soon afterwards, but I was afraid the wagons would get too far ahead of me if I should delay longer, and so I did not try to get a shot at them.

Two days after this I was hunting on foot, about two miles from the road, when I saw a pair of antelope feeding together on the sage plain.

I took advantage of a ravine which enabled me to crawl up within sixty or seventy yards of them and killed one. When the ball struck it, with a convulsive bound it dashed off a few leaps and fell dead.

This was the first antelope killed in the company. I dragged it to a pond of water nearby and butchered it. While I was dressing it, William Hovias, one of the Germans, came up on horseback and carried it to camp. We found the flesh tender, sweet, and delicious, although it was not fat—merely in good order for eating.

When Hovias got into camp with it, everybody examined it with great curiosity and asked him, "Why, Hovias, have you killed an antelope?"

"O, yes," he answered with a show of ostentatious pride, "it's nothing to kill an antelope."

I said nothing and they all thought that Hovias had killed it.

I had never seen the great jack rabbit of the Plains and, one day before I had seen an antelope, one of these rabbits started up before me and I thought it surely must be a young antelope. I did not get a chance to kill it and did not suspect my mistake till we got among the antelopes. The Germans killed a great many of these rabbits with their shot guns. They usually shot them on the run. I did not find them very good eating and so I wasted but little ammunition on them.

The Germans also killed a great many plovers with their shot guns and, when I got a good chance, I would knock one's head off with my rifle, for they are very fine eating. There are a great many of them along the valley of the Platte.

One day Bennett killed a large fat hawk and we cooked it and ate it. We found it very tough and we could not get it cooked tender, but it tasted very good.

We traveled up the rich and beautiful valley of the Kansas for about two hundred miles, or more, above the point where we crossed it, and then crossed over to the Platte River, which we struck somewhere not far above Grand Island.[11]

In passing over the divide between the two rivers, we crossed several of the main trails traveled by the buffaloes and the Indians in passing

---

11   Scott's estimate is close. There are two crossing points, one at today's Topeka, Kansas, and another twenty miles upstream. The trail entered the Platte River basin at trail mile 298.3. Aubrey Haines, *Historic Sites Along the Oregon Trail*, 4th ed. (Tucson, AZ: The Patrice Press, 1994), 39, 41, 56.

between the Kansas and the Platte. These trails were worn down into the ground, in some places, till they were two or three feet deep.

In traveling up the Platte, we found the plain full of buffaloes. At times the herds extended clear across the valley and as far along it as we could see, like dark, dense forests of timber. Here and there, a rising column of dust would mark the arena of some fiercely contested bull-fight. And long before we came near them, we could hear a deep, murmuring roar, unlike anything I had ever heard, but to some extent resembling the distant roar of a coming storm.

Just before we reached the crossing of the South Fork, three of us concluded to take a buffalo hunt. We started in the morning, and went to the hills to the left of the road keeping the train in sight.

In the afternoon, when we were six or eight miles from the train, a large herd came dashing past us. Two of us selected a fine cow and fired at her together. She ran a few jumps and fell. Both shots had taken effect in her vitals.

A fine, large bull ran up to the fallen cow and stopped. The rest of the herd soon passed out of sight among the sand hills. But the gallant bull stood his ground, showing a determined purpose to defend his fallen companion. He would lash his sides with his tail, lower his head in a threatening attitude, loll out his tongue, scrape, and paw up the ground, and make a variety of hostile movements, as though he were on the point of charging upon us. We were not more than fifty paces from him, and I can scarcely conjecture what we should have done if he had put his threats into execution. It would have been impossible to have escaped his vengeance. However, we did not dare to show the least disposition to retreat, for any exhibition of the white feather on our part would have brought the torrent of his wrath upon us, swift and terrible.

We stood still, loaded and fired four shots, each, into him—twelve balls in all—without bringing him down. But now his wounds sickened him so much that he went off, about a quarter of a mile, and lay down to die.

We skinned the cow's hump and cut off as much of the most choice flesh as we could carry with us. But by this time it was near sundown and the train was from twelve to fifteen miles away. We saw the wagons when they went into camp and stopped for the night and we could keep our course, even after dark.

After night came on, one of the men complained that his boots hurt his feet so that he could go no further. So we had to stop on the prairie till morning. We gathered a few "buffalo chips"—that is, the dried excrement of the buffalo—and some dried grass and weeds for kindling and made a miserable camp-fire.

We were now in a region of country that is nothing but a succession of sand hills with here and there a patch of grass. There was no timber except in the watercourses, and what was there was mostly small willows, but fuel could generally be found close along the Platte River in the drift-wood that came down from the mountains during high water.

Our situation was not at all pleasant, but we were very tired and slept soundly.

The country was full of big, white, buffalo wolves, and little coyotes, and, while we slept, they stole our buffalo meat from within a foot of our heads. The next morning, when we awoke, we found ourselves about five miles from the train, and, quite crest-fallen, we went into camp without any buffalo meat or anything else to show for the hard toil we had endured.

We brought into camp nothing but the story of our adventure, which would have been much more interesting if we could have told it around a liberal roast of the fine buffalo meat that the wolves had taken from us.

On reaching camp, we found that we were not the only ones who had suffered a buffalo hunt. There had been two others—James B. Stephens and Moses Eads—out the same day.[12]

When they got out into the sand hills, they saw a herd of buffaloes, feeding some distance away. They dismounted, tied their horses head and foot with the bridle reins, crept up close to the herd, fired into it, and killed one. Then one of them butchered while the other went to bring up the horses. He went back but could not find them.

When the meat was all ready for packing, they both hunted, but the horses could not be found. They continued their search till they barely

---

12   Stephens became a well-known figure in Oregon as the founder of East Portland. Corning, *Dictionary of Oregon History*, 234; Leslie M. Scott, "Beginnings of East Portland," *Oregon Historical Quarterly* 31, no. 4 (Dec. 1930), 351-59. Moses Eades was listed in Hubert Howe Bancroft, *History of Oregon, Vol. 1: 1834-1848*, (San Francisco: History Company, 1886), 465. Oregonpioneers.com lists thirteen members of the extended family of the brothers Moses and Solomon Eades.

had time to reach the train by the time it was dark when they abandoned the search and walked to camp without their horses or their meat.

They never saw nor heard of their horses, again, and, of course, the wolves got the full benefit of their buffalo hunt as well as ours.

There had probably been a small party of Indians watching and preparing to attack this same herd of buffalo, but when they witnessed the maneuvers of our hunters, came to the conclusion that a pair of good, well-equipped horses were a better prize than the beef which they could capture at any time. So, I think the Indians slyly slipped off with the horses.

Ash Hollow as sketched by Pherne Pringle, June 13-14, 1846. *Courtesy Stafford Hazelett.*

CHAPTER VI

ᴔ

Adventures on the Way to Oregon—
Ash Hollow to Fort Hall

The train had now reached the crossing of the South Fork of the Platte River, and stopped a day to look for the best ford. The more unfortunate party of buffalo hunters determined to spend the day in making another effort to find their horses. At their solicitation, I went with them. We got a late start, but soon came into the vicinity—or what they supposed to be the neighborhood—of where they had left them.

Here we found a large herd of buffaloes feeding on the hills. We rode up in gunshot of them and Stephens shot a fine bull which ran a short distance and fell.

When the herds are feeding, the cows and calves usually occupy a position in the center of the band while the bulls flank them as a safeguard against wolves, and it is not easy to get a cow or calf without dashing into their lines, or when the herd runs past you. When they are running the young bulls and heifers generally lead, the cows and calves come next, and then old bulls bring up the rear. We did not try to take the carcass to camp, but we skinned out enough for our supper and for breakfast next morning, for after having hunted all day without getting any trace of the missing horses, we camped for the night among the sand hills not very far from where Stephens killed the bull.

The meat was fat and good and it seemed to be a pity to leave so much of it for the wolves, but we could not take care of it under the circumstances, and were compelled to leave it to those predatory vandals of the plains.

This James B. Stephens afterwards settled on a section of land which is now covered by East Portland on the Willamette River. [13]

---

13   East Portland was annexed by the larger city of Portland in 1891. Corning, *Dictionary of Oregon History*, 201.

We hunted for the horses till noon the next day without finding any sign or vestige of them, whatever, or even the place where the men had been who lost them. The face of the country here is so uniform that it is difficult to distinguish one place from another.

We returned to the train late in the afternoon just as the last wagons were crossing the river.

In the evening a large herd of buffaloes appeared, feeding on the low hills about a mile from camp. Hedges and I went out to kill one. We got into a ravine and, having the wind of them, came easily in good range, when Hedges fired on a fine young cow and knocked her down in her tracks.

This frightened the herd, so that they dashed off at full speed in a little while leaving a number of the calves in the rear where a large, white, buffalo wolf rushing in cut off one of the calves and killed it.

The weather was very warm and, while we were butchering the cow, we suffered from excessive thirst. We saw a buffalo pond about a quarter of a mile away, and Hedges went to it and got a drink. I would not go but stuck to my butchering although I was very thirsty. He pulled off one of his boots and brought it back with him nearly filled with water. Although this could not be considered a very dainty drinking cup, I found the water very refreshing to me and took a deep draught of it without feeling any very nice qualms about the vessel from which I drank.

When we had skinned and cut up the cow, we went back to camp and sent out horsemen who brought in the nice beef.

By the time we reached the crossing of the South Fork of Platte, nearly every person in the train was more or less dissatisfied. Some complained of the Captain, some murmured against one man and some against another. When we would lay by a day to rest the teams, the children would fall out, and quarrel with each other. Some of the women disagreed and gossiped about each other, and sometimes they quarreled because their children quarreled. Some of the men were always finding fault, first with one thing and then with another, till it seemed like the Devil had broken loose among us.

Everybody had fallen out with the pilot. Even the Captain, who had held faith in him longer than any one else, refused to board him, or to have anything to do with him, and said he had no more use for him.

We crossed over the divide and struck the North Fork of the Platte at Ash Hollow. We traveled up this stream with but few incidents, except such as grow out of the quarreling and wrangling of some of the people, till we reached Fort Laramie.

We forded the Laramie River just above the fort, which is situated on the north side of that stream, a little above its junction with the North Platte. This Fort was in possession of the American Fur Company. There was a small village of Sioux Indians camped near the Post.

We lay by here for two days and then the train split up.[14] About half of the company stuck to Captain Ford. The rest traveled one day and then organized by electing me Captain.

We entered the Black Hills soon after passing the Fort and traveled on, now grumbling and growling, and scarcely any two agreeing about anything.

While we were in the Black Hills, Bennett and a man named Heck went off the road to hunt. They started a flock of mountain sheep in a canyon on a small stream and killed one of them. But they became so absorbed in the chase that they failed to get to camp that night but were compelled to camp in the canyon where they had killed the sheep. They did not come up with the train till after we had camped the next evening. But they stuck to their mutton and brought in as much of it as they could conveniently carry.

At the crossing of the North Platte we found a ferry boat made of buffalo skins. The raw hides had been nailed to small willows and then bent up in the shape of a boat with cross ties, or strips, of buffalo skin at the top to hold it in shape. We forded the river with our stock and wagons, but the water was so deep that we had to resort to the raw hide boat to get the most of our provisions and other goods over.

When we left the Black Hills we soon struck the Sweetwater, a clear, swift stream, about twenty yards wide and perhaps eighteen inches or two

---

14   This breakup is well-attested to by other participants. John Minto, "The Occasional Address," *Transactions of the Fourth Annual Reunion of the Oregon Pioneer Association* (hereafter, *OPAT*) 4 (1876) (Salem, OR: E. M. Waite, 1877): 39; "Reminiscences of Washington Smith Gilliam," *OPAT* 31 (1903) (Portland, OR: Peaslee Bros., 1904): 206; James R. Robertson, and Alanson Hinman, "Reminiscences of Alanson Hinman," *Quarterly of the Oregon Historical Society*, 2, no. 3 (Sept. 1901): 267.

feet deep. The lower part of the valley is rather sandy and covered with sage and greasewood.

The day we reached the Sweetwater, we passed the Independence Rock. This is a remarkable, isolated, granite rock, about two thousand feet long and about one hundred and fifty feet high, of an oval shape, standing out in the level plain on the left bank of the river. It has a crater-like depression on top which appears to be, sometimes, a small lake, but is evidently most of the time dry. It has a little earth in and around the edges of this depression that supports a few plants of sage and greasewood and a sickly, dwarf pine, not over eight or ten feet high. Aside from this it is entirely bare of vegetation.

On the side next to the river, this rock is covered with thousands of the names of persons who have visited it. Among these are found many, in fact, nearly all, the names of those who have a place in the history of the Rocky Mountains and the Pacific Slope who have gone west by this route either chiseled in or painted upon the Rock. Most of them, however, were painted, some of which were then nearly effaced and I have no doubt many of them have faded out entirely by this time. These records upon the Rock were an interesting study.[15]

The year before, in 1843, General A. L. Lovejoy, who afterwards settled at Oregon City, and is well known in the early history of Oregon, in company with another gentleman stopped here to paint their names upon the Rock while their train passed on.[16] Just as Lovejoy finished his name with the last touch of the brush, an Indian slapped him on the shoulder, and he turned suddenly, stunned with amazement to find himself and his companion prisoners in the hands of a small, straggling war party of Sioux Indians. They kept them at the Indian camp all night and held a council to determine whether they should kill them or hold them for ransom. The result was that they took them to their train the next day and sold them to their friends for a plug of tobacco, each. General Lovejoy, in concluding this anecdote of himself, would sometimes,

---

15   Levida Hileman and others have done Scott's "interesting study." Hileman, *In Tar and Paint and Stone* (Glendo, WY: High Plains Press, 2001), 30-31, 116.

16   The "other gentleman" was Lansford W. Hastings, whose own book described the incident. *The Emigrant's Guide to Oregon and California* (Cincinnati: George Conclin, 1845; facsimile reprint, Bedford, MA: Applewood Books, 2010), 11-17.

Devils Gate as viewed from the west, July 2011. *Courtesy Stafford Hazelett.*

humorously add that he felt like there would have been more glory in being tortured to death than in being sold so cheaply.[17]

We crossed the Sweetwater just above the Devil's Gate which is another place quite as remarkable as Independence Rock and almost five miles further up the river. Here the river makes a cut through the point of a granite ridge a distance of about a thousand feet and about one hundred feet wide with perpendicular and beetling walls four or five hundred feet high on either side. Through this gorge the waters foam and tumble over and among huge masses of rocks that have fallen from above. Viewed in connection with its surroundings, this place is certainly one of the wonders of the world.[18]

---

17 The year was 1842, not 1843. The story is embellished from the published version and may reflect Lovejoy's own telling. *See* Asa Lovejoy and Henry E. Reed, "Lovejoy's Pioneer Narrative, 1842-48," *Oregon Historical Quarterly* 31, no. 3 (Sept. 1930): 244-49.

18 The Sweetwater cut through the Sweetwater Rocks to form Devils Gate, a 370-foot-deep and 1500-foot-long granite gorge that narrows to a mere 50 feet. The trail crossed the river near Independence Rock.

Here we began to realize that we were in the Rocky Mountains, not on account of that roughness of our road, for that was smooth and level as we could desire it along the valley of the Sweetwater, but at the edge of the valley, from a half mile to a mile or, at most two miles, from the river, immense, picturesque ranges of granite rose sheer up from the plain to the very clouds, with scarcely a tree or shrub to relieve the glaring sublimity of their massive, grizzly terraces and escarpments. But our road rose with an easy grade along the stream till we reached the South Pass.

The South Pass is a wonderful roadway through these rugged mountains which is said to be about a mile and a quarter above the level of the Gulf of Mexico into which the waters running east from her flow.

We passed through the great plateau of the Pass which is about twenty miles wide along the ridge of the mountain north and south—around the north and west sides of the Table Rock—a remarkable fortress of rock whose perpendicular walls form the southern limit of the Pass, to the Sandy River, a tributary of Green River, which latter is called the Colorado where it enters the Gulf of California.[19]

All of this country from the South Pass to Green River is a barren, sandy plain, covered with sage and greasewood and a little scattering of grass which grows in small bunches among the sage, and which was now entirely dry and brown except immediately on the lowest lands along the margins of the watercourses.

The crossing of Green River is about seventy miles from the South Pass and was at this time within the boundaries of Mexico.[20] The river here is from four hundred to five hundred feet wide and from eighteen inches to three feet deep with a bold and dashing current running over pebbles and small boulders of a greenish granite. In many places below, it runs between high and precipitous banks, commonly of red or yellow sand-stone, with here and there a bluish green strata of argillaceous limestone.

---

19   "Table Rock" refers to Pacific Butte, "whose perpendicular walls" do indeed "form the southern limit of the [South] Pass." Will Bagley, *South Pass: Gateway to a Continent* (Norman: University of Oklahoma Press, 2014), 20, 26, photo 32.

20   Scott was technically correct about the northeastern boundary of Mexico, which had been settled at the 42nd parallel of latitude and the Rocky Mountains by the Transcontinental Treaty or Adams-Onis Treaty, in 1819. Fort Bridger and the crossing of the Green River were south of the 42nd parallel and west of the crest of the Rockies.

The waters are pure and clear, but this limestone and the granite pebbles and boulders in the bed of the stream give to its clear waters a strikingly greenish appearance. From which circumstance, possibly in connection with the green groves of large cottonwood trees growing along its banks, the Mexicans call the upper part of this stream, the "Rio Verde," or Green River.

This part of the Green River Valley is famous for the great number of sage hens—a species of prairie chicken—found here, and the Shoshone and Crow Indians call it the Prairie Hen River.[21]

In many places the current of this river is lashed into foam, and sweeps around in immense sucks and whirlpools, forming deep, funnel-shaped depressions in the surface, and then leaping up like the breaking surf on a rough sea coast that would seem to render navigation perilous if not impossible.

Some fifteen or twenty miles below this crossing, we came to a village of deserted huts and cabins, where a few years before had been a trading post, and great rendezvous of the hunters and trappers of the Rocky Mountains. Here were the little cottonwood cabins, daubed with mud, in which they had lived, and there was the race track where they had contended with each other and with the Indians in foot-racing and in trials of the speed of their mules and their wild mustang ponies, and in feats of personal strength and activity.[22]

---

21 This stream flows into today's Green River, which the Absarokas and the mountain men called the Seeds-ke-dee-agie, the River of the Prairie Hen. The Shoshones and Utes called it the Bitter Root River, "from a great abundance in its valley of a plant which affords them one of their favorite roots," John C. Frémont reported. Granville Stuart said they called it Can-na-ra o-gwa, "poor river," for its lack of trees and grass. But English swashbuckler Richard F. Burton said the Indians, "in their picturesque way, term this stream Wágáhongopá, or the Glistening Gravel Water." Bagley, *South Pass*, 26.

22 Collins and Scott are in error. The Green River rendezvous repeatedly took place at the confluence of Horse Creek and the Green River, which is not close by Scott's location. Scott instead seems to describe the Bridger-Fraeb post on Green River. Will Bagley, *So Rugged and Mountainous* (Norman: University of Oklahoma Press, 2010), 199: "Jim Bridger and Henry Fraeb had started a trading station on the west bank of Green River in August 1841, not long after Fraeb's encounter with the Bidwell-Bartleson party. When Indians killed Fraeb while he was in the mountains 'making meat' for winter, Bridger abandoned the site, moved to Blacks Fork, and started a trading post in partnership with Louis Vasquez."

Just below this place we left the river and, after passing over a broad, barren, sage plain, we entered some deep defiles in the mountains. Almost perpendicular walls rose on either hand, showing in many places strata of different colors. In some places white strata, several feet thick, runs like fillets of marble along the face of the yellow precipice. In some places little turrets, not more that twenty or thirty feet in diameter at the base, arose in almost perfect conic form to a height of fifty to one hundred feet from the perfectly level plain where the road wound like a paved street among the crags and upon nearly every one of these cones was an eagle's nest.

After passing for a short distance through this place, we came into a region where our road was more hilly and continued so till we reached Black's Fork of the Green River. This stream is, perhaps, a hundred feet wide and, at the time we reached it, contained scarcely water enough to cover the pebbles in its bed.

The next evening we camped on Ham's Fork, which is about half as large as Black's Fork, and did not contain water enough in many places to cover its bed.

Though the grass was all dried up, it was abundant on this stream and our stock fared very well. Here, where there is scarcely any rain in the summer time, the grass cures up like hay and stock like it much better than the best of hay and keep fat on it.

A portion of our way lay through some hills where we passed several ranges of perpendicular bluffs of various colored strata which some persons called the "Rainbow Hills," and, by a stretch of the imagination, one might trace some resemblance of a rainbow in the colors along the faces of the bluffs, but unfortunately for a person of no more vivid nor poetic imagination than myself, the lines of the different colors ran horizontally instead of with the graceful curve, and then in the colors and blendings, I could not, for the life of me, make a rainbow of them.[23]

On the head waters of Ham's Fork we came to Fort Bridger and by this time our company had dwindled down to fourteen wagons. One of our men, a German by the name of Grammaticher, was very ill with a fever and on this account we lay by here for three or four days.

---

23   Scott's "deep defiles in the mountains" are probably climbing out of the Green River Valley. His "Rainbow Hills" apparently describes the trail between the Hams Fork confluence with Blacks Fork at Granger, Wyoming, past Church Butte, and into Bridger Valley.

It was getting late in the season, and we were afraid that if we lost much time, we would be caught by the snows in the mountains. So I advised the families to go on, and as I had no family, and there was no family with our German friends, one of whom was the sick man, I would stay with them till he either recovered, or died. And we expected him to die soon, as there was no means of doctoring him, and he was very low.

Bennett and his wife got in with Barton Lee and went on.

We lay here two days longer, when Grammaticher died, and on the third day we buried him. The next day we resumed our journey. We were now three days in the rear of every other wagon on the road.[24]

We hurried on as rapidly as we could, feeling that we occupied the place of danger from the Indians as well as from the early frosts and snows of winter. The weather was warm and dry, the country hilly, and the road extremely dusty, so much so that it was often difficult for the driver to see the length of his team ahead of him.

Almost fifteen or twenty miles from Fort Bridger, we crossed a stream about twelve feet wide the waters of which seemed to be of a chalybeate nature and were also brackish with salt.

For almost three days after leaving Fort Bridger, our road lay among the hills when we found some pieces of coal lying on the surface of the ground apparently having been dug out by the rabbits and badgers. Then we came out upon a high, narrow ridge or causeway, as it would seem, of white argillaceous limestone which formed an excellent roadway a few rods wide but running almost, or quite, south breaking off precipitously on either hand but especially on the right where we could look almost straight down into the great and beautiful valley of Bear River.

After passing along this ridge for a short distance, we turned down to the right and soon found ourselves following a roadway which in

---

24   Clyman recorded a similar incident on the eastern side of South Pass, near the final crossing of the Sweetwater River, five days before arriving at Fort Bridger. According to Clyman, the Gilliam train left him on August 23 with a "Mr. Barnett" who was failing. Clyman noted that "Perkins and Scott came up with the rear of all the Emigrants on the route & we had their company during the night." The next day, "Mr Scotts company remain here to day..." and ladies of the company helped "Barnett." That night, August 26, "Barnett" died. Linda M. Hasselstrom, ed., *Journal of A Mountain Man, James Clyman* (Boise, ID: Tamarack Books, 1998), 108-10. Clyman's contemporary account has the name, date, and place right. Scott wrote from memory forty-five years later. Levi Scott is the only free adult named "Scott" in the 1844 lists.

some places seemed to have been cut out of the face of the white cliffs, going almost north, and descending with a steep grade towards the valley below.

From the foot of the bluffs, we crossed the valley and camped on Bear River, a beautiful stream about one hundred feet wide, well timbered at this point with cottonwood trees, and having rich prairie bottoms two miles or more wide.

We saw a great many Indian lodges in the valley along the river and a few of the Indians came to our camp in the evening. We felt the insecurity of our position, being only two wagons, and in the extreme rear of the emigration.[25] We could expect no reinforcements nor support from any quarter if we should be attacked. And we knew nothing of the temper of the Indians who swarmed in this part of the valley.

The next morning, while we were hitching up to resume our journey, a strapping young warrior rode up to us and accosted me, in very good English. He demanded to know of me whether there were any more white people coming. I promptly answered him, "Yes, there are a great many more coming."

"Then," he demanded, "what are you going to give the Indians for traveling through their country?"

"Nothing!" I responded.

"They always expect something from the white people when they travel through this country," he said.

"I have nothing to give," said I. "We are only traveling and have no more with us than we need for ourselves. We are not going to give the Indians anything."

"Then," said he, "the Indians may play hell with you, if you do not give them something!"

"Boys!" I commanded, "get your guns out of the wagons!" Then turning upon him with a stern countenance, I said, "You leave here! Or I will play hell with you!"

Now, really, I should have been afraid to molest him at all for there were hundreds of Indians in sight of us, but I thought he was sounding us and trying to see if he could intimidate us. So, I concluded, it might be best to put on a bold front and play the joke back on him.

---

25   Among 1844 overland diarists, only Clyman mentioned Scott's train.

He looked into my face with a searching gaze for a moment and then rode off without uttering another word. Not another Indian came near us while we were in Bear River Valley.

We traveled north down this charming valley and in the forenoon of the next day we crossed a beautiful, clear, swift stream about fifty or sixty feet wide, fringed with willows and cottonwoods.

Soon after crossing this stream we found the hills shut in, steep and rocky upon the river till the valley was in places less than a quarter of a mile wide, and in some places we crossed the hills to avoid the increased distance of following the river.

We crossed another tributary of Bear River about noon, larger than the one crossed in the morning. I believe this latter is called Thomas's River, and the one crossed in the morning Smith's River.

Although we were not again visited by any of the Indians, in the afternoon of the fourth or fifth day after coming into the valley we met a "White-Indian," that is, an unprincipled white man who had been living with the Indians for several years and had contracted their habits and embraced all of their lowest and worst vices as we afterwards learned. He said his name was Staggs.[26]

We had been without fresh meat for sometime and desired to get some. We asked him if he had any. He said, "No, but I shot an elk just back here a little way. I cared but little for it and did not follow it but I am sure I killed it and I can soon find it. I will go and hunt it up and meet you at your camping place tonight."

He then directed us to camp on a little creek that runs into Bear River at the Soda Springs. We drove in and camped at that place. After we had been a short time in camp, we saw him coming, but he was a long way off and on foot, leading his horse.

---

26   "It is said that many of the white men in the Mts. try to act as much like Indians as they can & would be glad if they really were so," missionary Mary Richardson Walker wrote near Green River on July 6, 1838. Fred R. Gowans, *Rocky Mountain Rendezvous* (Layton, UT: Peregrine Smith Books, 1985), 179. Marcus Whitman described the problem in 1843. Some of the Indians, he wrote, join "desperate white men" and "form bandits in the difficult passes, and are at all times ready to cut off some lagging emigrant." Whitman to Secretary of War, late 1843, in Clifford M. Drury, *Marcus and Narcissa Whitman, and the Opening of Old Oregon* (Glendale, CA: Arthur H. Clark Co., 1973), 2:397.

It was then almost sundown. We had prepared and eaten our supper before he reached us. He had his horse laden with elk meat and was walking and driving a cow and calf before him. He said he had bought the cow off some emigrants and had turned her over to a band of Indians he was with who had that morning started to go to Salt Lake and had agreed to drive his cow and calf, but had left them soon after they started and he would have to take them himself. We helped him to hang his meat up in a cedar tree under which we were camped and gave him his supper which we had cooked for him.

By the time he was done eating it was dark and he said he must go and look after his cow or the wolves would eat her calf before morning if he did not keep it close to camp. In about half and hour he came back and said he could not find her. "But," said he, "I must find her! I don't want the wolves to kill the calf."

Then he went and saddled his horse, which was picketed not far away, rode off in the darkness, and was gone for several hours. When he returned, towards midnight, he said he had been unable to find them and he felt confident that the wolves would eat them up before morning.

But the wolves did not molest them, for at daybreak there was the cow with her calf at her side almost in the same place where he had left them the evening before.

A little beyond the Soda Springs the road leaves the Bear River and turns rather to the northwest while the river turns nearly south and we understood that we would have a long, hard, day's drive to the next camping place. So we were up early and had our breakfast by the time it was light and were ready to gather our stock for an early start.

Staggs asked such an enormous price for his elk meat that we would not take any of it.

All hands turned out after our teams. But, when we drove the stock in, two of our horses were missing and could not be found anywhere in the vicinity of the camp.

We hitched up the teams and started them on while Charlie Zummordie and myself stopped to take another look for the missing animals. We had but little provisions cooked and did not keep any with us, supposing we would find the horses and come up with the wagons where they would stop at noon. But in this calculation we were mistaken.

Zummordie took the road and went back towards our camp of the night before, supposing that they had fed back in that direction, and that he could soon overtake them.

I went to where the horses had been turned out the evening before, intending to take their tracks and follow them, at least, till I should ascertain whether they had merely strayed away and the general direction in which they had gone.

I soon found their tracks and could follow them without much trouble. One of their long halter ropes had been tied to a billet of wood which dragged some thirty or forty feet behind the horses leaving a very plain trace upon the ground. But, after following their trail for about a quarter of a mile, I found the stick of wood and could see that the rope had been cut off near the knot.

Staggs was with me before I found the piece of wood, pretending, with a great show of earnestness, to help me. But he kept always before me, zigzagging about, and galloping hither and thither, making all the tracks he could with his horse and obscuring the trail I was trying to follow as much as possible, and trying, by every means that seemed to be in any way credible, to convince me that the horses must have gone in some other direction.

At length, I spoke to him very abruptly and ordered him to go behind me because he was doing more harm than good and, moreover, I told him very plainly that I should follow my own judgment and did not need any of his counsel or advice.

He soon galloped away towards the river, declaring that he was sure he saw the horses in that direction.

I trailed on for about two miles when I came to a nearly level, flat rock, about six hundred feet or more across in every direction. This rock is between two rather steep hills, buttes, or head-lands. I went around this place three or four times before I could find where the horses had left it. At length I found where they had gone straight up one of these buttes.

The soil on the side of the butte was loose, and there were some fragments of rock which had been started by the hoofs of the horses, and the way was so steep that they had ascended with so much effort as to leave a very plain trail that I could follow as fast as I could climb the hill which I found to be about a mile high.

When I reached the top of the butte, I soon came to a deep sink, or crater-like depression, down in the bottom of which I found the horses securely tied to a small cedar tree.

It was now about ten o'clock. I took the horses back to camp, gave them water, hobbled them, and turned them out to graze till Zummordie should come in.

I had almost made up my mind that I ought to shoot Staggs if I ever got sight of him again. About noon, the impudent scoundrel came riding up to the camp. I was sitting with my rifle lying across my lap. I was amazed at the rascal's audacity.

"Where in the world did you find your horses?" said he.

"I found them on top of the mountain, where they were tied."

After sitting for about twenty minutes, neither of us speaking another word, he said, "I must be going! For I have a long ride to make this afternoon."

"Oh, no!" said I, "wait till my comrade returns. When he comes, he will buy some of your elk meat."

He rose up, stood a few minutes, sat down again, and neither of us spoke for almost a quarter of an hour. He then rose to his feet, took up his gun without saying a word, mounted his horse, and spurring him suddenly into an Indian lope kept up this gait across the valley as far as I could see him.

By his time I was getting pretty hungry and could see no indication of Zummordie's return. I thought I would roast some of the elk meat. On examining it, I found it had good marrow bones in it. I cut four of these bones out of it with about as much flesh on them as I thought two men could eat and put them by the fire to roast by the time the Dutchman should come, for I did not suppose he would be out much longer.

I got them done to a turn, but no Dutchman came yet to help me eat them. I waited for him for some time longer and still he did not come.

I was very hungry and could wait on ceremony no longer. I divided the meat as equitably as I could and ate half of it, keeping the rest of it warm by the fire for my comrade when he should arrive.

Zummordie came in about two o'clock in the afternoon, having walked all day, and he was as hungry as a wolf. He had gone the entire distance back to our previous camp and returned which was equal to two days journey with the wagons. No wonder he was tired and hungry.

I gave him what I had cooked for him. With a sparkle of pleasure he picked the bones and then broke them and ate the marrow, as I had done.

During his repast, I related to him how I had tracked the horses into the old crater and found them tied up there. I related to him the extraordinary conduct of Staggs and told him what I thought of that bold and audacious scoundrel. He gnawed away at the bones and only responded once in a while with an exclamatory grunt.

"Vell!" he exclaimed, as he sucked the last bit of marrow from the bones, "I tidn't dink dot elg-meat vas so coot! I pelief it vas petter as fuffalo!"

"Yes," I replied, "I think so, too."

"Now, you petter pelief, dot vas coot!" he continued, eyeing the lot of meat as it hung in the tree.

"But," I reminded him, "we must get our horses and be off." I feared he would insist on cooking some more.

When we were read to start, he said, "Vell, I will take some of dis elg-meat mit me!"

He cut off almost fifty pounds. I told him that was too much, we had a hard ride before us and our ponies were poor. I cut off about ten pounds and gave it to him. He tied it to his saddle and we mounted and set off to overtake the wagons.

∾

CHAPTER VII

Fort Hall to The Dalles

After we had traveled two or three miles from the Soda Springs, we saw a cloud of crows, ravens, and buzzards rise and fly from some dead body not far from the road. We turned aside to see what it was and found the carcass of a three year old steer which had apparently died there. It had been skinned and the hide lay there by the side of it.

We could see just as plainly as though we had butchered it ourselves that the elk meat we had been eating had been cut from this carcass.

The Dutchman took a solemn, serious look at the carrion before us, then at the piece he was carrying, then turning, looked at me for a moment as though he would search the innermost workings of my stomach, and then he broke forth with, "Cot, tam! Hell, and 'nation! I carries dis meat no furder!"

He untied it from his saddle and dashed it down with an emphatic vigor that spoke the angry surgings of his soul more definitely than he could have done with the best and plainest English at his command.

Pretty soon we began to laugh at ourselves for being so badly fooled.

We rode on and reached camp about midnight. We roused up the other boys, told them the story of our troubles in finding the horses, and had a laugh over the villainously dirty trick the rascally Staggs had played on us about the elk meat besides stealing our horses.

While Staggs and I were holding Quaker meeting at the Soda Springs after I had found the horses, I made up my mind that when Zummordie should return we would bind the scoundrel and take him to Fort Hall with us and give him up to the officers of the Fort. I thought I should make a complaint to them against him and ask them to determine what ought to be done with him for the treatment we had received at his hands.

But, if we had taken him, I do not know whether we should ever have been able to have carried our prisoner further than the carcass of that dead steer where, I am inclined to think, the Dutchman, at least, would have insisted on turning him over to the buzzards that they might have held an inquest on him.

When we reached Fort Hall and related the circumstances, they told us they knew Staggs very well and that he was a villain.

When I was at Fort Hall, again, in 1847, Captain Grant, who had command of the Fort, told me that after Staggs left me at the Soda Springs in 1844 he fell in with a Spaniard—or rather, a Mexican—and they entered into a scheme together to rob a party of Indians who were coming to the Fort to dispose of a rich lot of furs.[27] Accordingly, they met the Indians in the mountains and Staggs, having several fresh horses, made a bargain with the Indians to help them on to the Fort with their peltries.

Under the pretense of helping them drive the pack-train, Staggs and the Mexican, after a while, managed to get some distance ahead of their employers when, starting the train in a run, they were soon out of the reach of their arrows and, being well provided with firearms, they kept the Indians at bay till they finally fell behind, apparently gave up the struggle, and were left out of sight.

But the Indians, although invisible to the robbers, kept upon their track and continuously and persistently followed them up for two days and nights. Then their horses were so hungry and jaded as to become unmanageable and they were compelled to stop and let them graze while they were themselves completely worn out with constant exertion and vigilance. Believing the Indians to have been left far behind, they camped, picketed out their horses, and rolled up in their blankets to dream of their rich booty, feeling themselves to be in perfect security.

But while they slept, their pursuers, who were more than a match for them in vigilance, endurance, and cunning, crept into their camp,

---

27   Grant worked as a fur trader for the Northwest Company and then Hudson's Bay Company after the merger in 1821. He was assigned to Fort Hall as Chief Trader in 1841. He was quickly in competition with Fort Bridger. He originally carried out the company's orders to discourage emigration to Oregon, but eventually siezed the opportunity to make money off the American emigrants. He famously opined that wagons could not make the journey all the way to the Willamette Valley, an assertion modified by 1844. According to John Minto, he said, "You [damned] Yankees will do anything you like," referring to the previous two years' emigrations' disregard of his advice. Bagley, *So Rugged and Mountainous*, 182-86, 203.

seized Staggs and recovered all their property while the Mexican made his escape by flight, so the Indians reported.

They then went to the fort, sold their furs, and gave Staggs up to Captain Grant, requesting him to deal with him as he thought best. Captain Grant proposed to Staggs that if he would leave the Mountains, go to the Willamette Valley, and behave himself, he would let him go, but if he would not do this, he would give him up to the Indians, and give them permission to do as they pleased with him. Staggs agreed to do as the Captain desired, evidently well pleased with Grant's decision and advice.

The Captain said they let him go and that was the last they had seen or heard of Staggs in the Rocky Mountains.

Before we started the next morning, a large band of Indians rode up to our camp. They had an abundance of service berries to trade us for anything we had to offer them. These are very nice berries and excellent, sustaining food and we were very glad to buy them.

There are great quantities of red haws in this part of the country as well as service berries. This Bear River Valley got its name legitimately, for its mountains are full of bears. They live pretty much altogether on the service berries and haws in the latter part of the summer and in the fall. The are extremely fond of the red haw, as we could see, for, in and about the thickets, the ground and the rocks were literally covered with their discharges which had settled down into flat cakes and dried, having almost or quite the appearance of pure dried haws.

We purchased several nice lots of berries from the Indians and were preparing to start and were just about ready to proceed on our journey. As we were on the point of starting, here comes a squaw, all in a rush and a flush of anxiety and business earnestness, with about a bushel of berries in an old buckskin shirt. She had sewed up the tail and filled it with fruit. This was more than we had intended to buy and we thought rather more than we needed after what we had already purchased. So, we hesitated, thought we did not need them, but when we took a peep into the bosom of her shirt, her berries appeared to be so large and fine and so much nicer than any we had just bought, that we began to waver, and finally concluded that we might do well to embrace the contents of her vestment in our acquisitions. For we had never seen such plump and fine looking sweetness in an old buckskin shirt before.

She, possibly being a belle of the tribe, woman-like, had an eye to the toilet and proposed to take a pocket-comb for the lot.

We concluded the treaty without hesitation and got a vessel to empty our purchase into, but she seized the old shirt, convulsively, and made signs to us that we should lift it into the wagon, that it was ours, also, as well as its contents. So we took it up, set it into the wagon, and drove off, elated with the bargain we had made.

When we halted at noon, we thought we did not exactly like the looks of this sweaty old buckskin shirt with our nice berries in it, so we got a clean sack and poured them into it. There was about a quart of the nicest berries the squaw had been able to find on top and all the rest we found to be *dried bear patties*, such as we had seen lying in great profusion about the thickets and places where the bears had resorted.

And here we were, again, confronted with the unsavory evidence of the need of Missionary effort in the Rocky Mountains. We could have required no further testimony to convince us that this unfair belle of the Mountains had never been trained up as a Sunday School teacher. And we mentally resolved that we would, ever after this, mistrust the contents of the most sacred garment of the sex.

Two days after this, we reached Snake River a short distance above Fort Hall. This was a trading post of the Hudson's Bay Company, a British firm extensively engaged in the fur trade throughout the Northwest. This Fort was commanded by Captain Grant, a very affable, free spoken gentleman, who gave us a great deal of valuable and interesting information about Oregon as well as concerning the road and distance we had to travel to reach the place of our destination. He was trading horses, flour, or anything else he had to spare, that the emigrants wanted, as they passed, for cattle.

Our cattle had become so exhausted and it was getting so late in the season that we feared we might be caught by the winter snows in the mountains which must necessarily be dangerous if not a fatal misfortune to us. So we proposed to trade them for horses and pack-rigging with which we could advance more rapidly than was possible with our poor and jaded teams.

The Captain ordered his horses to be driven up and I soon found that I could trade with him, but he and the Germans could not agree upon an exchange of property.

I had traveled with these Germans all the way from Missouri, where we had first met, and we had agreed, before reaching the Kansas River, to stay with each other all the way across. I had never been acquainted with a more agreeable company of men and did not wish to leave them. And, as they could not trade, I declined to do so. We moved on with our ox teams to the American Falls on the Snake River, twenty-five miles from the Fort.

Between Fort Hall and the Falls, we crossed the Portneuf, a very clear and beautiful river about three hundred feet wide and about three feet deep in which sported great numbers of the finest mountain trout. The soil along its banks seemed to be very rich and deep. It was fringed with willows and a few fine cottonwood trees grew along its margin. Its broad bottom lands were covered with an abundance of the finest pasture grass.

Between the Portneuf and the Falls of Snake River,[28] we crossed a deep narrow stream called the Pannanax [Bannock Creek], near the mouth of which, below where we crossed it, there seems to be some lakes and swamps, which appear to be favorite resorts for multitudes of waterfowl. Long lines of swans, pelicans—with their great haversacks, or pouches, in which they are said to carry their provisions of water and fish upon their migratory flights—multitudes of wild geese and other aquatic birds passed over our heads, filling the air with the rustling of their pinions and the songs of their flight.

Snake River, above the Falls, is about a thousand feet wide with several low islands covered with willows. The banks of the river are low, perpendicular walls of basaltic lava, increasing in height and the channel narrowing on approaching the Falls from above. At the Falls, the river pours over a great precipice of trap rock, not exactly with a sheer leap, but it is sufficiently retarded by terraces and parted by a rugged tower of rock, rising in the center about half way down, to lash the waters into white foam and to give variety and increased sublimity to the scene. I had never before witnessed a scene of such rough and naked grandeur.

---

28   American Falls is twenty-four trail miles beyond Fort Hall. Frémont measured the face of the falls at 870 feet in 1843 and emigrants estimated the combined drop at about fifty feet. It was one of the last major landmarks before the final "parting of the ways" for Oregon and California emigrants. Haines, *Historic Sites Along the Oregon Trail*, 305, 319-20.

The dark and barren rocks around the Falls rise in their treeless majesty with only here and there a tuft of willows near the water's edge or a stray plume of the gray sage clinging upon the crags like the eagle crest of a savage warrior.

Our cattle scattered when we camped here for the ground was rocky and bare offering them but little feed, so they wandered away in groups and hid themselves in the willows where they lay concealed the next morning. We were detained all day hunting for them.

When we got them gathered up again, we resolved to go back to the Fort and trade with Captain Grant for we saw that our oxen were so jaded and worn out that they would hide themselves whenever they could, that they might get a little rest, and might thus delay us very much in the remainder of our journey and probably cause us to be snowed under in the mountains. So we thought it best to exchange our jaded cattle for fresh horses.

So, the next day, one of the Germans and myself went back to the Fort on foot and traded with the Captain. He agreed take our stock where it was, at the Falls, without requiring us to go to the trouble of delivering it to him at the Post.

We got our ponies and outfit together as soon as we could and, about sunset, Captain Grant, with three Canadians and ourselves, mounted and started for our camp at the Falls.

I had nothing but an indifferent bit of string for a bridle and a pack saddle to ride upon, which, without stirrups upon which to rest much of the weight of the rider and without cushion or covering, is much worse to ride upon than the bare back of the horse.

Captain Grant and his men took the lead almost at full speed as is usual among the mountaineers and, of course, we had to follow at the same rate or be left out of sight behind in a very short time.

The misery of riding at such a gait, on such a saddle as I had under me, for a quarter of a hundred miles, in three dark hours, cannot be known to any one—may not be understood by any one—who has never suffered the fearful experience. I have never seen a dictionary that contained words adequate to the description of it.

Mazeppa must have enjoyed a delightful canter in comparison with my ride between Fort Hall and the American Falls. All I can do is just to note it down as it was the severest experience of my long life.[29]

Sometimes I was clinging to one side of my horse, sometimes to the other, sometimes I was humped up and leaning forward, sometimes backwards, and every change of attitude seemed only to augment the pain. But I must drop the subject. It pains me, yet, even to think of it.

We reached our camp before midnight and, after picketing out our ponies securely, we rolled up in our blankets, and slept till morning. When I awoke I could scarcely roll over. I was so jammed and bruised and sore from the effects of my ride as to be hardly able to get upon my feet. But, after stirring around a while, and getting warmed with exercise, I felt a little better, but it was a week, or more, before I ceased to be a sufferer from the effects of that ride.

Paul Revere's ride and Sheridan's ride have both become famous in history. But those patriotic heroes each had a good saddle and a strapping stallion, worth about five thousand dollars, under him. If either of them had attempted the feat on an old pack saddle and a Rocky Mountain mustang, history would, perhaps, never have noted his experience and he would have felt much worse the next day.

After breakfast, we got up our cattle and delivered them. When Captain Grant and I had first talked of trading at the Fort, I had an ox that was tender footed and so lame that it was with great effort he could keep along with the wagons. Before leaving there I had sold him this ox for a sack of flour. Now, when we made our last trade, neither of us mentioned this former transaction. So when Grant had looked over and counted the stock, he turned to me and inquired, "Where is the other steer?"

"Didn't you get him for the flour?" I answered.

"Yes, but I paid for him then," he replied.

"Certainly." I responded. "If you had not paid for him, I should not have left him at the Fort."

---

29 "Mazeppa" was a poem by Lord Byron which became popularly known through a play performed by traveling actors in the mid-nineteenth century. Mazeppa was "bound to the back of a wild Tartar horse...and the horse is turned loose." *Oregonian*, "Amusements," December 12, 1870, 3.

"Aye, aye!" said he, "but I thought I was getting six head in this trade."

"Why didn't you mention that before we traded?" said I. "You know what stock I had. All I could do so as to give you all I had and you have got them. I wish you had spoken about this before we traded and put ourselves to so much trouble. Now, after we have exchanged property, I think it rather late, under the circumstances, to raise this question."

"Well, well." said he, "I thought I was getting six head and there are but five. But I suppose it must go so, under the circumstances."

So he took our stock and returned to the Fort and we addressed ourselves to the new and unpracticed situation in which we were now placed. We were compelled to abandon our wagons as we could get nothing for them. When the Hudson's Bay Company's officer got our teams, he knew that he would get our wagons by right of prior occupancy after we had abandoned them. They got a great many valuable wagons that were abandoned by the emigrants and they purchased many lame cattle for almost nothing.

Not one of us knew anything about packing on horses and I am sure our first efforts were very awkward. However, we did the best we could. We packed up and traveled about five miles that day, camping early, so that we should have time to overhaul our baggage and get it in a little better shape for packing the next day.

In the morning we packed our animals and got ready to start before our German friends were quite ready. We started on, traveling slowly, so that they might overtake us. But we afterwards learned that soon after having started, one of their pack-horses stampeded, causing them a great deal of trouble and delay.

We stopped to noon, early, and waited for them till two o'clock and they were not yet in sight. Then, we concluded that we had better go on to the next watering place and camp, where, we felt confident, they would join us before night as we supposed we should only have to go a few miles to find a good camping place. But we were compelled to drive till ten o'clock that night before we came to water or anything like a suitable place to camp. Here we came up with our friends who had left us at Fort Bridger who were camped here with their wagons.

As our German friends did not come up, we concluded, finally, that they had resolved to take it slowly till they should have better learned the art of packing their goods upon animals. So we went on again the next day and did not see them, again, until we met at Oregon City, into which village they came several days after we had arrived there.

When we bade farewell to our friends with the wagons at this camp, we traveled on at a pretty good rate, for we had hardy ponies that were fresh and in good order. We passed emigrant wagons nearly every day, all the way through, so much had the two great companies of Captain Ford and Captain Gilliam become broken up and scattered by this time.

At the crossing of Snake River we came up with a party of emigrants who had hired an Indian to pilot them across, for the ford was dangerous and not directly across the stream but running diagonally across and against the current and a little deviation from the proper course which the oxen were liable to make by their disposition to yield to the current was likely to be fraught with disaster.

The water was a little more than waist deep. All the dress the pilot had on was a strip of cloth about an inch wide passing over one shoulder and down between his thighs, being tied in a bow knot around his limb in front; besides this, he was as naked as he was born.

We thought it a ridiculous comedy to see him wade the stream in this plight in the presence of so many ladies but he acted with as much nonchalance, and seemed to be as proud of his position, as if he had been a prince giving a grand drawing-room reception to a concourse of distinguished foreigners. He received twenty-five cents for his services which to him was, simply, *wealth.*

At every camp and stopping place, now, the Indians brought us abundance of salmon which we gladly traded for as our stock of provisions was getting low and we relished the famous fish as an agreeable change and improvement of our diet.

We thought the fish very fine. But we had not yet learned much about salmon, their habits, their seasons, and their runs. At this season of the year, a white person who knows anything about salmon will not catch them nor eat them. They were floating down the river, all run-down, poor, and exhausted with their long run from the sea, their spawning, and fighting, and dashing against the rocks at the numerous rapids, cascades, and waterfalls. Many of them were floating, dead, upon the stream, and many of them, with the scales nearly all sluffed off, were scarcely able to wiggle a fin. In places, they were lying dead in piles along the margin of the river and in the eddies. But we knew nothing about all this, or, at most, not enough to put us on our guard against being swindled by the Indians, to some extent, in the fresh fish they traded us. We bought what we thought we could eat of such fish as they brought to us and we ate them with a relish.

The Indians along the river are said to be the most shiftless, indolent, and poverty stricken race on the continent. During the salmon season they have plenty, get fat and extremely lazy, and good natured. But, it is said, they know nothing of frugality and will not put up provisions for a time of scarcity or famine. But few of them will take the trouble to dry the fish when they are plenty and many of them suffer severely during the winter season for food.

There is no game in the country to amount to anything and they have not even skins of which to make clothing and the cold winters must be very severe on these naked, starving people. But they forget it all and are perfectly happy when the salmon comes again.

When we reached Boise River, I rode along its banks one day, making observations and taking in everything new that came under my eye. At length I came to an Indian fish-trap. It consisted of a large log reaching across, from bank to bank, with poles set in the water, slanting up stream to the bottom, the tops resting against the log about two inches apart, entirely across the river. This prevented any fish from passing down stream. And I suppose there must have been three or four wagon loads of salmon piled in against that rack. Some were dead, some could scarcely wiggle, and some were playing around quite lively, and could, possibly, have reached the sea again, if they could have passed that trap. After this we bought no more fish from the Indians.

When we reached Fort Boise, another Hudson's Bay trading post, we got a lot of dried salmon skins upon an order of Captain Grant of Fort Hall, which he had given us in our trade with him, upon the commander of Fort Boise. "Salmon skins" was what the order called for. Grant had assured us that these were excellent food which we found to be true.

We found the "Salmon skins" to be the bellies of salmon taken during the spring run—when they are very fat and excellent—and nicely dried. We found them very much better than the fresh fish we had been buying from the Indians.

Here we crossed back to the south side of Snake River and traveled down it to the Malheur River on which we camped where we struck it.

'The next night we camped on Burnt River, up which we traveled one day, and the next day we struck Powder River. In one day from Powder River, we reached the Grande Ronde Valley. This is the finest valley we had seen since leaving that in which Fort Hall is situated.

In the Grande Ronde Valley, we killed a small elk and lay by a day to dry the meat which we found excellent. This was the first elk we had ever seen and the first elk meat I have ever tasted—if we except that which Staggs had played off on us at the Soda Springs.

From the Grande Ronde Valley we crossed the Blue Mountains and in two days came to the Umatilla River. Here we found a great many Indians who seemed to have plenty of good horses and, in every way, appeared to be superior to and in better circumstances than the fish-eaters we had met with along the rugged banks of the lava-walled Snake River.

These Indians appeared to know something about the cultivation of the soil to which the Snake Indians did not give any attention. The land along the Umatilla and at the base of the Blue Mountains is very fertile while much of the country along Snake River is barren sand and rocks.

Some of the Cayuse Indians who dwelt along the Umatilla came to our camp with Irish potatoes to trade. One of them took from under his blanket a little sack of very small potatoes, not more than one man could eat, which we eagerly bought at the price he asked for them. After sitting a few minutes, as if making a very important calculation, he gravely drew out a sack of very nice large ones. Of course we could not resist the temptation and we bought these also.

It seemed to tickle him immensely, that he had played his small potatoes on us before we suspected him of having any better. It was a very safe and judicious method of testing the market, to ascertain the value of potatoes.

The next day we reached the Columbia River just above the mouth of the Umatilla. Going down the Columbia along a sandy barren looking sage plain we crossed John Day River and proceeded to the River Des Chutes without the occurrence of any incident worth recording. We found the Des Chutes a rough and rapid stream with a dangerous ford near its confluence with the Columbia and we had to hire an Indian to pilot us across it.

From here we followed an Indian trail over an uneven country of grass-covered, sandy hills and camped within about four miles of the Dalles where we ate the last of our stock of provisions.

❧

CHAPTER VIII

Exploring a New Country

When we reached the Methodist Mission at the Dalles, we found that there was plenty of provisions here to sell but there was no flour. We got all the fresh beef, potatoes, and wheat we wanted. The Missionaries had a large iron hand-mill—something like a large coffee-mill—on which, with great labor, we ground some of the wheat which we bought from them. But, then, we had to eat our bread, bran and all together, for they had neither bolt nor sieve. The potatoes were excellent and the beef was fat, tender, sweet, and juicy, and the bread, although very sweet and good, was very coarse. No doubt, the dietetic reformer, Graham, would have enjoyed it as the *ne plus ultra* of the staff of life; yet, we would have been glad to get the coarse, rough bran out of it.

The first night we lay here, the Indians stole one of our horses. I hunted for him all the next day but could not find him. While hunting for him the second day, I found another one of our horses, which we had not yet missed, tied up in the bushes a mile or two from camp. I felt now that I would like to commence killing Indians. But this was a pastime I did not dare to indulge in. The joke would have been turned on me too easily, for there were Indians everywhere. So, all I could do, under the circumstances, was to shake my scalp-lock and thank the Lord that matters were no worse with me. This was on Wednesday and I hunted faithfully till Sunday without getting any trace, whatever, of the missing animal.

There were two Methodist clergymen in charge of the Dalles Mission—the Rev. A. F. Waller, and Rev. H. B. Brewer. The Rev. Mr. Waller afterwards settled at Salem, in the Willamette Valley, and there built a lasting monument to his memory in the foundations of the Willamette University.[30]

I thought it might be well to inform these gentlemen of our loss and give them a description of the missing horse; that, possibly, they might be able to aid us in finding him. When I rode up to the Mission, they were both sitting in the house. I spoke to them and the Rev. Mr. Waller came out to where I was. I told him of our loss and described the animal to him, adding that I should hunt the balance of the day and then go on without the horse if I failed to find him.

"What!" said he, "hunting your horse on Sunday! I should not be surprised if you never find him!"

I was not religious and had not given the matter a religious thought. All I had thought about was the loss I had sustained and the great inconvenience it was to me. His speech, at the time, struck me as a cruel lack of sympathy with me and I answered him hotly, "Neither would I be surprised if you stole my horse yourself!"

I turned angrily away without exchanging another word with him. I was too wroth to give him credit for piety at the time. I could only see in it a canting rebuke which I was in no frame of mind to relish. But, the truth is, the Rev. A. F. Waller was a genuine, self-sacrificing Christian, whose first thought was always God and his laws. Temporal interests, however great—and he could appreciate them as much as they deserved—were always secondary considerations with him. Those who knew him least were likely to misjudge him most.

I put in all the balance of that Sunday in unavailing search. But when I returned to camp, I found the horse there. An Indian had driven up a band of ponies near our camp and my horse was among them. John and Hedges recognized him and caught him. But his tail had been shaved and his legs were badly cut by hobbles.

The Indians had shaved his tail for the double purpose of disfiguring him so that we would not be likely to recognize him and to get the hair. They make the small ropes which they use instead of bridles and their *cinches*—saddle girths—mostly of horse hair.

---

30   The oldest building on the Willamette University campus is Waller Hall. *See* biography of Waller in Corning, *Dictionary of Oregon History*, 257; Herbert O. Lang, *History of the Willamette Valley* (Portland, OR: G. H. Himes, 1885) 897. *See* biography of Brewer in John M. Canse, "The Diary of Henry Bridgeman Brewer," *Oregon Historical Quarterly* 29, no. 2 (June 1928): introduction, 189-90.

On the third day after we lost the horse, when I came in from hunting him, there was a crowd of Indians at the door of our tent. I was very hungry, weary, and angry, and I said to them, "Go away from here! The damned Indians have stolen my horse and I don't want them about me!" One of the Indians responded very indignantly, "You say I steal? You go, talk to Mr. Brewer. He tell you, me pray every night. Me no steal horse!" He drew his blanket about him firmly and strode away with an air of deeply wounded sensibility, insulted honor, and injured innocence.

When we started from the Dalles to cross the Cascade Mountains, a party of three or four white men and several Indians started with us and we traveled together about four or five miles when they turned off on a trail to the right to go to the mouth of Dog River,[31] which is about a day's journey below the Dalles, while we kept the left-hand trail—which had previously only been traveled by the Indians except that a party of emigrants, consisting of a few families with about a hundred and fifty head of stock, had taken this trail a day or two ahead of us with the hope of finding a better way through the mountains than that hitherto traveled by emigrants.[32] This trail crossed Dog River several miles above its mouth.

Before we separated from the party going to the mouth of Dog River, an Indian rode up to me several times, repeatedly, and in an indignant and reproachful tone and manner reiterated what I had said to the Indians at the Dalles. "The damned Indians stole my horse! The damned Indians stole my horse!"

I really cannot say whether he intended to pick a quarrel with me or only to reprove me for publishing such a bad opinion of his race. But I took no notice of his evident desire to discuss the matter with me and was careful not to give him any further pretext to be offended.

When we reached Dog River, we found it to be not a large stream but it was up—swimming. So, we carried our baggage across on a log and made our horses swim. My son, John, mounted his horse to drive the others into the river and, when they were all safely over, he concluded to

---

31 Today's Hood River.

32 The route had also been traveled by the Methodist missionaries for a decade between their stations in the Willamette Valley and The Dalles. For an extended and graphic emigrant reminiscence of this route in 1845, *see* Sarah J. Cummins, "Autobiography and Reminiscences of Sarah J. Cummins," Oregon Historical Society Research Library, Mss 1508; reprint, Fairfield, WA: Ye Galleon Press, Fairfield, 1999.

ride his animal across, just for the fun of it—as boys sometimes do reckless things just for the novelty, adventure, and fun of the risk. The horse went to the bottom with him and he lost his seat but still held on to the saddle. After a desperate struggle in the cold, swift current, the horse came ashore with John clinging to the rigging.

After having traveled about five miles further, we camped where there were some tall, green, fine-looking tussocks of grass—each bunch large enough to feed a horse. But to our astonishment, our horses would not touch it, tired and hungry as they were, but they stood by it all night without tasting a bite of it.

The next day we traveled in sight of Mount Hood, passing closely under the northern base of it. Opposite the foot of this snow peak and in sight of it, on Dog River, which heads among its glaciers, we came to a place where the trail passed along a narrow ledge not more than five feet wide and, in places, not more than three feet—with the perpendicular walls on the left dropping down a hundred feet to where the rushing waters of the swollen river foamed and fretted against them, while on the right the beetling escarpment rose for a hundred feet above our heads for half a mile or more, when we came out upon the summit of the Cascade Range.[33]

Here we found the snow about a foot deep, which had fallen since the party in advance of us had passed, and we had great difficulty in finding and following the trail for a distance of three or four miles when we came out of the snow down on the western slope of the mountain. This was in the early part of November.

We camped that night on a small tributary of the Sandy River which runs into the Columbia near the western base of the mountains. Here we found but very little grass, but the frosts had caused the leaves of the willows and alders to fall which lay upon the ground in deep piles. So our horses filled themselves principally with leaves—for there was next to no grass, at all—and they had worked very hard now for three days without anything to eat.

---

33   This place is called Lolo Pass, and is located ten miles northeast of Zigzag,
      Oregon, not to be confused with the Lolo Pass on the Idaho-Montana border.
      Scott refers to the "summit of the Cascade Range" when he was clearly referring to
      the pass. Scott used this terminology consistently in describing crossings of ridges
      and mountain ranges at their passes.

The next day, after passing a great number of horses and cattle—mostly cattle—along the trail, some dead and some exhausted and unable to proceed further, we came up with a party of emigrants who had preceded us encamped on the Sandy River. They had lost about one half of their stock in crossing the mountains.

Elijah Bunton was one of the principal men of this party. He afterward settled in the western edge of Camas Prairie, in the Umpqua Valley, not far from the present village and College of Wilbur. He had sent his son, William, down the Columbia River in a canoe to get some horses and provisions and meet him on the way as soon as possible.[34]

In crossing the mountains, Mr. Bunton had lost all of his stock except one ox and one pony. He was accompanied by his wife and two small children. He packed the ox and the pony with their beds, clothing, and provisions, while he and his wife walked and each carried one of the children. He came to me to get me to carry some of his goods so that Mrs. Bunton could have the pony to ride. I let him have one of my horses to pack on the day we started from this camp and then they got along much more comfortably. Towards evening, we met his son with a supply of fresh horses and provisions. So he returned my horse as he had no further need of him and the next day we went on and left them.

In three days, after leaving them, we reached Oregon City, at the Falls of the Willamette, on the 8th day of November 1844. This place seemed to be head-quarters and the objective point of all the immigration. Here we met only one man with whom I had been acquainted before starting to Oregon. This was a gentleman from Illinois by the name of Straight.

Oregon City was a new town and the only one in the Willamette Valley. Every one who had any property here was trying to improve it and this made work for all who wished to labor. But there was no money in the country to pay the laborers. They had to take just whatever they could get. Sometimes we could get one thing and sometimes another for our work.

---

34   Bunton eventually settled near Roseburg, at Bunton's Gap, close to the junction
     of the Old Scottsburg Military Road with the Southern Route to Oregon after it
     also became a military road. R. A. Booth, "History of Umpqua Academy," *Oregon
     Historical Quarterly* 19, no. 1 (March 1918): 23. Bunton was enumerated among
     the emigrants of 1844 by John Minto at the reunion of pioneers in 1876. Minto,
     "The Occasional Address," *OPAT* 4 (1876) (Salem, OR: E.M. Waite, 1877): 41.

There was plenty of wheat but we had no flour. There was not a mill in the country. Most people ate boiled wheat or peas instead of bread. The Canadians had a small field-pea which was very prolific and made excellent food. Nearly everybody used this pea as a substitute for coffee and it was not a bad one, either. Potatoes grew well and were excellent with salmon. Salt salmon was the principal substitute for bacon. There were but few hogs, yet, in the country.

A dollar and a half was the measure of a day's wages but scarcely anyone had a dollar and a half in money; that was merely the nominal statement of the case.

What goods there were for sale were very high and of an inferior quality—except those held by the Hudson's Bay Company, and they usually refused to sell to American settlers for anything but cash. They had no disposition to encourage the settlement of the country by Americans and they soon absorbed pretty much all the money the immigrants brought with them.

Everyone was compelled to board and lodge himself. That is, he must look out for his own provisions and blankets. These necessaries a traveler always carried with him for he could not expect to be accommodated in these things among the settlers. The people were kind, hospitable, and obliging as their circumstances would allow but they were poor. Each felt like a camper in a wilderness and could not be expected to provided food or bedding for anyone but himself and his family if he had one.

The first job I got after reaching Oregon City was that of putting up a plank fence for a man by the name of Moss. This took two day's work and came to three dollars. When I finished it, I asked Moss if he knew anyone who would like to hire me to work for him. I was poor and felt that I must keep busy, if possible, so as to make a living.

"No," said he, "I do not know of anyone who would like to hire a hand."

"Well," said I, "I wish you would inquire for me, if you have an opportunity, for I would like to get a job."

"I will do it," he replied.

The next day he sent me word that Dr. McLoughlin wished to get out a lot of hewn timbers for building a mill and that I could get the job. I went to the Dr. and got his order for the timbers.

After I had finished this work for Dr. McLoughlin, I called on Moss to get my pay for the work I had done for him. I presented my bill for "2 days work in building a fence—$3.00."

"That's all right," said he, "but I have a bill against you."

"What is that for?" I inquired.

"For contracting—$3.00," said he.

"What does that mean? I don't understand it," said I.

"Why, for getting you that job of work from Dr. McLoughlin," he replied.

"But that did not cost you anything, not even the least effort," said I. "I am willing to pay you a fair compensation for anything you have done for me but, it seems to me, you charge too much. I never employed you to make any contract for me and you never made any. I merely asked, as a favor, that if you knew of anyone who wanted work done, you would be kind enough to let me know about it."

"Well, well!" said he, "that is all the way we have of getting along here—to make one hand wash the other!"

And so, our accounts never received any further adjustment.

Sometime after this, T. W. Berry, a very intelligent, affable, and free spoken gentleman, went to have a settlement with Moss about some matter of business between them. Moss attempted to play about as small a trick on Berry as he had on me when the latter, looking him in the face with a mingled expression of astonishment and contempt, exclaimed in a burst of honest indignation, "Moss, you are the meanest man in Oregon!"

"Oh! you'll not get a quarrel out of me on that question," coolly replied Moss. "I could prove that myself by a least twenty men right here."

He was pretty generally known, after this, as "The meanest man in Oregon."[35]

We turned our horses out on the Clackamas River bottom, for we had nothing to feed them on, and were compelled to leave them to make their own living on the wild grass, like the ponies of the Indians, and we lost two of them during the winter.

---

35   This story of Scott's business dealing with Sidney Moss was extracted by Collins from a much later point in Scott's original. Moss was an emigrant of 1842 and well-known businessman in Oregon City. *See* Moss biography in Corning, *Dictionary of Oregon History*, 170-71.

We built a little shanty on the bank of the Willamette River between Oregon City and the mouth of the Clackamas River consisting of three rude walls against the bluff of the second bank of the river forming a sort of wigwam, or temporary hut, in which we passed the winter.

The waters of the Willamette rose this winter, it was said, about three feet higher than usual. The Clackamas Indians said that the unusual rise in the river was because we had built our shanty in that place and that the "Spirit of the River" was angry and was trying to wash it away. However, their "River God" was not able to get the waters quite up to our habitation.

During the winter we made some shingles and hewed out a lot of building timbers. Then we did a few jobs of carpenter's work and, finally, to employ our time we bought a lot and built a small house on it. By the time we had finished this, the winter was over.[36]

When spring opened, I went down to Astoria, the principal trading post established on this coast by the American Fur Company, at the mouth of the Columbia River, but which was now in the possession of the Hudson's Bay Company. I went to see what the prospect was, there, for burning lime. I supposed, from what I had heard about it, that this was a good place to start a lime kiln. There was no lime in the Willamette Valley and I concluded that there would be a sufficient demand for it in a short time to make it a profitable and growing business.

But I found the quantity of limestone at Astoria entirely insufficient to justify me in attempting to start the business. I found the rock about the mouth of the Columbia to be pretty much all of basaltic formation and what little indication of lime could be found consisted of small pebbles scattered in the soil of the bluffs without any stratification.

On returning to Oregon City, I took a trip up the Willamette Valley about fifty miles to the Rickreall which is a beautiful little river flowing almost directly east from the Coast Range of mountains into the Willamette.[37]

By this time, the waters were down so that they could be forded. I procured a horse and saddle and rode throughout the settlements. I had

---

36   According to deeds retained by his descendants, Scott developed this property and sold it to Hugh Burns in December 1844. Fred Lockley, "Impressions and Observations of the Journal Man [Mrs. R. E. Dersham, daughter of William J. J. Scott]," *Oregon Journal*, Nov. 25, 1926, 10, col. 6-7.

37   Rickreal Creek in Polk County enters the Willamette west of Salem at Eola.

only come to look at the country and I did not wish to take up a land claim. So I went through the scanty settlements of the Willamette Valley, charmed with the beauty of the country and the excellence of the soil at every step.

About the middle of May 1845, I met with Heck, Hovias, and Zummordie, three Germans who had crossed the Plains with me, and who, also, wished to explore the country. So I procured an outfit and we started up the Willamette Valley, intending to go as far beyond the settlements as we should deem it safe for so small a party to venture. The more we saw of the country, the more we were enchanted with the magnificent beauty of its scenery and the richness of the soil.

I had never seen a "bucking" horse and did not exactly understand the meaning of that term as a modifier of the "mustang" until I started on this trip. I traded for a mare that had the reputation of being a "bucker." She was a pretty, clean limbed, nice looking pony, with fine action, and I knew from her motions that she could move under a rider as smoothly as a whirligig. So I concluded to ride her and pack my other one.

When I mounted into the saddle, she set in to bucking. First, she stood up on her hind-feet, then, vigorously shaking her head with a vicious little squeal, she dropped it suddenly between her fore-legs, at the same time thrusting them out as straight and stiff as if they had been iron posts without a joint in them, then, with a high curvette, suddenly flinging her heels into the air, she came down in almost a vertical line, like an arrow that had been shot over a church steeple, my hat flying off and my head almost going with it, she struck the ground like a thunderbolt.

Before I had time to take in the slack, with a sudden whirl to the right, she gave a second and more rapidly executed exhibition of the same trick. Now, spinning to the left, with increasing velocity and wickedness, she gave me an encore; and then, gathering all her strength and cussedness, she executed a tremendous *da capo* movement that brought down the saddle and the rider with a stunning accent all in a heap upon the hard ground.

This was my first experience with a bucking horse. I knew all about it now. I didn't wish to study the subject further.

I then put the pack on her and concluded to lead her and ride the other horse. She went along with the pack, meekly enough, in a sort of reflective mood, as if she felt deeply penitent for her wickedness, till we got out into the broad open prairie near the Yamhill River, a little above where McMinnville now is, when the little vixen set in to bucking again and she never stopped till she had completely stripped herself of her pack, pack-saddle, bridle, and halter.

We could no more catch her on the prairie than we could have caught a wild elk. So we were compelled to distribute her burden among the other horses and to drive her along with them, loose, till we came to the house of Jesse Applegate at the head of Salt Creek Valley where we drove her into a corral and lassoed her.[38]

We wanted some butter to take with us but we had no money to buy it with. Mr. Applegate had a good many cows and made plenty of butter. He wanted rails to fence a field and told us that we could have all the butter we needed if we would make rails for it.[39]

We concluded to make two hundred rails for him and take our pay in butter. So the four of us went out into the timber and, after a hard day's work, succeeded in getting two hundred rails made. This was a very poor result for so many men for we afterwards learned that a good rail-maker could cut and split from one hundred and fifty to two hundred rails in a day, alone, in good timber. But we had not yet learned how to select good timber, as we had never made rails in fir timber before, and we frequently chose the very worst timber in the grove.

The next day we packed up, again, and proceeded on our way towards the head of the Willamette Valley. About four or five miles from Mr. Applegate's, we crossed the Rickreall where the town of Dallas, the county-seat of Polk County, now stands.

About fifteen miles from the crossing of the Rickreall, after having passed through what is now the beautiful Monmouth prairie, we forded the Luckiamute River two or three miles below the forks at a place afterwards owned by Mr. M. M. Nealley.

---

38   This is the first meeting of these two men in spring 1845. Scott and Applegate cooperated on several other projects described in the original manuscript, including an attempt to get help from the U.S. Army in California after the Whitman incident and an exploration of an improved Southern Route between Roseburg and Medford. Applegate also tried unsuccessfully to include Scott in his Klamath Commonwealth community.

39   Later, the Garrison family sought to make a similar arrangement for food but Applegate no longer accepted barter. Abraham Henry Garrison, "Reminiscences of A. H. Garrison, His Early Life, and Across the Plains and of Oregon from 1846 to 1903," Oregon Historical Society Research Library, Mss 847.

Five or six miles, perhaps, south of the Luckiamute, we came to a small muddy stream, in crossing which one of our pack-horses mired down and we were compelled to remove his pack before we could get him out. The water in this creek looked so much like dirty soapsuds and the sticky clay so much like soap that we always, afterwards, spoke of it as "Soap Creek," and it retains the name to the present time.[40]

We stopped for several days on a little mountain branch or brook three or four miles south of Soap Creek for the purpose of examining the country in the vicinity more thoroughly as that was the main object of the journey.

While we were camped here, three of us were out one day, together, and had separated from one another a short distance when a coyote sprang up in the long grass a little way from me. I fired and broke its back when it dropped down in the grass and lay there, unable to get upon its feet, again.

I called to the other two men who, on hearing the shot and the call, came towards me. Zummordie was not far from me and the wolf lay on a line between us. So I kept looking up in a tree, as though the object of interest were there, all the time keeping such a position as to have him come directly to where the wolf lay. He kept his eyes up, trying to see what was attracting such earnest attention from me. When he came near the wolf, it rose upon its fore feet and snapped at him, viciously, at the same time uttering a fierce growl. He sprang back with a frightened expression of horror on his face. He took in the situation as soon as I began to laugh at him and, recovering himself, exclaimed good-naturedly, "Now! ve blays dot same dhrick on Hovias!"

So we got into the right position to bring Hovias to the coyote and called him, earnestly, to come. But, when he came up to the wolf, its fierce snap and growl frightened him so much that he flew into a passion when

---

40   The creek flows north and east from a valley north of Corvallis through Benton and Polk Counties into the Willamette River. The Davis family, emigrants of 1847 by the Southern Route to Oregon, settled in the valley. Charles George Davis, *The South Road and the Route Across Southern Oregon: Short Studies in the History of the Oregon Country, Including Strategies in the Cold War Over the Far West Frontier* (North Plains, OR: EmigrantsWest.com, 2000), and *The Oskaloosa Company: Last Wagon Train to Skinner's in 1847* (Portland, OR: Frontier Publishing, 1996). Lewis A. McArthur & Lewis L. McArthur, *Oregon Geographic Names,* 7th ed. (Portland, OR: Historical Society Press, 2003), 893-94.

we laughed at him and retorted angrily, "You big fools! ven you play such tam foolishness mit a wolf! He woot joust so soon pite a man as notting!"

From this camp, on Reed's branch, we went to the mouth of Mary's River, where the city of Corvallis now is, and camped there for three or four days.[41] While we were camped here, two of us went upon Mary's Peak, which is the highest anywhere in this part of the Coast Range.[42] It's generally crowned with snow till after midsummer. It is about twelve miles west of Corvallis and has always been the finest hunting ground, especially for the black-tailed deer, in this part of Oregon. But at that time it was not at all necessary to go to the mountains for game as we could kill all the deer we needed anywhere around our camp.

While we were on the excursion to Mary's Peak, we visited what is now called Blodgett's Valley, which is a very beautiful region of country lying between the main valley of Mary's River and the upper end of King's Valley on the Luckiamute. I thought the country between the Yamhill and Mary's River the finest I had ever seen.

While we were camped on Mary's River, Heck went out near a knoll three or four miles west of our camp where he saw a large cougar lying in the long grass under an oak tree. He did not know what kind of an animal it was so he got into a ravine and crept up within fifty yards of it. When he raised up to shoot, he saw another one of the same kind. He took a look at the majestic animals and then he skulked back down the ravine and returned to camp, overawed by the leonine bearing of the beasts.

He told of the occurrence that night at the camp-fire and asked me if I knew what kind of animals they were and what would have been the probable consequence if he had shot one of them.

I told him I had never seen a cougar but what I had heard about them corresponded so well with his description that I felt sure the animal he had seen was the great lion of the Pacific Slope.

We crossed Mary's River and went up the Willamette Valley as far as the Buttes, about sixteen or seventeen miles further south. This was as far beyond the settlements as was then thought safe for so small a party to venture on account of the Indians who were wild and thought to be dangerous.

---

41   Scott named it for the man who jumped his claim in 1846 and settled there. Reed's Branch is now called Arbor Creek.

42   Mary's Peak, highest peak in the Coast Range, has an elevation of 4,097 feet.

There was no one settled at that time south of the Rickreall except that Gen. Cornelius Gilliam was then living on the south bank of the stream at the present site of the town of Dallas.

We found the country delightful. There was the green range of the Cascade Mountains to the east, crowned with white peaks of perpetual snow—the grandest on the continent, the low evergreen mountains of the Coast Range to the west—with their western bases washed by the Pacific Ocean, while between these two ranges of mountains stretched out seventy or eighty miles of the most beautiful prairie lands, crossed by numerous well-wooded streams of clear, pure water, flowing from the east and from the west into the beautiful Willamette, which flows through the center of its valley for a hundred and fifty miles from the Calapooya Mountains to the Columbia River.

The soil was rich and deep and covered with a luxuriant growth of the finest pasture grasses and bright with beautiful flowers. The ruffed grouse—one of the finest game birds in the world—was hooting everywhere and the pheasants were drumming through the woods. Deer were plenty and tame and we easily killed all the wild meat we wanted. We could kill a deer anywhere in the valley, whenever we needed meat, with nearly as much ease as a farmer in Iowa could go into his pasture and kill a sheep.

I was so charmed with the country, the excellence of its climate, and the surpassing beauty of the scenery, that the more I roamed about, the more I wished to roam. It seemed as though I never could exhaust the interest of this enchanting valley. But I found that my means were about exhausted and I must go to work.

On our return to the settlements, I took a job to build a house for Lindsay Applegate who had settled near the head of Salt Creek, a small tributary of the Yamhill River. The three brothers, Jesse, Lindsay, and Charles, with their families had settled here almost exactly on the forty-fifth parallel of north latitude. After having finished this job of building, I got out some staves and headings, cut some whoop-poles, and coopered for awhile during the fall and winter of 1845 at Lindsay Applegate's where I remained until the next spring.[43]

---

43   Scott was making barrels.

During this time, my son, John, was at work with J. W. Nesmith and
A. F. Hedges at the house-carpentering business in Oregon City which
place was now improving very rapidly if we may take into consideration
all the embarrassing circumstances.

James W. Nesmith was then a young man about twenty-five years
old, full of good sense and energy, and had reached Oregon a year before
I came. He was born in the State of Maine, July 23rd, 1820. Like myself,
he was an orphan boy, having lost both his parents in early childhood.
With that self-reliant and industrious energy which always gives promise
of a man of worthy deeds when directed by the sterling principles that
ruled his character, Mr. Nesmith had acquired a fair education with a
genuine love of books and a taste for social intercourse with educated and
experienced men which had a strong tendency to bring him to the front.
He had worked his way with intrepid independence all the way across
the continent from Maine to Oregon and that, too, at a time and under
circumstances of hardship and daring that might have crowned a veteran
brow with distinguished honors...[44]

---

44   An extensive biography of James Nesmith was added by Collins at this point in
his manuscript. It has been deleted from the text because of having little relevance
to Scott's account. Nesmith married David Goff's daughter, Pauline, a few days
before the June departure of the Southern Route exploring party. They had seven
children. Nesmith went on to a distinguished career in Oregon politics as a Union
Democrat and U.S. Senator during the Civil War. He was the only Democrat
senator to vote in favor of the Thirteenth Amendment of the U.S. Constitution
abolishing slavery. He died at home near Rickreall, Oregon, in 1885. His daughter,
Harriet N. McArthur, became a pillar of the Oregon Pioneer Association and
Oregon Historical Society, and her son, Lewis A. McArthur, began the assembly
of the history of the geographic names of Oregon as a hobby to collect the
names of all the post offices and railroad stations. Corning, *Dictionary of Oregon
History*, 174; Harriet K. (Nesmith) McArthur, "Biographical Sketch of Hon. J. W.
Nesmith," *OPAT* 14 (1886) (Portland: Press of Geo. H. Himes, 1887); Richard H.
Engeman, *The Oregon Companion* (Portland, OR: Timber Press, 2009), 265.

CHAPTER IX

༄

1846 Trail Explorations

Now there was no road across the Cascade Mountains better than the wretched Indian trail by which we had crossed them and they must be crossed in order to reach the Willamette Valley. The only known way to get a wagon into the valley was down the Columbia River by water. And, by this way, a difficult, dangerous, and laborious portage of several miles must be made around the Cascade Falls where that river passes between the two great snow peaks of the range, Mount St. Helens on the north and Mount Hood on the south.

The emigrants were compelled to abandon their wagons at the Dalles, a hundred miles above the mouth of the Willamette, at which place they embarked in bateaux and canoes to make the passage through the mountains to the valley. The loss of their wagons, which were needed by them in making their farms, was seriously felt in addition to the peril and difficulty of a voyage down the river in such miserable boats as they were able to get and sometimes they were compelled to make it on rudely constructed rafts. Several lamentable disasters had occurred on the river and some lives had been lost. There seemed to be a deep and general impression that we must have a road across the Cascade Mountains.

There had been a Provisional Government organized during the summer of 1843 to stand off the Hudson's Bay Company which was endeavoring to claim and hold the country as a possession of the British crown. Hon. George Abernethy, one of the most excellent men in the country, was elected governor in 1845 and did everything in his power to carry out the objects of the new and daring little government and to encourage the settlement of the country by brave and hardy Americans to the utmost of his ability and to the extent of the scanty means under his control.[45]

---

45 *See* biographies of George Abernethy in Corning, *Dictionary of Oregon History*, 1; Engeman, *The Oregon Companion*, 16; Medorem Crawford, "Gov. George Abernethy," *OPAT* 14 (1886) (Portland, OR: Press of Geo. H. Hines): 37-40.

But, the Provisional Government looks a great deal larger, now, at this distance of time and on paper than it really was, then, in fact. It had next to no revenues nor any means to do anything towards making a road across the mountains and the settlers, although possessed of incomparable pluck and energy, had scarcely anything to contribute towards such an enterprise.[46]

In the spring of 1846, there was a sort of popular call for volunteers to view out and locate an emigrant road across the mountains. A company of fifteen men was raised. Each must furnish his own horses, arms, ammunition, blankets, and provisions, and all to take the risk of hostile encounter with the Indians, to spend the time and endure the hardships of a campaign in a wild, mountainous, and unexplored country, for the consideration of pure patriotism and the gratification of adventurous curiosity.[47]

On the 15th of May 1846, Cornelius Gilliam, B. F. Burch, Solomon Tetherow, Robert Smith, Wm. Wilson, Wm. G. Parker, John Owens, Bennett Osborn, John M. Scott, Jack Jones, Black Harris, William Sportsman, David Goff, S. H. Goodhue, and myself, started on this enterprise.[48] We traveled southward up the Willamette Valley supposing we would be likely to find a pass across the mountains near the head of the river. After having gone about a hundred miles up the valley on the west side, we concluded to cross to the east side of the Willamette River and follow some of its eastern branches into the Cascade Mountains.

---

46   For a brief review of the early days of government in Oregon, *See* Frederick V. Holman, "A Brief History of the Oregon Provisional Government and What Caused Its Formation," *Quarterly of the Oregon Historical Society*, 13, no. 2 (June 1912): 89-139. As a non-participant, Scott's assessment was rather less heroic than the recollections of some of the participants.

47   Scott did not mention the subscription exceeding $2,000 which was promised to reimburse the men of the exploring party for their costs. Jesse Looney Papers, Oregon Historical Society Research Library, Mss 2263. There is strong evidence that the subscribers did not honor their pledges. Rev. A.E. Garrison claimed to have paid $21 to Scott. Abraham Ellison Garrison, "Forty-two Years in Oregon," Oregon Historical Society Research Library, Mss 1009, 29. An anonymous writer thought Scott received $14. [Oregonian], "New Roads to Oregon, No. 2," *Oregon Spectator*, March 18, 1847, 2-3.

48   Gilliam, Tetherow, and Wilson were the only ones who did not participate in the second, successful, exploring party for the far southern route as explorers. Tetherow joined the road building party at Canyon Creek Canyon upon learning of the arrival of the first of the road hunting party. Emigrant of '46 [Truman Powers], "A Pioneer's Reminiscence," *Oregonian*, March 12, 1879, 1, col. 2.

In crossing the valley from the upper waters of the Long Tom River, we camped one night on the side of a prominent butte rising out of a range of hills near the middle of the valley.[49] From the tops of this peak to the verge of the horizon in every direction we had one of the most delightful views of the country I have ever seen. Its beauty and grandeur are beyond the descriptive powers of my pen.

Gen. Gilliam said he wished to call this charming peak "Spencer's Butte," in honor of a distinguished friend of his and he stated the reasons why he wished to honor that name but I have now forgotten what his reasons were. However, we always afterwards spoke of it as Spencer's Butte and it still retains that name.[50] This butte is about three miles south and in plain view from Eugene City and the State University, but at that time the country was a wilderness, some sixty or seventy miles from any civilized settlement.

From Spencer's Butte we went in a south-easterly direction with the intention of striking the Middle Fork of the Willamette River where it comes out of the mountains. From the top of the butte, the valley lay spread out under the eye like a great map on which we could plainly trace the courses of all the streams and we could see where each of the three forks of the Willamette seemed to emerge from the mountains and the Middle Fork gave the most promising appearance of a practicable pass across them.

We crossed the Coast Fork about three miles above its junction with the Middle Fork and went up by Mount Pleasant, crossing Rattlesnake and Lost Creeks, small tributaries of the Middle Fork, and continued on up the valley to where the mountains seemed to close in upon the river from each side. We lay here one day and several of us went up the mountains but could make no satisfactory or favorable discovery of a route across the Cascades, that grim and formidable barrier between the Willamette Valley and the east.

---

49 This branch of the Long Tom River is now known as Coyote Creek. *See* McArthur, *Oregon Geographic Names*, 242-43, 590.

50 Dr. Elijah White claimed to have named the butte in 1845 for the Secretary of War at the time. Elijah White, comp. A. J. Allen, *Ten Years in Oregon* (Ithaca, NY: Press of Andrus, Gauntlett, & Co., 1850), 267-69. McArthur, *Oregon Geographic Names*, 900-01, has White's version, a Hudson's Bay Company version, and another version, but not Scott's attribution to Gilliam.

The next day we came back down the river about three or four miles and attempted to cross it, but the waters were very high and we found it difficult to get over. We stopped at this camp a day and W. G. Parker, Robert Smith, and myself got across to the northeast side of the river.[51] There we found a wide, low bottom, and the river runs through it in several branches or streams. When we reached what we concluded must be the main channel, we found it swimming to our horses. But after searching for some time, we found a drift on which we crossed, carrying our saddles and baggage on our backs. After a while, we succeeded in getting a rope across and stationed a man to lead the horses over. We were afraid to turn them loose, apprehending that they might be drawn under the drift by the swift current, for we were compelled to cross above and close to it.

With some difficulty we got our baggage over and then took the horses across one at a time, a man holding to the rope to lead and help them to stem the rushing current. We got two of the horses over without accident when Bob Smith concluded to ride his horse across to save himself the trouble of going down to the drift and crossing there. But when he rode into the water, the horse refused to swim. They were both rolled over in the cold, swift waters, giving Bob a most uncomfortable ducking. Parker and I held on to the rope and pulled with all our might. At length the horse, being pretty well suffocated with water, rose to the surface and began to swim. We landed both the horse and his unhappy rider safely, but very wet, Smith having barely escaped with his life by clinging to the animal.

From here we went up the river a few miles to the top of Butte Disappointment but, being unable to make any favorable discovery of a way into the mountains, we returned to camp, hardly knowing what would be the best move to make next.

---

51   William Parker was a brother of Cynthia Parker Applegate, wife of Jesse, and also an 1843 emigrant. He married a daughter of Solomon Tetherow, another road explorer and emigrant of 1845 by the Meek Cutoff. Parker purchased Duncan's Half-Way House in 1877 which he renamed "Parker Station." It was located on the Southern Oregon Wagon Road at a convenient mid-point between the major settlements at Ashland and Linkville, now Klamath Falls. Devere Helfrich, "Stagecoach to Linkville," *Klamath Echoes* 11 (1973), 25 (map), 27, 29, 32, 36, 38; Lindsay Applegate, "Notes and Reminiscences of Laying Out and Establishing the Old Emigrant Road into Southern Oregon in the Year 1846," *Quarterly of the Oregon Historical Society* 22, no. 1 (March 1921): 44.

From this camp we returned to the Coast Fork and went up that stream about ten miles when we suddenly came upon two Indians fishing in the river. They ran into the bushes when they saw us, as though they were frightened out of their wits, and concealed themselves. A short distance further on we came upon an Indian camp which was deserted by all its inhabitants except two very old people—a man and a squaw. The man had on an old pair of pants and an old hat and could talk the jargon—a sort of non-descript *talkee talkee*, used by the traders and trappers in their intercourse with the Indian tribes of the Northwest, the principal constituent of which is the language of the Chinook Indians. His dress and speech showed that he had held some intercourse with white people, but they were both very much frightened and we could get no information from them.

We camped two or three miles above here which was as far up the river as there was any prairie or open ground.

In the evening, the old Indian, having shaken off his fear, came to our camp. He still seemed to know nothing about any way across the mountains, at least he would tell us nothing that was of any value or that gave us any satisfaction.

From this camp we returned down the Coast Fork about ten miles where we crossed to the west side and camped that night on its most westerly branch. Here, we struck a well-beaten Indian trail and met with some Indians who informed us that this trail led across the Calapooya Mountains into the Umpqua Valley.

Here, Gen. Gilliam left us and returned home. We had no guide nor leader and our party was without any organization. In starting out we had overlooked the important principle that an organized plan with a head and leader is essential to the success of almost every undertaking.

We took the Indian trail and continued on our journey in a southerly direction across the Calapooya Mountains—a transverse chain of densely timbered mountains separating the Willamette and Umpqua valleys and connecting the Cascade and Coast ranges. In the north side of the Calapooyas are most of the sources of the West, or Coast, Fork of the Willamette River, and on the south side the source of Elk Creek, a tributary of the Umpqua River.

We struck Elk Creek near its head but the company were divided in opinion as to whether it were a tributary of the Umpqua or of the Willamette.

Tetherow and Wilson were in favor of abandoning the enterprise and returning home. They were not quite sure that it would be safe for them to do as Gen. Gilliam had and attempt to return alone, so they talked the subject up till about noon when we came to a small stream with very steep banks. Bob Smith, who was riding a very small mule, on going down the bank suffered the misfortune to break his crupper,[52] when away went Bob, saddle, gun, and all, over the mule's head into the water which was about knee deep. This was fun for all but Bob who got the ducking. He was almost fighting mad and the more we laughed at him, the more he became disgusted with the whole business, till, finally, he swore he would go home with Wilson and Tetherow.

We took our noon lunch here and when we started on, again, the three discouraged explorers took the back track for home.

It was cloudy all the afternoon and we did not get so much as a glimpse of the sun and it was difficult to tell in what direction we were traveling as we wound among the logs and timber and along the ridges and canyons of the mountains.

The question arose in our camp that night as to the true points of the compass from our position. Each one pointed out the course which he supposed to be north—no two exactly agreeing in their judgment. I took out a small pocket compass—the only one in the company—which proved that every one of us was at fault.[53] And Black Harris—who had assumed the role of guide—most of any. He was completely turned around and insisted that south was north. I had not lost my reckoning very much for I had been careful to observe that the ridge we had followed during the afternoon curved gradually but constantly to the left which, in the course of a few hours travel, must have nearly reversed our bearings.

---

52   A crupper is a leather loop passing under a horse's tail and buckled to the saddle to help keep it in place.

53   Scott carried a pocket compass. In the next exploring party, the only equipment was a pocket compass, a pocket watch, and a spyglass. One of the Road Hunters, "For the Oregon Spectator," *Oregon Spectator*, April 15, 1847, 2-3.

We continued our journey south for two days more which brought us to Calapooya Creek in the Umpqua Valley just above where the town of Oakland now is and almost a hundred and fifty miles from the settlements. Here we concluded to return home, having apparently accomplished nothing towards finding a pass through the Cascade Mountains.

On returning to the Willamette, I stopped at a place where I had determined to settle, some six or eight miles north of the mouth of Mary's River and about twenty-five miles south of any other habitation in the valley.

The rest of the company went on to the settlements. We had talked the matter over and thought it likely that a new company could be raised to push the exploration further. I told them that if this could be done, I would join the expedition and that I should keep my outfit in readiness and be prepared to go at a moment's notice.

I took up my claim and went to work to improve it and make me a home. This engaged my entire energy and attention till early in June when Jesse Applegate, having raised another company to prosecute further the enterprise which had occupied the other company during a portion of the month of May, came to my place and requested me to join the expedition.

I dropped my work and fell in with them at once. But this expedition cost me my land claim for, while I was gone, Tom Reed jumped it. When I returned the next winter, he had possession and seemed to be determined to "hold the fort." He had a family and I had none. I felt confident that I could soon raise a force that would dispossess him and restore to me my rights but that would probably work a hardship upon his family and I had seen so many vacant places that I liked better and could have for the taking that, finally, on his paying me twenty dollars for the improvements I had made, I gave up my claim to the place and let him take it. He secured a patent to it from the government.[54] It made him a fine home. He kept a sort of wayside inn here for many years and became a wealthy farmer. I believe he still lives there now in the year 1888.

Captain Applegate's company consisted of Jesse Applegate, Lindsay Applegate, Wm. G. Parker, B. F. Burch, David Goff, John Owens, Robert

---

54 Tom Read's (corrected spelling according to the General Land Office records) claim was mapped and patented in Township 10 South, Range 4 West, Section 31. The patent was issued in July 1867.

Smith,[55] Bennett Osborn, S. H. Goodhue, Jack Jones, John Bogus,[56] William Sportsman, Black Harris, John M. Scott, and myself. Fifteen of us, all together.

We started from my place about the middle of June 1846, and we traveled nearly the same route as that by which the former party returned till we reached the Umpqua Valley.

Captain Applegate had obtained a map made by Peter Ogden, a member of the Hudson's Bay Company, who had been through a portion of the country we expected to explore. This map had been made from observations taken by Ogden wherever he had traveled and outside of these limits its delineations were mere guess work and of no practical value. But as long as we were upon Ogden's line of travel, we found it very accurate and of great benefit to us.

After crossing the Calapooya Mountains into the Umpqua Valley we struck the California Trail which was the route that had been most generally traveled by the few persons who had passed between the Sacramento and the Columbia valleys.

We were delighted with the Umpqua Valley. The air was soft and balmy, the water plenty, clear and pure, and the grass was very fine. There was plenty of timber, fir, pine, red-oak, alder, laurel, yew, balm, myrtle, white oak, etc. There is some red-oak—most people, I believe, call it black-oak—in the head of the Willamette Valley, but I believe there is none lower down than the Long Tom River. Yet, there is a species of this white oak, as tough as hickory, and very valuable for wagon timbers, or for any purpose that requires tough, strong wood, in both the Umpqua and Willamette valleys. The yellow fir makes a fine wagon tongue, or a ship

---

55   Smith returned in spite of his near-disasters on the first exploring trip. Smith had been a companion on one of Scott's adventures before the May 1846 exploration. Scott and Collins described their earlier journey on pages 173-75, below. Smith came west in 1843 with the Applegate party, lived with the Applegates near Dallas, took up a Donation Land Act claim in the Yoncalla valley in 1850, and married Susan, a daughter of Charles Applegate, in 1851. He lived on his farm at Yoncalla, except for occasional service in the Indian Wars, until his death in May 1888. *Portrait and Biographical Record of Western Oregon,* "Robert Smith" (Chicago: Chapman Publishing Co., 1904), 485.

56   Scott's "John Bogus" is identified as "Henry Boygus" in Lindsay Applegate, "Notes and Reminiscences," 14, 39, 43. Jesse Applegate thought his name was "Henry Boggs." Dale Morgan, ed., *Overland in 1846: Diaries and Letters of the California-Oregon Trail* (Georgetown, CA: Talisman Press, 1963), 637-38.

mast, or anything else that requires a wood combining strength, lightness, and elasticity. Fir wood never warps, but if it be seasoned straight, which is natural to it, no matter how much it may be bent, when the bending force is withdrawn, it regains its original straight line, at once. There is a great deal of this timber, now, shipped to China, India, South America, and Europe, from the Columbia River and Puget Sound, and there are many places along the coast of Oregon and Washington from which it might be shipped with great profit.

We found game more plenty, if possible, than in the Willamette Valley, but we gave little attention to it, for we regarded our enterprise as one of the first importance, and our time too precious to be frittered away in the sport of the chase.

We met with but few Indians in the Umpqua Valley, and they were very shy and wild. We crossed the North Fork of the Umpqua River about three miles below the present Winchester ferry, and struck the South Fork a few miles above the junction.

We traveled up the South Umpqua, till we came near the foot of the Umpqua Mountains, where we met a party of eight or ten immigrants coming from California. I think they consisted of a Mr. Hess and his family, who afterwards settled in the lower end of the Chehalem Valley, in Yamhill County, and Hess's son-in-law, John Chamberlain, who settled on the Little Luckiamute in Polk County.[57]

They had some cattle with them, and a lot of Mexican horses. They said the Indians had killed one of their cows at the creek just across the mountains. This creek has ever since been called Cow Creek.[58] They informed us, it was about ten miles across the mountains, and that the trail was very rough and difficult. They said that while they were crossing the mountain, the Indians had wounded one of them with an arrow, and had run off one of their pack-horses down the steep mountain side into a wooded thicket, where they dared not follow them.

---

57   While Chamberlain did emigrate north from California to Oregon in 1846, he was already in Oregon City on June 17 to sign an affidavit about conditions in California. *See Oregon Spectator*, "Public Meeting," June 25, 1846. Chamberlain later settled near the Scott families in Polk County.

58   McArthur, *Oregon Geographic Names*, 240-41, records this story as an update to an earlier version published in A.G. Walling, *History of Southern Oregon* (Portland, OR: A.G. Walling, 1884), 424.

They said a wagon road never could be made across the mountain; that it could scarcely be crossed with pack-horses, and that any party, in crossing, would be constantly in danger from the Indians.

Having thus been forewarned by these unfortunate travelers, and taking every precaution against surprise, we crossed, without either accident or incident worthy of note, to a small branch of Cow Creek. The trail by which we crossed, on leaving the valley of the Umpqua, passed up a deep gorge, or canyon, for about two miles, and then turned up a ridge to the right, which we followed to the summit. While crossing, we could see from the trail on the heights, that the deep cut of the canyon we had left, seemed to extend entirely through the mountain. So we lay by a day, to examine this canyon, and see if a road could be made through it.

Captain Applegate, W. G. Parker, B. F. Burch, and myself went up the branch of Cow Creek, that flows from this pass on the south side of the mountain, to its head, and down Canyon Creek, flowing into the Umpqua, until we came to the trail by which we had crossed the mountain the day before. We found the grade for a road much better than we had expected, but with some very steep places.[59]

The Canyon was very bushy, so much so, that we were frequently compelled to clamber over masses of vine-maple, and other bushes, which grew so densely that a man could not crawl through among them. And there were great quantities of logs and boulders choking up the pass, which would have to be removed, in opening a road.

While we were floundering in the thickest, deepest, darkest, and most impenetrable gorge of this canyon, where we felt sure no human being, either civilized or uncivilized had ever been before, we were suddenly almost stupefied with amazement by finding a leaf that had been torn from a printed book. The penetrating enterprise of the press had entered

---

59   According to Elisha Applegate, recalling his father's retelling, Jesse Applegate and Moses Harris were sent to follow down Cow Creek while Lindsay Applegate and William Parker went up over the divide from Cow Creek to Canyon Creek and discovered the route that was opened by the emigrants later that year. By the Applegates' story, Scott was not involved in the exploration for the route through the Umpqua Mountains. Reese Kendall, *Pacific Trail Camp-Fires* (Chicago: Scroll Publishing Co., 1901), 133-35. According to the 1877 Applegate reminiscence, one party was sent to explore Canyon Creek while the rest stayed with the horses at their camp near Azalea. Applegate, "Notes and Reminiscences," 17.

this wild pass in advance of us. Finally we accounted for the presence of this unquestionable evidence of civilized refinement in this wild and lonely place, by concluding that it must have been borne hither by the winds, from the California Trail upon the mountain side far above.

That evening we returned to camp on the south side of the mountain, by the trail in which we had crossed the day before. We made our report to the rest of the company, and all of us together gravely and carefully discussed the possibility of making a wagon road through the canyon, with its probable cost, and the time it would take to accomplish it. We had no difficulty in arriving at the conclusion that it could be done, and was a better place for a road than we had hoped to find, but the other questions were not so easily, nor satisfactorily settled.

The next day we went on, crossing Cow Creek three or four miles from our camp, we passed over the range of hills west of Wolf Creek, and struck Grave Creek, about where the road now crosses it. We crossed the latter creek and went down it, till we struck a small branch running into it from the south, and going up this, crossed over the divide to the Jump-Off-Joe. This stream gets its rather singular and uncouth name from an incident which occurred upon its banks a year or two before, near the place where we reached it. Jo. McLoughlin, a half-breed son of Dr. John McLoughlin—the Chief Factor of the Hudson's Bay Company, in Oregon—being out on the stream alone, some distance from his camp and comrades, was surprised and so closely pursued by a party of hostile savages, that, to save himself, he was forced to jump from a precipitous bluff about twenty-feet high into a thicket of bushes growing on the margin of the stream. Being uninjured by this flying leap, he was able to rejoin his party, which was camped near by, and to escape the scalping-knife of his pursuers. The stream has ever since been called Jump-Off-Joe.[60]

Just after crossing this stream, we saw a small party of Indians, and started to go to them. But they ran like wild beasts, and concealing themselves in the woods, we could not get to speak with them.

We next came to a very pretty little creek, that was then known among the trappers as "Butcher-knife" Creek, and by the natives, who dwelt along its banks, it was called the "Tetalum,"—which signifies the "sunflower,"

---

60   McArthur, *Oregon Geographic Names*, 521.

and is a very fitting and appropriate name, but by some unaccountable outrage on good sense and good taste, it is now called, "Louse Creek."[61]

About nine years after we reached this creek, the Wagner family was murdered by the Indians at the crossing. Mrs. Wagner and her little girl were killed, and the houses burned. Mr. Wagner made his escape, as he was not at the house when the attack was made. This took place in the autumn of 1855.[62]

When we stopped for dinner after leaving this creek, we saw an Indian approaching us. We thought it best not to permit him to come to us, so Captain Applegate and several others went out to meet him with guns in their hands. They made signs to him not to come, and he turned away.

On reaching Rogue River, several of us rode up to an Indian village, about a quarter of a mile above the crossing. The inhabitants all fled, and hid themselves. After awhile one of the Indians showed himself, and we beckoned him to come to us, which he did with great caution and trepidation. We soon satisfied him that we entertained no hostile feeling towards his people, and only wished to cross the river before us. He soon rallied one of his men and got a canoe, which was not more than ten or twelve feet long, and very flat and wide for a canoe, indeed, it was about as rude a boat of this kind as I had ever seen. They managed it with poles, and two of them could run it almost straight across the swift current.

We unpacked our animals, and after having sent two armed men across in the canoe, we drove the horses—of which there were more than thirty head—into the stream, and compelled them to swim over. Then we transported our packs, and other things, taking one man at each passage. We kept an armed guard stationed on the bank to keep back the Indians, who now showed some disposition to come to us, since we had employed their leaders as ferrymen.

---

61   An old pioneer settler in the area attributed the name to a story of miners infested with lice who held a contest with the parasites at the location. Robert Earl, Oregon Historical Society Research Library, Mss 793, 50. According to McArthur, *Oregon Geographic Names*, 595, the creek was named for "an Indian camp on its banks that was infested with vermin."

62   Multiple correspondents sent reports, *Oregon Statesman*, Oct. 20, 1-3, and Oct. 27, 1855, 1-2; and *The Oregon Weekly Times*, "Indian Hostilities South," Oct. 13, 1855, 2. *Oregonian*, "The Rogue River Massacre, Story of the Killing of Nineteen Persons on October 9, 1855," Dec. 20, 1885, 3, col. 4-6; The Manzanita rest areas along Interstate 5 between exits 61 and 66 north of Grants Pass have interpretive monuments relating this history.

When we got everything and all the men over, the next thing was to settle for our ferriage. So we tore a tent in two and gave each of the Indians half of it. They drew it around their shoulders and shivered, making their teeth chatter, and by their signs informed us that the tent was not as warm clothing as they would like, but that they would much prefer to have a pair of blankets. We gave them to understand that we had no blankets to spare, and finally, we satisfied them by giving each a plug of tobacco, in addition to the tent cloth.

We traveled up the south side of Rogue River, to the Willow Springs, whence we crossed the valley and struck Bear Creek, just below where the town of Phoenix now is.

While going up this creek we overtook a party of Canadians—French and half-breeds—on their way to California. Upon information received from them, we took a more easterly direction, went up Emigrant Creek, and striking a spur of the Siskiyou Mountains, crossed them some distance east of the California Trail.[63]

In about five or six miles after we struck the mountains, we found ourselves on the other side, where we camped on a small stream flowing into the Klamath River. Captain Applegate and myself found a beaver dam on the creek, and I shot one of the beavers, but it sank in the water, and we did not get it. We called the stream Beaver Creek. We followed it down, nearly as far as the timber line extends down the mountain side.[64]

To avoid the heavy timber on the Siskiyou Mountains, we bore too much towards the south, which course we kept, over pretty rough ground, till we struck the Klamath River. We turned up the river, which was more in the direction we wished to go, and followed its north bank till we came to where it runs through an impassible canyon.

---

63 The men clearly knew the way, as it had been traveled by Ogden in 1826-27, and MacLeod and McKay in 1829, and described to Dr. Elijah White in 1845. This was the last assistance the South Road Exploring Party received from the Hudson's Bay Company employees. Lindsay Applegate described this meeting, and a subsequent battle the "Canadians" had with Indians, to his son, Jesse A. Applegate, in 1886. Jesse A. Applegate, "A Scrap of Early History," *Oregon Statesman*, May 7, 1886, 8. The location is near Pilot Rock, about ten miles southeast of Ashland, and neither the landmark nor the battle that occurred are mentioned in the Scott or Applegate reminiscences. For Pilot Rock, *see* McArthur, *Oregon Geographic Names*, 762-63.

64 McArthur, *Oregon Geographic Names*, 65 (Beaver Creek), mentions this location as described by Ogden in April 1827.

As we could not pass up through this canyon, we concluded to return down the river till we should find a place where we could ford it, when we would go over and try to find a way up on the other side. We came to this conclusion reluctantly, as this course turned us in the opposite direction, from that in which we wished to travel.

We had not retired down the river more than a half a mile, when we came to a place that seemed to me to be a good point to leave the river, and make our way out a little to the mouth of the stream, in the direction we wished to go. I suggested that we stop here a day or two to let the horses graze and rest, while some of us should go on foot and search out the prospect for a way through the timber, along the bench lands further back from the river.

Captain Applegate approved of this suggestion, at once, but some of the others objected. However, on taking a vote, it was approved by all except Lindsay Applegate and Jack Jones, who were so much dissatisfied as to threaten that they would abandon the enterprise altogether, and return home.

We found a good place to camp, and after having pitched our camp and turned our stock out to graze, four of us started out in the direction we wished to go, keeping back on the terraces, or benches, at a considerable distance from the river. Some six or eight miles from camp we came to a high butte, or peak, rising clear above the timber line of the mountains. We went to the top of it, from which we could see out beyond the forest, into the open country. From the camp to this point we found good ground for a road, and as far as we could see further on, the prospect was very flattering.[65]

We returned to camp in glowing spirits, and reported our discoveries. The following day we moved on through the timber, and at noon found ourselves on the Klamath River, above the canyon that had given us so much trouble and concern, and eight miles below where it runs out of the Lower, or Little Klamath Lake. We went up the river nearly to the lake, where we crossed it, and camped for the night.

We were now on the east side of the Cascade Mountains, but there was not one of us who had the slightest suspicion that we had accomplished

---

65   This incident was not included in the Applegates's two published reminiscences. The description of the butte suggests they climbed Parker Mountain, named after Applegate's brother-in-law, William Parker.

so much. We were now in an open country and could keep our course without difficulty. We were compelled to bear a little to the south to get around the south end of the lake, on the east side of which we camped for the night.[66]

From this camp we traveled in a northeasterly direction, till we struck Tule Lake, where we found a great many wild Indians. As we came down from the hills towards the lake, we saw them running in every direction, in the most frantic confusion. Some hid in the tall grass, some ran into the tules along the lake shore, and some crowded into the canoes and shoved out into the lake.

We rode up to one of the wigwams, where there was a very old squaw, who seemed to be the only person left in the village. Frenzied with despair, she came running towards us, with a stick of dried fish in her hand, presenting them to us as an offering of peace and hospitality, at the same time shaking and trembling as though she were dying with fright.

We took her offering, examined it, returned it to her, and then rode away, in a northerly direction along the margin of the lake, leaving her rooted to the spot with terror and amazement.

A short distance from here, we saw two Indians, one on horseback, and the other on foot leading a pack-horse, coming directly meeting us. They paused a moment when they first saw us. Then they came on a short distance, where they paused again, took another look at us, dashed off their packs, mounted their ponies, and leaving the trail, fled at their utmost speed through the tall grass, as far as we could see them. We went to the packs they had left, which we found to be roots and seeds, such as they use for food. We left their property as we found it, and continued our course around the lake.

In a little while after the fugitives had disappeared from our sight, we saw a dense signal smoke arise, in the quarter where they had vanished.

---

66   Lower Klamath Lake.

∾

CHAPTER X

Finding a Way to the Humboldt River

As soon as the two Indians, who had thrown away their packs and fled from us, had raised their smoke, we saw similar responsive signals curling up from the hills in every direction all around us. And, by this means, the Klamath and Modoc Indians throughout all the vast extent of their territories knew, as well, that strangers and, perhaps, formidable foes were in their midst, as civilized people learn a similar fact by telegraph.

By the color of the smoke, which could be changed and varied in several ways, and by its intermissions and renewals and many variations in the management of its appearance, a multitude of facts could be communicated and directions and orders given to the scattered members of the tribe.

The several tribes of this part of the country were almost constantly at war with each other and each tribe or confederation of tribes had a system of signals made by smoke in the daytime and fire at night by which any warlike intelligence could be almost instantly telegraphed all over the country.

We continued on our way, bearing more easterly around the lake, till we came to a deep, narrow river with steep banks and with scarcely any perceptible current which emptied into the lake.

As we traveled up this stream in search of a place to cross it, we came suddenly upon a family of Indians, taking them so completely by surprise that they seemed to be rooted to the spot with amazement and so paralyzed with fear that they did not attempt to fly although they were on the opposite side of the river which was not more than half a bow-shot in width and entirely destitute of timber or bushes in which they could hide from us. We were so close to them before they saw us that they were afraid to run. But pretty soon the *paterfamilias* came towards us making every sign of peace and friendship he knew. We gave him to understand by signs that we wished to cross the river. He showed us immediately that, by going up the stream some distance, we would find a place where we could cross it, measuring the depth of the ford on his ankle.

By gestures we signified to him our thanks and, on proceeding up the river about a mile, were gratified to find his information correct. There was a ledge of volcanic rock crossing the stream at right angles over which it poured in a beautiful waterfall for about eight feet, perpendicularly down, onto another steppe of the ledge which formed a smooth, flat roadway across the river, over which the water rippled, swift and clear, about six inches deep.

At the lower edge of this roadway which was, perhaps, not over one hundred feet wide, the current seemed to cease and the river to suddenly assume an unfathomable depth with scarcely any perceptible current in all its course to its entrance into the lake below.

This was the finest natural crossing I ever saw on any stream anywhere. But I have heard that about twenty years after we discovered this ford, the steppe, on which we passed the stream, and which was the crossing place of the emigrants afterwards, disappeared, supposed to have been shaken down into the abyss below by volcanic violence.

We crossed the river on this natural bridge and turned our horses out to rest and graze while we ate our noonday lunch.[67] There was an extensive level plain lying before us in the direction we desired to go. We could see a green looking spot at the foot of the hills on the farther side of this sandy, sage-plain which we supposed to be rendered verdant by grass and willows which we thought indicated plenty of water and a good place to camp. We discussed the matter thoroughly and all agreed that this green patch should be our next camping place. We did not suppose it to be more than five or six miles away and were in no hurry to start. So, we let our horses feed till pretty well along in the afternoon when we packed up and started for our selected camping place.

---

67   This natural bridge allowed the explorers and, later, the emigrants' wagons to cross the Lost River south of Merrill, east of Klamath Falls. The rock is now the foundation of the Bureau of Reclamation's Anderson-Rose Diversion Dam. There is a monument to the explorers of 1846 at the dam.

But we found on traveling over the plain towards it that we had mistaken the distance and that it was fully ten miles or more from where we had crossed Lost River on the rock bridge and it was after dark when we reached it.

We found the place to be a grove of juniper trees growing on a dry, sandy tract of land without so much as a suggestion of water anywhere in the neighborhood of it. This was a sore disappointment to us after having toiled so far over the dry, hot sand during the afternoon.

We could not think of camping here on this dry, barren sand, so we turned to the south along the foot of the hills and, after traveling three or four miles further, were compelled to camp in a dry gulch without having found a drop of water. Many of the men inconsiderately vented their disappointment in bitter curses and complaints against the Captain for leading us into such a place.

These evergreen junipers were a species of tree none of us had ever seen before. They grow from twenty to thirty feet high on barren sand ridges where scarcely anything else, unless it be cactus, will grow. Their umbrageous tops very much resemble the foliage of the red alder and are formed by a dense cluster of limbs at the top of the naked trunk. These green tree tops had deceived us all alike.[68]

The rest of us were just as much responsible for the mistake as Captain Applegate, nevertheless, some of the men continued to grumble and complain and mutter against him.

We started very early the next morning and, after having traveled about two miles, came to an excellent spring of water where we got breakfast and let our hungry horses graze till about ten o'clock.[69]

The men seemed to have all regained their wonted good humor and fine spirits except the Captain. He had suffered such unjust and unreasonable complaint that it made a deep and gloomy impression upon him. After breakfast, he said to us, "Now, boys, I want you to choose another

---

68   This was their first experience of a juniper tree. As they learned, the presence of a
      juniper tree means there is not likely to be any water on the surface nearby since
      it is capable of existing in very dry circumstances and keeps virtually all other
      vegetation except sage from growing within its range.
69   The distances and description suggest that they found what is now called Bull
      Spring, east of Tulelake, California.

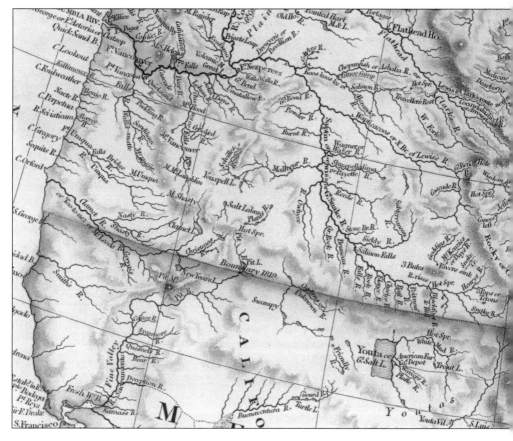

Detail of John Arrowsmith's 1844 Map of British North America based on information provided by explorers of the Hudson's Bay Company.

"Pit L." became "Goose Lake" and the river labeled "Swampy" or "Ogdens or Unknown" became "Mary's" and then "Humboldt." "New Years L." became Clear Lake. "Pit Mt." became Mount Shasta. "Mt. Shasty" became Mount McLoughlin.

Scott believed Ogden had mistaken Sprague River for the Swampy or Ogden's river, but Arrowsmith's map has "Christmas" River in about the correct place for Sprague River.

This published map should approximate the manuscript map provided by Ogden to Jesse Applegate before the South Road Exploring Party began its journey in June 1846.

From David Rumsey Collection, accessed August 6, 2015: www.davidrumsey.com/luna/servlet/detail/RUMSEY~8~1~2755~260040.

leader if you wish to have any leader at all, for I will have nothing more to do with the control of this crowd."[70]

The men, as if they were astonished that he had taken any notice of their unreasonable murmurings, insisted that he should continue in the command of the company. But he would not consent to it. At length, I proposed to him that he should choose two men from the company as his aides and counselors or staff and continue as Captain, himself, with them to share the responsibility.

He consented to this settlement of the difficulty and chose David Goff and myself as his counselors. This seemed to give entire satisfaction to all and everything went on smoothly, as before.

We had lost the route traveled by Ogden when he made his map which was now of no use to us but we did the best we could without any map or guide.[71]

From here we went in an easterly direction around the south side of the mountains where our way was pretty level but very rocky. Its rocky nature increased until at length we struck a sort of lava-bed, or pavement of rock, when we turned obliquely to the south for a few miles over better ground and camped at a magnificent spring of fresh cold water which we called Goff's Spring, in honor of the newly elected Lieutenant of the company.[72]

---

70 This incident was not included in the Applegates's two published reminiscences. Perhaps this event and speech were what Jesse Applegate had in mind when he recounted for Bancroft a conversation with British Lt. William Peel. Lt. Peel was astonished that the United States government had allowed unescorted citizens to conduct themselves across the continent, saying, "the Government should at least have sent an officer to command each party." Applegate recalled replying, "I told him he was somewhat mistaken in the character of the people—they were probably brave enough, but could never submit to discipline as soldiers. If the President himself had started across the plains to command a company, the first time he should choose a bad camp or in any other way offend them, they would turn him out and elect some one among themselves who would suit them better." Jesse Applegate, "Views of Oregon History, 1878," Bancroft Library, Mss P-A 2, microfilm, 14-15. Applegate was unsure of the date he met Lt. Peel, but it was 1845. Dorothy Morrison, *Outpost: John McLoughlin and the Far Northwest* (Portland, OR: Oregon Historical Society Press, 1999), 417.

71 Scott was precisely correct in locating this area as the place where they left Ogden's paths as Ogden could have mapped it for them. *See*, Jeff LaLande, *First Over the Siskiyous* (Portland, OR: Oregon Historical Society Press, 1987), 111-20.

72 Goff's Spring was later renamed Pothole Spring.

Goff's, now Pothole, Spring. The photo shows a marker placed by Trails West over the grave marker of Lloyd Dean Shook, 1851. *Photo courtesy Stafford Hazelett.*

I will here take occasion to remark that David Goff was a man of excellent spirit and temper, with sound judgment, and in whom we all reposed the utmost confidence. Much of the success of our enterprise may justly be attributed to his good sense and wise suggestions.[73] He was the father-in-law of Gen. J. W. Nesmith who served Oregon with so much credit as her Senator at Washington City during the Civil War.

On leaving Goff's Spring, we traveled in an easterly direction until we came to a *coulee*, or bed of a small river, with well defined and, in some places, precipitous banks, but there was no water in it except here and there a hole, or pit, and there were larger round clumps of willows growing along in the middle of the *coulee*. It seemed that the water had not run in this channel for a long time. It appeared to be an abandoned river bed. But the puzzle is where do the waters now run that once flowed here?[74]

---

73   Harriett K. McArthur (Nesmith), "David Goff," in DAR, *Polk County Pioneer Sketches*, 1:65-67.

74   Scott described the bed of Fletcher Creek with excellent precision. Water is present only sporadically. Pringle called it "Pool Creek."

As we were passing around one of the patches of willows growing in the *coulee*, we suddenly, and unexpectedly to both sides, met an Indian. We were within a few steps of him before he was aware of our presence. He stood for a moment as if transfixed with horror. Then he ran to us, holding out at arms length and presenting to us a half grown ground-hog—all the time shuddering with fright. We took his ground-hog and, after looking at it, gave it back to him with a little piece of tobacco to quell his fears and made signs to him that he was at liberty to go. He started off slowly, looking back at every step as though he feared he would be shot down. The further he went, the faster he went, till he passed out of our sight on a dead run.

From here we crossed a very rocky, flat ridge with scattering pine trees growing upon it—some of which were very large and would make excellent timber. Then we came to an extensive flat with a large, shallow lake in it. We saw some wild geese and a great many goose quills on the beach and we called it Goose Lake, which name it still bears. This seems to be a place where the wild geese resort in large numbers, during the molting season.[75]

We passed around the south end of the lake to the east side of it and camped on a clear little branch running out of a large, cold spring a short distance above, down into the lake.

From here we traveled over broken ground for a few miles and then crossed a pine-covered ridge into another large flat, now known as Surprise Valley, where we camped on a small creek with plum bushes growing along its banks.

About thirty miles east of here we came to High Rock Canyon. This is one of the most remarkable places I ever was in. After crossing a wide sage plain from Surprise Valley, we came to the head of a small branch with a few little alders and quaking asp bushes growing along it. We go down this creek, which sinks in the sand a little way from its source, but the gorge deepens as we advance till we find ourselves in a deep canyon about one-hundred yards wide, almost as level as a pavement, and strewn with the skulls and immense horns of the mountain sheep, along

---

75   McArthur, *Oregon Geographic Names*, 413, does not give a source for the name. Scott's story and Jesse Applegate's letter have been submitted for the next edition. Jesse Applegate [Z], "Road to Oregon, No. 3," *Oregon Spectator*, March 18, 1847, 2, col. 1.

High Rock Canyon, looking north along the wagon road entrance. *Photo courtesy Stafford Hazelett.*

the dry bed of a small branch winding through it, which must be filled with water at times—perhaps when the snows melt in the spring. A perpendicular wall of lava rises up on either side two or three hundred feet high. We traveled some ten or twelve miles through this wonderful place which seemed like passing through the street of some dead and silent city—silent, except when its massive walls would send the echo of some sound made by the passing travelers reverberating from side to side and diminishing in force till it seemed to lose itself in the clouds. The walls on either side seemed like the plastered walls of buildings and abandoned fortifications.[76]

When we emerged from the east end of this canyon, we passed over some low, broken hills for a few miles to a flat, with a small brook of

---

76   Scott's description of Upper High Rock Canyon and High Rock Canyon suggests there is one long continuous canyon. There is a separating sage plain between them of approximately four miles. Upper High Rock Canyon is very narrow and the cliffs appear to be volcanic. High Rock Canyon is not so narrow and the cliff walls are higher and more like the "walls of buildings and abandoned fortifications."

Black Rock Desert, looking south as Levi Scott would have approached the Black Rock and Black Rock Spring in 1846, 1847, and 1849. *Photo courtesy Stafford Hazelett.*

good, clear water running through it towards the south for a short distance when it disappeared in the sand, at the edge of an extensive sage plain. Here we were compelled to bear more towards the south than we had been traveling for some time, in order to get around the spur of a mountain.[77]

In about twenty miles, we came to Black Rock which is a high point or mountain spur of black scoria from the base of which gushes an immense spring of boiling water running off in a large brook bordered with coarse wire-grass growing about two feet, or more, high. The black slag and pyrites of its peak were, in some places, so hot that a person could scarcely stand upon them and, on being rolled down the steep side of the mountain, they would strike each other with a metallic ring like pot shurds.

---

77   They came out of the canyon country into the area now known as Mud Meadows at the north extremity of the north arm of the Black Rock Desert.

We had been, now, for two weeks, expecting every day to find a stream laid down on Ogden's map as Mary's River but still we did not reach it. I am satisfied from later explorations made by me that Ogden passed much further north, around the north end of the Big Klamath Lake, and struck Sprague River which he laid down correctly on his map but called it "Mary's River."

This stream, Sprague River, empties into the Big Klamath Lake. It runs in the same general course as the stream laid down on Ogden's map and is the only stream in all this region of country which answers to his description. We mistook the Humboldt for this river when we afterwards struck it.[78]

We all thought the river we were in search of was still south of us. We wished to go east but, if we could strike this river as laid down on the map, we could go east by traveling along its banks with better camping places where there was plenty of grass and water. This would be preferable to traveling over the extensive desert lying all around us and stretching away to the east of Black Rock as far as we could see. I think this was an exceptionally dry season—a drought, in this dry and barren country.[79]

We were afraid we should suffer for water and were at a loss which way we ought to go from Black Rock, so we took a vote of the whole company on this question. Captain Applegate did not vote, but, when we voted to go south, he was not satisfied with the decision and requested that he be permitted to take all the men who would volunteer to accompany him and go southeast towards what appeared to be a gap in the

---

78 Scott was mistaken about the river shown on Ogden's map as he remembered it forty-some years later. Arrowsmith's maps of 1837 and 1844, based on Hudson's Bay Company reports, showed the Humboldt River in a fair approximation of its relationship to the other known features of the area: the Klamath Lakes basin on the west and Ogden's river between it and Great Salt Lake to the east. Sprague River flows west for about 60 miles across central Klamath County into the Williamson River just before it flows into Agency Lake. See reproduction of Arrowsmith map (p. 80).

79 While precipitation varies by season in the Black Rock Desert area, experience over the last one hundred fifty years has shown that summer seasons do not offer sufficient quantity of retained moisture to produce vegetation of any consequence. Scott's expectations of finding good water, wood, and vegetation along the Humboldt River were also based on his past experience, and the valley of the Humboldt was, and remains, more barren for more of its length than almost any river of similar size. A comparison of the diaries of emigrants to California on the Lassen and Nobles trails for any year will reveal the true nature of the area.

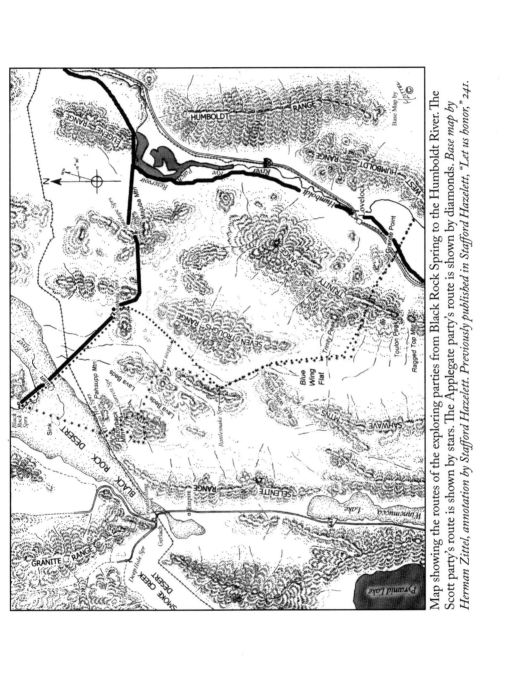

Map showing the routes of the exploring parties from Black Rock Spring to the Humboldt River. The Scott party's route is shown by stars. The Applegate party's route is shown by diamonds. Base map by Herman Zittel, annotation by Stafford Hazelett. Previously published in Stafford Hazelett, "Let us honor," 241.

mountains in that direction and, when we should find the river for which we had been searching so long, we would meet again on its banks.[80]

We all agreed to this, and five men,—Lindsay Applegate, Bob Smith, John Bogus, Wm. Sportsman, and Black Harris,—volunteered to go with him.[81] David Goff, B. F. Burch, W. G. Parker, John Owens, Bennett Osborn, S. H. Goodhue, Jack Jones, John M. Scott, and myself, resolved to go south.

We now separated, six of them and nine of us. We traveled south for about twelve miles over a dry, level plain covered with volcanic ash, which had apparently at some time been the bottom of a vast lake, till we came to the hills which seemed to surround the desert.[82] Here we found a little water, which was not good but we could use it, and we stopped here for our midday lunch.

In the afternoon we continued on south between the high mountains and over low, barren, sandy hills. After having traveled six or seven miles, we stopped and, leaving two men with our pack animals, all the rest of us scattered out along the foot of the mountains in search of water and a place to pitch our camp.

B. F. Burch, Jack Jones, and myself were not very far apart when we came into a flat hollow, or gulch, in the mountain side where we saw before us a green bunch of low willows. We all three started towards these willows and, when we were about a hundred yards below them, had approached each other near enough to begin to talk in a loud tone. As soon as we commenced talking, an Indian rose up from behind the willows and looked at us for a moment. Then he turned and ran up the mountain side as fast as he could. We called to him and tried to prevail on him to stop, but the more we called, the faster he ran until he disappeared from our sight.

---

80 A fuller explanation of the four days of this exploration and the routes traveled can be found in Stafford Hazelett, "'Let us honor those to whom honor is due': The Discovery of the Final Link in Southern Route to Oregon," *Oregon Historical Quarterly* 111, no. 2 (June 2010): 220-48.

81 The 1877 Applegate reminiscence reported seven men in their party and identified only the two Applegates and Robert Smith as members of the party. Lindsay Applegate, "Notes and Reminiscences," 31-35.

82 These suspicions of Collins were borne out years later with the discovery that the Black Rock Desert was a portion of prehistoric Lake Lahontan. Scott's party had arrived at Trego Springs by his direction, distance, and description. Hazelett, "Let us honor," 230, 235.

We went to the place from which he ran where we found an excellent spring of good, cool, fresh water. There we found a small fire of willow sticks and, nearby it, the skin of a badger spread out upon the ground with the flesh of the animal, all neatly stripped from the bones, lying upon it while the bones were arranged around the fire roasting.

We went back to where we had left the pack horses when we all soon got together again. We went to the spring and camped for the night. This was an excellent camp both for ourselves and our animals.

We did not molest the poor, frightened Indian's property but left everything just as we found it. He might have remained and enjoyed his badger feast and our company in perfect safety if he had only known it.

The next morning before we started from this camp, Parker and myself went up on a high ridge of granite—the only mass of hard granite rock I had noticed since we started on this journey. The best route for us to travel seemed to lie to the southeast from here, which course we took. Far away to the west was a vast, level plain which seemed to have a lake in the midst of it, but the distance was so great that we could not be sure of it. We could not determine whether there was a mountain on the west side of it or not.

We were compelled to turn more and more to the east as we proceeded on our journey to keep between the mountains which did not seem to rise in ranges, as usual, but to be scattered in promiscuous heaps and piles all over the country.

After having traveled about twelve miles, we came to a small branch, or stream, of spring water where we camped. We seemed to be in the midst of a vast, sandy desert, without the least indication of water in any direction except in the stream on which we had camped and which sinks in the sands of the desert but a little way from the hills.[83]

So, the next morning we fortified ourselves for a day in the desert without water by breakfasting on bread, coffee, and water without eating any bacon. As we had no vessel in which we could carry water, we were compelled to start without any and to do without it after leaving this brook until we should reach water again. The outlook was not at all promising that we should be able to reach water, again, in one day. Our course lay to the south across a vast sandy desert and this proved to be

---

83   Rattlesnake Spring. Hazelett, "Let us honor," 237-38.

as hot a day as I ever experienced in my life. The sand was so hot that it would almost blister a man's feet through his shoes.

We traveled on till about three o'clock in the afternoon without any indication of water anywhere when we struck the tracks of some Indians. Where they had walked through the sand, their tracks were as distinct as if there had been snow on the ground. They appeared to be fresh, as if the Indians had just passed, but, in this dry desert, they may have shown as freshly if they had been made a month or more before. We supposed that these tracks would certainly lead us to water and we resolved at once to follow them.

The Indian tracks led us in an easterly direction, the way we really wished to go, and directly towards a gulch in the side of the mountain where we confidently expected to find water.[84] But to our unutterable disappointment on reaching this gorge, we found it as dry as any part of the desert we had traversed.

The Indians had scraped out a basin in the sand and had lain there, I suppose, during the night, for the impressions of their bodies were perfectly distinct in the sand and reminded me of a wild-hogs bed. From here they had crossed the mountain. We could only track them a short distance up the mountain side, it was too rocky, dry, and hard for them to leave any very distinct impression of their footsteps. But we could see, here and there, traces of an old foot path all the way over the mountain.

We reached the summit of the mountain just a little before sunset. The sun was shining brightly on the vast level plain to the east and in front of us. There, to our great joy, we could plainly see unmistakable indications of an abundance of grass and water. But, it was so far away that we could not hope to reach it till long after dark.[85] We were suffering intensely from heat and thirst and our animals were ready to sink down from the fatigue of their toils through the hot sand and upon the hot, steep mountain for so long a time without water or food.

---

84   They had been traveling south in Granite Springs Valley when they saw the tracks. There is a gorge in the west side of the Trinity Mountains which looks like the sort of place that ought to have a spring and which generally has green vegetation. There is a historic spring and well at the head of the gorge, but there is no water at the surface in the summer months. The view from the valley floor does reveal a pass at the top of the range. Hazelett, "Let us honor," 237-42.

85   Scott and the party were standing at the top of the pass in the Trinity Range between Toulon and Trinity Mountains. Hazelett, "Let us honor," 242.

View from the top of the pass in the Trinity Range between Toulon and Trinity Mountains. Scott and his party crossed at this place and saw this view in July 1846, and the Applegate party followed Scott's tracks and crossed over the next day. *Photo courtesy Stafford Hazelett.*

We rejoiced in sight of deliverance. At a glance, it seemed so near! But when we looked more closely over the weary stretch of intervening desert, it seemed so far away! Our throats were dry and our tongues were thick, but the end was a green spot on the horizon.

We selected two of the best horses we had and sent Jack Jones and John Scott forward who were to travel in the direction of the apparent watering place as rapidly as their animals could advance, while we should follow with the others at a slower pace till it became dark, when they were to make a light by burning greasewood, which is a stiff, prickly, vining plant which grows in abundance in some places on these deserts and that burns with a quick, oily flash, for us to steer our course by.

But, by the time they reached the foot of the mountain, it was dark and, having reflected on the risks they were running of falling into trouble with the Indians in the night, they did not enter upon the journey across the plain but halted at the base of the mountain till we came up with them.

We all concluded that there might be danger ahead if we attempted to reach that green spot in the night, for we might ride into the midst of an Indian camp in the darkness on reaching the water; so, we stopped near the foot of the mountain, unpacked our animals, tied them to the largest and strongest sage bushes we could find, spread our blankets on the ground, and lay down to rest, if possible, until the morning sun should light us on to deliverance.

Both men and horses were suffering intensely. We had neither eaten nor drunk anything since early in the morning, but we did not suffer so much for want of food, it was water! Water! Water! We would have given the world for water! But, after we had lain still for a while in the shadows of the night, our blood cooled a little and its hot, rushing current quieted down till we began to feel more comfortable, and, finally, fell asleep, to dream of floating and bathing in a broad clear river of pure, cool water from which we could not drink although we plunged deep into its waves and struggled to take in the waters that would never rise quite to our lips and a draught of empty air was all that we could get.

Whoever has marched all day and slept all night without water in a hot sandy desert during the dog-days will understand our situation and our dreams better than we can describe them with a pen.

Jack Jones had two loose horses, one of which he would not tie up, but insisted that it would not leave the other horses and, if it were allowed to be at large, might be able to find a few bunches of dry grass or browse a little from the greasewood, and, so, out of compassion, he let it go loose. We all told Jack that his horse would be gone in the morning, that a horse could smell water at a long distance, and he would be sure to go to it. Sure enough, in the morning, this horse was gone and Jones started on his track to follow him up.

The rest of us took our course for the supposed water. It was cool now and we moved on cheerfully, for a little while, till we came into a broad, level plain, part of which was evidently, at intervals, inundated with water and bore a luxuriant growth of vegetation.

The floods had washed the sand and loam over the wide flat till it had filled and raised from one to three inches deep all over the level land. The decayed vegetable matter, mixed with this sediment, formed a sort of peat. The drought had been so great this year that it had dried out and was now on fire. Where the fire had passed, it had left a mass of loose sand and ashes and we found our way very much like traveling through snow, only it was dry and hot, and in places the fire could be seen and here and there little columns of smoke were seen rising out of the ground.

About seven o'clock in the morning, near the middle of July 1846, we reached the Humboldt River. It was a very deep, sluggish stream where we struck it, perhaps eight feet wide, with perpendicular banks, and so full that we could lie down and drink out of it and our horses could drink from the top of the bank. A mule stepped off into the water and went down out of sight. The river was so deep and the banks so abrupt that he could not get out till we threw a lasso over his head and drew him out. He would most likely have drowned without help.

This was evidently the low water channel, for at a high stage of water the river must have been fully ten miles wide at this place. We struck the river but a short distance above the Lake or Sink. This river has no outlet to the sea but runs into a lake and sinks like Bear River at Great Salt Lake. Ten or twelve miles above here, we found the river standing in holes and pools in some places, and, in others, running over the gravel in a very shallow stream.

There was not a stick of wood in sight, not even a willow nor a piece of driftwood. So we could get no fuel, but there was plenty of excellent grass for our animals on a low flat, or bottom, near the river. There was a great deal of green flag and tule along the margin. This was the green we had seen from the top of the mountain the evening before which gave us the welcome assurance that we were approaching water again.

We had plenty of bread baked and raw bacon for our dinner, so it was not really necessary that we should have a fire and the absence of fuel gave us but little inconvenience. We only remained here long enough to enjoy the luxury of a bountiful supply of water and to allow our weary, hungry animals to rest a little and fill themselves with the rich green grass.

But where was Jack Jones? Where was Captain Applegate and his party? We could not content ourselves to be still longer than we deemed absolutely necessary for the temporary refreshment of ourselves and horses.

CHAPTER XI

❧

The Final Link and Recruiting Emigrants

Captain Applegate and his party who separated from us at Black Rock traveled southeast about twenty miles when they came to a low gap in the mountains which surround the Black Rock desert where they found a little water in holes in the ground six or eight inches in diameter resembling the burrows, or dens, of the jack rabbit. The water stood in these holes several inches below the surface of the ground without any branch or discharging stream as is usual with springs. The water was not good and seeped in very slowly when it had been taken out as low as it could be reached by a horse or dipped out with a cup.[86]

These "Rabbit-Hole Springs," or "Jack Rabbit Springs," as they have since been called by different parties, were evidently kept open by wild animals which resorted to them to drink. There were five or six of these holes, close together, and, weak as they were, all together would afford water enough for a large number of animals provided they did not all take a notion to drink at the same time. But a half dozen men and twice as many horses that had toiled through the hot, ashy, sandy desert for twenty miles were a little more company than could be immediately supplied at these springs and they failed to get water enough for their horses.

Discouraged with the prospect here and in this direction, they turned southward in the hope of falling in with us. After passing over a high mountain and being nearly on the point of perishing from thirst, with their horses almost exhausted as they had not all had as much water as

---

86   Scott's description matches the Applegates' and other travelers' description of the place. J. Goldsborough Bruff saw it with dead cattle head-down in the water pits and made a famous drawing. Georgia Willis Read and Ruth Gaines, eds., *Gold Rush: The Journals, Drawings, and Other Papers of J. Goldsborough Bruff, Captain, Washington City and California Mining Association, April 2, 1849–July 20, 1851*, 2 vols. (New York: Columbia University Press, 1944); 1:332-33.

they could drink at any time since leaving Black Rock, they found a place where a weak little vein of water comes out of a crevice in the rock so slowly that it took a long time for themselves and their horses all to get a drink. It seeped out into a small basin, or depression, in the bed-rock where they could save every drop of it; otherwise, they could not have even secured a drink for the men.

They had made up their minds to camp here, but, before they had succeeded in watering their horses, they saw some Indians furtively watching them from the heights and, fearing an attack from them, they packed up after it became dark and started again upon their travels in order to elude the Indians and, if possible, to find our camp, going south as nearly as they could in the night.

About seven o'clock in the morning, on the third day after parting with us at Black Rock, they saw our camp from the summit of a high mountain just as we were leaving it. But we did not see them and they were too far away to give us any signal with fire-arms. They had a field-glass and could see us, who had none, farther than we could see them.[87]

They reached our camp at the little branch about ten o'clock in the forenoon, but we were gone out of sight or hearing of them. Having turned their weary animals out to graze, they cooked a hearty meal of fresh meat, which they had killed during the morning, and rested here till midday when they packed up again and followed our trail through the desert to the foot of the mountain where the Indians had slept in the sand.

Night overtook them here and they were compelled to camp without water, as we had done on the other side of the mountain. They could track us no further and could not tell which way we had gone, but they crossed the mountain the next morning very nearly on the same route we had taken. They crossed early in the morning while we crossed late in the evening. We had the sun at our backs and could see the green valley of the Humboldt in the distance before us, while they had the fierce rays of the morning sun shining directly in their faces and could see nothing. They were weary, thirsty, and disheartened, and could not decide which way they ought to go to get out of this terrible desert. They could not tell

87   Scott's report of the field glass was corroborated in the reminiscence of Elisha Applegate and the letter published by "One of the Road Hunters" in the *Oregon Spectator* dated April 15, 1847. Kendall, *Pacific Trail*, 138. The field glass was not mentioned by the Applegates in their 1877-78 published reminiscence.

whether we had gone to the east or to the south. They knew that we were trying to make our way south where we hoped to strike the river laid down on Ogden's map. But, the desert in that direction presented such a forbidding aspect that they could agree on nothing except the terrible conclusion that they must all perish. They could see no promise of deliverance in any direction.[88]

In a sort of aimless way, they wandered on down the eastern side of the mountain. There was not a tree nor a shrub to offer them the least shelter from the burning, blinding rays of the sun. There was nothing, anywhere, but a few precipitous points of jagged rocks here and there along the foot of the mountain to give them a particle of shade. They had lost our trail and could see no hope within the circle of the desolate, brassy horizon. All had given up that they must perish except Bogus and Sportsman, who, with unfaltering courage, cheered the others on as best they could, and encouraged them to make another resolute effort to extricate themselves from their perilous situation.

At last, Bob Smith concluded that he could go no further and lay down in the shadow of a great rock to die. His comrades tied his horse to the rock and left him.[89] Their lips were cracked and their tongues were swollen and they wandered away, apparently in a distracted condition, some going one way and some another.

After refreshing ourselves and our animals at the margin of the stream, we started up the river but soon found that where the peat of the river bottom had not been burned it was dried out and cracked open, till it presented a succession of fissures gaping about two feet wide at the surface of the ground and from six to eight feet deep, extending in every

---

88   The Applegates reported that the valley was filled with smoke when they crossed the mountain range. Applegate, "Notes and Reminiscences, etc.," 35. Edwin Bryant, diarist of the lead company packing across Hastings Cutoff, also commented on the smoke from the peat fires in the Humboldt drainage at that time: "August 13, The smoke in the valley continues very dense, and the coppery hue of the heavens increases—the atmosphere feeling as it looks, heated almost to blistering." *What I Saw in California* (New York: D. Appleton & Company, 1848; reprint, Lincoln: University of Nebraska Press, 1985), 203.

89   The Elisha Applegate version of the reminiscence told a very similar story of a man giving up, lying down in the shade of a rock, and the rest of the party continuing on, except the man left behind was Jesse Applegate, and Robert Smith was one of the rescuers. Kendall, *Pacific Trail Camp-Fires*, 138-39. There is no similar story in the 1877-78 Applegate reminiscence.

direction over the flat. These crevasses were but a few feet apart and rendered it most difficult and dangerous to travel with horses near the river. So we left the bottom and went back towards the mountains in search of a wagon trail which we had crossed in approaching the stream and to see if we could find any gap, or pass, through which wagons might be driven from this valley to Black Rock.

As we approached the mountains, we saw Bogus and Sportsman at some distance on the plain and directed our course towards them, supposing them to belong to a party of men from California. We did not expect to meet our friends in this direction nor at this time, but supposed they would strike the river some twenty or thirty miles further up where we expected to find them in a day or two, waiting for us.

They were not together and, when they saw us, both of them came to meet us and reported a man left in a dying condition, pointing to the place where he lay as nearly as they could.

Before leaving the river, Bennett Osborn had emptied a tea canister, filled it with water, and brought it with him. It was small and held but little. The two suffering men refused to touch a drop of it till Bob Smith should first have a drink.

Osborn went with them as fast as they could urge on their jaded horses to the relief of our suffering companion who had been left at the foot of the rock to die. But Bob Smith was too gritty to give up entirely as long as he was capable of making any exertion. After he had lain in the shade a little while and his blood began to cool a little, his strength came to him, again, and he arose to make another struggle for life. They met him and his suffering beast staggering on in another feeble effort to reach water. The contents of Osborn's can soon drove the mists from his eyes and sent the life-blood in a refreshed and refreshing current through his veins.

Jack Jones had followed the tracks of his lost horse to a spring of fresh water close by the emigrant trail to California a few miles from where we had bivouacked the night before, where he found the sagacious truant contentedly filling himself with the long, rank grass, and who greeted his master with a triumphant and happy neigh.[90]

---

90   The Applegates reported the spring "was almost as bad as one could imagine," corroborated by other diarists who passed through the area in later years.

About three miles from here, he fell in with some of the rest of the stragglers of Captain Applegate's party. He directed them to where they could find water and started to find the rest of the party, saying that, if it were necessary, when he found them he would kill one of his horses and refresh them with its blood and the water it had in its stomach. But we had succored the others before we met Jones. We were soon all together again at the spring where Jones had found his horse. And it was a very good camp for both water and grass.[91]

Captain Applegate and his party were a sadly dejected lot of men. We learned from them that Captain Applegate, himself, would have given up and lain down to die had it not been for Bogus and Sportsman who, by the most determined and heroic efforts, kept him and the rest of the men who were with them upon their horses and still struggling to find water.

After we all got together in camp, Captain Applegate went aside, by himself, and spread his blankets in the poor shadow of a large sage bush and lay there, wrapped in meditation for a long time. After a while, the Captain proposed to us that we ought to all get together and kneel down and give thanks to God for our deliverance. But there was not religious sentiment enough in that crowd of sun-browned men to second his motion. Some quietly smiled, while some openly ridiculed what they were pleased to look upon as a puerile proposition and only befitting women and priests, while two or three quietly looked grave and did not give expression to what they felt upon the subject.[92]

But the next morning the usual spirit and tone of cheerfulness was restored to our camp when we again took up our march. We traveled up the Humboldt about sixty miles in the direction we wished to go in the belief that we had struck the "Mary's River" of Ogden's map.

Our intention was to view out a road to Fort Hall. By the wagon tracks we found along the Humboldt and in the direction of the Fort we knew that we had struck the emigrant road to California. We knew that we were too far south for it to be the road heretofore traveled to Oregon and, when we had gone up the river for about sixty-miles, we

91 No diarists of the California overland emigration recorded such a place in that area along the Humboldt River.

92 These incidents among the men of the Applegate party from Rabbit Hole Springs to the Humboldt River as they followed the tracks of the Scott party were not included in the Applegates's reminiscences.

thought we had reached a good point to leave it and go west towards Black Rock.[93]

By this time we found ourselves getting short of provisions. We made a careful estimate of how much work it would require to open a road by this way to the Willamette Valley from the notes we had taken all along as we came out. We came to the conclusion that it would take at least thirty able and well appointed hands to open the road as fast as the wagons would travel. We agreed, too, that the emigrants must furnish these thirty men with sufficient provisions and tools to go ahead and prepare the way, otherwise, we would not aid nor advise any of them to attempt to reach the Willamette by this route at all.

I was appointed by a vote of our party to act as guide to the emigrants and to lead them through in case they should furnish the necessary force and equipment to open the road and we should finally determine to advise them to take this route. I accepted the appointment upon the condition that I might select a man to act with me as my assistant. This was agreed to and I chose Wm. G. Parker to be my aid.

Captain Applegate took our written estimate and with three men started for Fort Hall to get supplies for us to go home on and to interview the emigrants as to the thirty men with provisions and tools to open the road and to ascertain, as far as possible, whether it would be wise to advise the emigrants to take this new and untraveled route.[94] It was distinctly and emphatically understood that the Captain was to exhibit our estimate to the emigrants and, if they would comply with its requirements and furnish the force and supplies necessary to open the road, then he was to turn them this way, but, if they failed in these things, he was not to induce or advise any one to attempt this route but to advise them to continue upon the old road down the Snake and Columbia Rivers. And he was to procure a supply of provisions for our party at Fort Hall, and return to us and, if the emigrants could not open the road this season, we would return at once to our homes and see if some means could be devised for opening our new road the next summer.

---

93   The party camped at what became known as Lassens Meadows at the great bend of the Humboldt River about sixty miles above the Sink.

94   There were five men in the company according to the Applegates. Scott must have forgotten Bogus. None of the emigrants of 1846 saw the "written estimate" nor heard of it.

All of these requirements were not carefully complied with which caused a great deal of censure, much of which was not deserved by him, to fall upon the Captain's head afterwards. His sanguine temperament certainly led him to risk a little too much but most of the harsh abuse that was heaped upon him for turning the emigrants in this direction was unjust to him.[95]

After the Captain left us, Parker and myself started to view the route from the Humboldt to Black Rock.[96] We traveled about fifteen miles across the valley of the Humboldt and into the hills on very good ground for a road when we came to a spring on the hillside near the head of a dry, shallow ravine.[97]

About twenty-five miles further on we came to the "Rabbit-Holes," where we could look across the level stretch of twenty miles or more of ashy, sandy desert to Black Rock.

---

95   Scott refers to the failure of obtaining the required thirty men, with necessary equipment, before recruiting emigrants to follow the new route. Moses Harris and David Goff traveled separately from Applegate on this mission. They traveled west of Fort Hall and met wagon companies farther down the road to Oregon. According to the witnesses, Harris and Goff also made no effort to recruit road builders, only describing the ease of the new route without suggesting that any effort would be required of the emigrants themselves.

96   The published and well-known Applegate reminiscence of 1877 indicated that Jesse left the road-exploring party after Scott and Parker found the route between the Humboldt River and the Black Rock. Scott's original manuscript was very clear that Jesse left the party for Fort Hall before the final link was discovered between the great bend of the Humboldt River at Lassen's Meadows and the Black Rock by way of Rabbit Hole Springs. Scott's reminiscence is corroborated by Elisha Applegate's recollection of his father's story of the exploration. Kendall, *Pacific Trail Camp-Fires*, 141. The implication of this difference is much greater than it might at first appear. If the Applegate reminiscence of 1877 were correct, then the viable wagon route had been fully explored when the party of five men left to recruit people to try the new route. If Scott's and Elisha Applegate's reminiscences are correct, then Harris, Goff, and Applegate presented information to the emigrants that was dangerously false based on their own near-fatal experiences a few days earlier. Goff himself admitted that he had not seen the safe passage but claimed he relied on Applegate's assertion that there was one. J. Quinn Thornton, *Oregon and California in 1848*, 2 vols. (New York: Harper & Bros., 1949) 1:187. Applegate was so optimistic that he persuaded Captain Grant "to put those behind on the right track." Morgan, *Overland in 1846*, 2:637.

97   Scott described what has become known as Big Antelope Spring. There are three springs in close proximity.

We found the way very good for a wagon road, the principal embarrassment being the scarcity of water, for there was none between the Humboldt and Black Rock except the two springs I have mentioned, the distance being about sixty miles and the country a sandy, sage desert with, perhaps, half of the distance in the hills. These hills, though not very rough or steep, were very sandy and the road would have to be broken through the sage brush which is very laborious work for the teams and especially for the jaded oxen of the emigrants.[98]

We did not consider it worth our time to go across to Black Rock, so we camped for the night at the Rabbit Holes. Having accomplished our object more satisfactorily, and in much less time than we had even hoped to do it, we returned the next morning in the direction of our camp on the Humboldt where we had left the rest of the company with the horses and camp equipage to await our return.

As we approached the spring which we had discovered the day before, we saw an antelope feeding to the south of our trail about a quarter of a mile from the spring. Parker said he thought he could kill it. So, leaving his horse with me, he went down a little ravine that led him close to the spot where it was grazing and kept him well concealed till he came within easy gunshot of it. He fired from the ravine and knocked it dead in its tracks. By the time I came up with his horse, he had it almost butchered, when, each of us taking half of it on our horse, we went to the spring to get water for ourselves and our horses. I believe this place has ever since been called the Antelope Springs.[99]

This was an excellent, clear, bold, running spring with a branch about a foot wide and perhaps eighteen inches deep in which the water ran for about three or four hundred feet from the spring where it sank in the sand of the desert. Here we found an Indian *blind*, or *ambush*, constructed by them so as to conceal the hunter from his game when the animals came to the spring for water. They had filled and covered the branch,

---

98   Scott noted the poor condition of the draft animals after struggling down the Humboldt River valley and crossing from the river to the Black Rock Spring. The description of the condition of the stock of the Oregon emigrants of 1846 was not worse at this point in the journey than that of draft animals subjected to the haul along the Humboldt River in later years.

99   The 1877 Applegate reminiscence referred to it as Diamond Spring.

or channel which led off the waters from the spring, with sage brush so completely that nothing at all could drink from it, anywhere, except at the head where the spring issues from the ground, at which point they had left a space from a foot to a foot-and-a-half in diameter where access to the water was easy. About ten or twelve feet from the spring, they had dug out a pit in the sand from six to eight feet square and eighteen to twenty inches deep which they had first covered with willow poles, which must have been brought hither from a distance since there was nothing of the kind to be found nearer than the Humboldt River, which was at least fifteen miles away. This, again, they had covered with willow twigs and over these was spread a layer of earth so as to make it appear like the natural surface of the ground. There was an embrasure on the side next to the spring, about eight inches square, and at the opposite end from the spring they had left an opening through which a man, by lying down, might crawl into the pit. Here the poor, hungry Indian might lie concealed and shoot jack rabbits, badgers, birds, and, possibly, once in a while, an antelope as they came panting to the water brook.

After getting water for ourselves and our horses, we went on that night to the camp on the Humboldt. The boys had moved camp about half a mile further up the river from the place where we left them. So when we reached the old camp, we found it deserted. It was now ten or eleven o'clock in the night. We could see no trace of them in the darkness and could not tell whether they had been driven from the camp or had left it voluntarily. We conjectured the latter, as we felt confident that no force which the wild Digger Indians of this region would be likely to bring against us could have driven them from the camp. We fired a signal gun to which they responded with another almost instantly. So, in a short time, after having traveled about forty miles that day, we found ourselves safely back in camp again with our comrades a little before midnight.

The boys at camp had killed an antelope, which, with the one we brought in, added very materially to our rapidly diminishing stock of provisions, for we were nearly out of bacon and were getting very short of flour. Before we left the Humboldt, as we proceeded towards Fort Hall, we got so near out of meat that we boiled the last piece of bacon rind we had three times and made soup by thickening the broth with flour; the third time we boiled it we ate the piece of bacon skin with the soup, and then we were entirely out of even an apology for meat.[100]

We moved on slowly every day, resting and recruiting ourselves and our jaded animals as much as possible. After having advanced in this way about sixty miles, we were met by two of the men who had gone forward to Fort Hall for provisions and they were accompanied by fourteen emigrant wagons.[101]

Medders Vanderpool, who had previously been several years with the traders and trappers in the Rocky Mountains, was Captain of this company. Black Harris, who had known Vanderpool when he was in the mountains a few years before, heard that he was leading a company down Snake River, so he went down Goose Creek and met the company at the mouth of that stream.

Harris told them that they could drive right along into Oregon on this new route without any trouble at all. Having induced them to take the new route, he led them up Goose Creek till they struck the California Trail and met us.[102]

Having agreed to act as guide to the emigrants, I went to their camp and asked them if they understood the conditions upon which we had agreed to conduct them through on this route. They said they did not.

---

100 The 1877 Applegate reminiscence does not mention these extreme circumstances, nor any other incidents, after leaving the junction with the California Trail.

101 The two men would have been Moses Harris and David Goff. Sometime before meeting the first wagons, the remnant of the exploring party met diarist Edwin Bryant on August 9. Bryant, *What I Saw in California*, 195-97. Neither Scott nor the 1877 Applegate reminiscence mention the meeting with Bryant, though Elisha Applegate remembered that his father told him about meeting Bryant. Kendall, *Pacific Trail Camp-Fires*, 140. This was the same as Jesse Applegate's first full day at Fort Hall: "I arrived here yesterday alone and on foot from the Willamette valley at the head of a party to meet the emigration." Maude A. Rucker, *The Oregon Trail and Some of its Blazers* (New York: Walter Neale, 1930): 239.

102 Later, Harris and Goff vilified everyone who reported the representations used to induce them to take the new route and the conditions of the Southern Route as they traveled it. Moses Harris, "For the Oregon Spectator," *Oregon Spectator*, November 26, 1846, 3, col. 1-2; and David Goff [James W. Nesmith], "For the Oregon Spectator," *Oregon Spectator*, April 29, 1847, 4, col. 1-4. Goff's letter was actually written, and acknowledged, by James W. Nesmith, Goff's son-in-law. Stafford Hazelett, "'To The World!!' The Story Behind the Vitriol," *Oregon Historical Quarterly* 116, no. 2 (Summer 2015): 196-219.

I stated to them fully the terms we had agreed upon. They snuffed at this and made light of it. I told them it was impossible for them to get through without more help than was now at hand and, if no more assistance came, they must go back and take the old road or they would surely perish in the mountains during the winter.

Moved by my earnestness, they stopped till the next day when seven more wagons came up bringing a note to me from Captain Applegate in which he stated that he was confident of getting the requisite number of hands to open the road, that I had better go on with the wagons that had come to me, and in two days he would overtake us with the working party and the provisions.

Captain Applegate overtook us about the time he said he would but he only had five or six men with him instead of thirty.[103]

I was both astonished and gratified to meet my son, William, whom I had left in Iowa more than two years before, in the company the Captain had with him. They had met at Fort Hall and, hearing from Captain Applegate that myself and John were a little way back, he required no persuasion to induce him to join the company of road-workers.[104]

The emigrants heard of us and our recent discovery of a new road into the Willamette Valley as they arrived at Fort Hall and pretty much all of them turned in after us and continued to overtake us until, in a little while, we had seventy-five wagons with us. But, by several of our party of explorers falling in, we could only raise twelve men, all told, to open the

---

103 Scott remembered the number of men recruited from the emigration and equipped to build the road, which also matches the recollection of Truman Powers. *Emigrant of '46*, *Oregonian*, March 12, 1879. Lindsay Applegate remembered a party of twenty-one. "Notes and Reminiscences," 39-40. Joseph Burke wrote on October 17, 1846, that the party leaving for the Willamette Valley numbered twenty-four altogether but he did not name any and did not specify who was expected to work on opening the new road. Joseph Burke, "Letter to Sir William Hooker," in Morgan, *Overland in 1846*, 767.

104 William Scott wrote a letter dated August 14 at Fort Hall without mentioning Applegate. Oregon, August 14, 1846, Andre De Coppet Collection, Box 27, Folder 12, Manuscripts Division, Department of Rare Books and Special Collections, Princeton University Library; and Morgan, *Overland in 1846*, 638. William simply wrote a wrong date, because we know from Joseph Burke that the party left Fort Hall on August 11. Joseph Burke, "Letter to Sir William Hooker," in Morgan, *Overland in 1846*, 767.

road, and these were not well equipped with tools, and were but poorly supplied with provisions.[105]

I shuddered at the possible result of this rashness but we had started in, the column was pressing upon us from the rear, and we could do no better than to go forward and get through the best we could. I felt that the position of guide to the emigrants which had been thrust upon me was one of very trying importance and responsibility.

Those who had turned aside to follow us were the extreme rear of the emigration, and a large percentage of them had poor teams, and were more slothful and indolent men than those who had pressed forward and gone on down the Snake River before we could meet them.[106] We

---

105 In Scott's original manuscript, he recalled that only two or three men of the road exploring party joined the emigrants to make up a party of twelve road builders and one of those would have been his son, John. The road-clearing party actually numbered between twenty-one and twenty-four, but by the time the men crossed the Cascades, their number had been reduced to no more than thirteen workers counting all the explorers and the emigrants and including his two sons.

106 Scott was wrong. While the folks who followed Jesse Applegate were necessarily behind some wagon companies, they were, in fact, well ahead of the pace set by prior years' emigrations. Judge J. Quinn Thornton reached Fort Hall on August 7, almost a month before the date the Applegates reached Fort Hall in 1843. Thornton, *Oregon and California in 1848*, 1:160. James W. Nesmith kept a diary of the 1843 emigration and noted the Applegate company when they were near each other. Nesmith's party left the Applegate's behind on August 22 on Bear River and the Applegates had not caught up by September 1 when Nesmith left Fort Hall. James W. Nesmith, "Diary of the Emigration of 1843," *Quarterly of the Oregon Historical Society* 7, No. 4 (Dec. 1906): 348-50. The emigrants of 1846 who traveled with Scott drove farther and faster getting to the southern border of Oregon than the wagon companies following the traditional Oregon Trail did to reach Oregon City. Virgil Pringle's brother-in-law, Orus Brown, who was six days ahead of the Pringles and Tabitha Brown at Fort Hall, reached Barlow's Gate on September 28 and should have reached Oregon City, 715 miles from Fort Hall, a week later. Tabitha Brown, "A Brimfield Heroine: Tabitha Brown," in *Covered Wagon Women, Diaries and Letters from the Western Trails, 1840-1849*, ed. and comp. Kenneth L. Holmes, 11 vols. (Glendale, CA: Arthur H. Clark Co., 1983), 1:52; Fred Lockley, "Impressions and Observations of the Journal Man [Barlow Road]," *Oregon Journal*, August 28, 1928, 10, col. 6. Virgil Pringle and his family reached the Klamath River on October 3, having covered 736 miles from Fort Hall. Virgil Pringle, "Diary," Pacific University Archives, Forest Grove, OR; Oregon Historical Society Research Library, Mss Microfilm 1194; "Diary of Virgil K. Pringle, 1846," *OPAT* 48 [1920], (Portland, OR: Chausse-Prudhomme Co., 1923); reprint, in Morgan, *Overland in 1846*, 184. (The Pringle diary as reprinted in Morgan, *Overland in 1846*, is used for reference in the notes due to its greater availability.)

were frequently detained for an hour or two by some man being slow and careless about getting ready to start and it would not do to leave a family alone among the hostile Indians, who were very numerous and were watching us all the time.[107]

We were seldom more than half a mile from camp in the morning until it would be filled with Indians in search of whatever they could pick up. They were wild and shy, and it was not often we could get to see one of them, yet we frequently had damaging proof of their proximity. By carefully abstaining from any interference with their interests and keeping a close watch, a strong party could travel through their country with a reasonable degree of safety, although, they think it right to kill any one who is not a member of their tribe, and not only right but a distinguishing deed of heroism to slay a white man under almost any circumstances, and they would as soon kill a white man for his shirt as a deer for his skin. When they have the power, they believe in extermination, and slaughter men, women and children with the most unfeeling cruelty.

These Indians along the new route were barbarians of the most ignorant, bloody, and treacherous type. So we were compelled to stick together and keep a strong guard over our stock, and, yet, we scarcely ever saw an

---

The troubles that followed were closely related to the extra time and distance required to travel by the new, unopened route.

107 Whatever Scott may have thought about the character of the emigrants of 1846, he never lived nor traveled in company with so many people at any other time. They may have seemed quarrelsome and recalcitrant, but his description is a pretty fair summation of virtually every diary and reminiscence of large wagon companies, including those in 1843 and 1844, and Scott's. For example, *see* Scott's recollection of his 1843 migration on pages 20-21 herein. Whatever their qualities, all had been induced to join him because they were promised an easier, shorter, better route without any required effort to open the road. When they discovered they had been misled, and the men who misled them had "left us to the depredations of Indians, wild beasts, and to starvation," it was too late to return to the already opened and known safe route. Tabitha Brown, "A Brimfield Heroine," 52. When the work required to open the new road became apparent, their bitterness at being misled multiplied with their distresses. *See* MacKenzie K. L. Moore, "Making Place and Nation: Geographic Meaning and the Americanization of Oregon: 1834-1859," University of California (Berkeley), Fall 2012, 78-81, 83. "I will say here that such a journey has a tendency to destroy in nature much of its benevolence and sympathy for distress of all kinds, until we are almost devoid of those essential humane characteristics. Those who have never been through such ordeals may conclude this is not true, but it is true nevertheless." Tolbert Carter, "Pioneer Days," *OPAT* 34 (1906) (Portland, OR: Peaslee Bros. & Chausse, 1907), 79.

Indian. Some of us well knew that where there was the least sign of Indians, there was the most danger. But seeing no Indians made some of the men careless and negligent about guarding or taking care of their stock. And this bred dissatisfaction in our camp.

I had traveled with emigrants before and could make allowance for many things that an inexperienced person might not have been so patient with. These people had traveled together so long that they had learned each others foibles and frequently took delight in playing upon each others weaknesses; they sometimes quarreled and many of them held some petty grudge against nearly everybody else; they were, at least, disgusted with each other in many instances. They became reckless of wounding each others feelings; they would frequently speak out without due reflection; they gossiped about each other; and there was nearly always a wrangle of some kind in the camp.

All this was extremely disagreeable to me as it must have been even to many of the parties engaged in it. But I would not be understood to intimate that there were no exceptions. There were some as perfect ladies and gentlemen among the emigrants as I ever met with or could wish to meet anywhere. And I shall treasure the memory of their virtues and shall cherish their friendship as long as I live.

But, many circumstances conspired to make this the most difficult crowd to manage I ever got into. Although they usually treated me with becoming deference and respect, sometimes they would not follow my directions and suggestions which almost invariably resulted in some hindrance and embarrassment to the whole company.

I sometimes felt like I ought to kick myself for being so stupid as to board myself and work for nothing in all of these hazardous and laborious efforts to serve the interests of such an insolent and ungrateful crowd.

I was always very careful not to exaggerate anything or to make any effort to flatter any one. When we came to a difficult or dangerous place, they always found that I had not deceived them.[108] I never made a suggestion or gave a direction to them that I did not believe, after mature reflection, to be best for them and, after a while, they began to obey my

---

108 Applegate, Goff, and Harris had induced the emigrants to try the new road by representing that there were no such places and continued to insist afterwards that the factual reports of the emigrants themselves were untrue.

directions without talking back or questioning the wisdom or propriety of them.

Had it not been that they improved in this respect as we advanced and perils gathered more threateningly about us, I feel confident that the suffering would have been much greater than it was.

Now, since more than forty years have fled, I look back upon these perilous and gratuitous services to Oregon and its early pioneers with the most lively pleasure; indeed, with a satisfaction that is above all price.

CHAPTER XII

☙

Scott Leads the Emigrants into Southern Oregon

For three or four hundred miles our way lay through an open country which was comparatively level but much of it was rocky and of rather a barren and desert character. A great portion of it was covered with sage of which there are several different varieties, some growing but a few inches high, while some grow to a height of eight or ten feet. But that which mostly grew in our way and gave us the most trouble usually grows from a foot-and-a-half to three or four feet high and is very tough and stiff.

The road-workers, who had gone ahead of us, had not attempted to clear away the sage and we frequently had vast fields of it to drive over and to break down, day after day, through much of the open country. This was very hard on the teams, straining on the wagons, and rough on the people. One who has never had the experience can have but a poor idea of the difficulties and hardships of breaking a wagon road through a dense sage plain.[109]

On our way out, we had not marked out a wagon road but had only taken a careful view of the country sufficient to satisfy us that such a road could be made and the probable amount of cutting that must be done where the way would pass through the timber.

Captain Applegate had promised me, when he went forward and left me with the wagons, that he and his men would view and mark out the best route for me to follow by blazing in the timber, and marking with stakes and stones where there was no timber to blaze, so far as he could and, where he could not mark it out in any of these ways, the whole party were to travel over it in single file with all their animals and thus

---

109 Scott and Collins here mentioned the difficulties for the draft animals and equipment, in contrast to other statements suggesting the emigrants' stock was deficient. This strain was dismissed by those who were not with the emigrants in 1846, and overlooked and minimized by subsequent commentators.

make the way as plain as it was possible for them to make a trail. And he promised to leave written notes of instruction for my guidance wherever it would seem to be necessary and wherever it would aid me in following him, or in selecting the best way for the wagons, or in avoiding the perils of attack or annoyance from the Indians.

This, for the most part, he neglected to do, for which the most bitter anathemas were heaped upon him by the emigrants and which I do not think were justly deserved by him.[110] For, after leaving us, he and his party came to the conclusion that it would be best for him to go on into the settlements and stir up all the interest he could and get people to meet the emigrants with provisions and men to help open the road and assist them in reaching the settlements before the winter rains should set in. In accordance with this plan, he went forward, leaving the direction of the road-working party to another who did not, perhaps, take the necessary pains to carry out his instructions.[111]

The party of road-workers pushed on, doing but little to aid those behind them, till they came to the heavy timber on the Siskiyou Mountains when they blazed through it doing but little cutting where a great deal of work ought to have been done, most of which the emigrants were compelled to stop and do as they came to it.[112]

---

110   Compare Lucy Henderson Deady's recollection that "there was no road" and "We had been eight months on the road, instead of five, so we were out of food and our cattle were nearly worn out." Fred Lockley, "Impressions and Observations of the Journal Man [Lucy Henderson Deady]," *Oregon Journal*, January 25, 1923, 8, col. 6, and January 26, 1923, 8, col. 6. Jesse Applegate promised to mark and open the road and to leave directions. He performed neither. The emigrants lost time and effort doing what Applegate had promised them he would do. Applegate may not deserve all the blame for the failures of the advance crew, but he made the claims for the nonexistent road and promised to open the way, then blamed the emigrants for the time it took to find and make a road for themselves in the absence of evidence of his passing before them.

111   The assertion that Applegate went forward to get help to open the road and relieve the emigrants was contradicted by Moses Harris and by James Nesmith writing for David Goff. *Oregon Spectator*, November 26, 1846, and April 15, 1847. Truman Powers remembered that an Applegate was sent ahead out of the road-building party to get help and supplies. Emigrant of '46, "A Pioneer's Reminiscence," *Oregonian*, March 12, 1879. Rev. Garrison wrote: "Mr. Applegate left soon after turning that portion of the emigration that followed him, saying that he would send assistance from the Willamette to open the road which if he did I never knew it." "Forty-two Years in Oregon," 28.

112   David Goff's letter attributed the difficulty finding and making a road from the Klamath River to the valley of the Rogue to a fire. *Oregon Spectator*, April 15, 1847.

I found one note from Captain Applegate when we came near Goff's Spring at the first very difficult place we reached. This note was buried at the root of a large pine tree on which he had made a very large and conspicuous blaze and had written on it with a pencil directions where to find the note. These directions could not be understood by the Indians who probably regarded them as some potent *medicine* or *hoodoo* in connection with the white man's God which they would do well to avoid as much as possible. So the note was not found nor disturbed by them. This was the last note or word I had from the Captain till I reached the settlements the next winter.

So I had the unexpected and laborious task upon me of searching out in advance of the wagons the particular track to be pursued, which sometimes caused delay and imposed upon me, constantly, an immense amount of work. Indeed, my labors were more than doubled, especially since I had given up the valuable service and assistance of Mr. Parker, and, in consequence of the scarcity of road-workers, had consented for him to go forward with them. This left upon myself the whole burden of the duties which I had calculated would employ the constant and active services of us both.[113]

There were many natural landmarks that I remembered by which I could usually keep my course, but there were a multitude of obstacles to the convenient passage of wagons which had escaped my attention in first passing through the country which now met me *vis a vis*. I was compelled to look out for these things and to avoid them in the best way I could, which kept me constantly going and coming.

Some of the emigrants seemed to think me under obligations to furnish them a good, easy road, with plenty of grass and water all the way through.[114] These demands were extravagant and foolish, for they knew as well as I did that there was no road at all till we should make it. There were long stretches of unwatered desert, as had been explained to them, and we encountered one most serious embarrassment that we had not

---

113 Scott did not mention David Goff and apparently did not consider Goff of much service.

114 Scott was not present when Harris, Goff, and Applegate made these promises, but he heard about them from the emigrants. Applegate's letters published in 1847 describing the Southern Route carried the same descriptions. Applegate, "Road to Oregon No. 3,"; Jesse Applegate [Z], "Road to Oregon No. 4," *Oregon Spectator*, April 15, 1847, 1, col. 1-3. His private correspondence was similarly sanguine.

thought of. In many of the camping places the Indians had burned the grass before we reached them for the purpose of harassing us.[115] In fact, for a great portion of the way, we were passing through a savage and treacherous enemy's country and in a state of *quasi* siege by them much of the time.

Sometimes, a few of the most worthless and ungovernable persons in the company whispered among themselves about the justice and propriety of hanging me. But, as I was the only person in the crowd who knew where we were or the way to go anywhere else, they could not very well dispense with my services, and, as I never lied to them nor misrepresented anything in the least, I had the confidence and respect of the better class of people and so I got along without much open complaint. Indeed, I found the respect of the better and more intelligent class, for me, was constantly increasing as our difficulties and dangers thickened around us all along the way.[116]

One of our exploring party, John Owens, and his father had come to Oregon in 1844, or 1845, and John's mother was coming across the plains this year, 1846.[117] John went forward with Captain Applegate after we struck the Humboldt River and met his mother near Fort Hall. She had a light two horse carriage, or hack, and they thought they could come through with the road-working party. So, they went forward with that party and were in advance of the party of emigrant wagons which I was conducting as we traveled down the Humboldt. John Owens and another

115 Indians in southern and western Oregon burnt the grasses regularly as a form of game and vegetation management, which they had practiced for millennia. Robert Boyd, ed., *Indians, Fire, and the Land* (Corvallis: Oregon State University Press, 1999). *Also see* Samuel A. Clarke, "Pioneer Days, No. VIII," *Sunday Oregonian,* June 7, 1885, 2, col. 3; J. Henry Brown, "Settlement of the Willamette Valley," 2, BANC MSS P-A 8, Bancroft Library, Berkeley, California.

116 Rev. A. E. Garrison's reminiscence corroborates Scott's concern and the stated reason for his anticipation of surviving the trip. "Forty-two Years in Oregon," 28-29.

117 A "John Owens" was recorded by Sutter as having arrived at his place on July 10, 1845, as one of the men accompanying Clyman. Hasselstrom, ed., *Journal of a Mountain Man, James Clyman,* 197.

man came back and met us where we struck the Big Meadows about thirty miles above where we left this river.[118]

They said that the Indians had shot one of their horses and stolen another and they wanted a few men from our company to go with them to the Indian camp where those people were digging roots and gathering seeds, which they store away for food, about a mile and a half or two miles from the road, to see if their stolen horse could be recovered.

I told them that we did not wish to lay by nor make any delay, but that I would help them if the company would go on to their camp, about four miles further down the river, and I would take with me such men of our company as would volunteer to go with us.

Five of our men offered to go with me, so there were eight of us altogether, who started across the valley towards the Indians whom we saw on the opposite side of the river. After proceeding about a half mile, we came into a marshy tract of land covered with high tules where we unexpectedly came upon a party of squaws digging roots in the swampy ground. They ran and hid in the tules leaving a little child in the edge of a small open place which was not more than thirty or forty feet wide. A young man by the name of Thomas saw the child, which could not have been more than one or two years old, and cried out: "There is an Indian! Shoot him!"

But we could see that it was a mere child and passed on without molesting it. I called to Thomas not to shoot, that it was only a child.

We soon found we were getting into ground that was too marshy to ride over, so we turned further south, where we found better ground, and directed our course towards a body of about fifty Indians. Three of those Indians came running towards us and yelling at the top of their voices. One of them came directly towards us while the other two circled a little to one side as if they would flank us.

We moved on slowly till we came close enough to make signs to the one who was coming directly towards us when we stopped and beckoned him to come to us. He halted at the same time and all that we could

---

118 The name "Big Meadows" has generally been applied to the meadow along the Humboldt River at present-day Lovelock, Nevada, downstream from the turnoff to Oregon. The Scott-Collins description of the meeting location is thirty miles upriver of that turnoff, or somewhere around present-day Winnemucca, where there were also extensive meadows.

understand from him was the emphatically repeated sign that we should go away.

We stood still and, again, beckoned him to come to us. After some hesitation he came up in about thirty feet of us. Then, by signs, we tried to make him understand that we wanted the stolen horse. He would not recognize any of our signs but continued by his gesticulations to insist that we should leave. In response to every sign, suggestion, or movement on our part, he only continued to repeat his signs that we must go back and that we should by no means advance any further in the direction of their camp.

Some of the boys proposed to shoot him. I objected to the folly of so rash a course and told them that, in addition to its being a bloody and needless crime on our part, it would endanger the safety of other emigrants behind us even if it did not bring down immediate disaster with the merited vengeance of the Indians upon us.

Then, as we saw that our little party was not strong enough to fight them, I proposed that we go back to the wagons and report the situation and, if the company should think it advisable, they could send out a party strong enough to give them a sound thrashing.

We turned back. I told the men to ride off slowly for, if the Indians should get the impression that we were afraid of them and were running from them, they would be certain to follow us and attack us if they could overtake us.

Contrary to my advice, the men turned their horses and started back at a rapid pace except John Owens and myself, who remained behind with Dan Toole who was the only man of our party who had come out on foot. The rest of the men rode on a full run to the river. We called to them to stop. They replied that they would stop when they got to the river, which was about a mile away.

Toole then asked us to take him up behind one of us. Owens's mule refused to allow them both to ride him at the same time and I told Toole that my animal was not able to carry both of us but that Owens and I would stay with him, that we would cover his retreat, and not leave him under any circumstances. I told him to get on afoot as fast as he could walk and we would keep between him and the Indians.

The Indian we had been trying to treat with came running after us and soon began shooting arrows at us. Several of his arrows having missed us, struck in the ground before us.

By this time, about ten of the warriors came running towards us, shouting the war-hoop. We moved steadily on till we reached the Humboldt River where the other men had crossed and paused on the opposite bank. As soon as Toole came up with them, one of them took him on his horse behind him. Then one of them fired off his gun, when they all turned and started off again as fast as they could ride, leaving Owens and myself on the river bank.

The Indian who had been shooting at us was now within about a hundred yards of us and seemed to feel that he had put our whole party to flight. The other Indians were further away but running towards us as fast as they could, still yelling their war-hoop. We stopped and dismounted.

The Brave who was leading the Indians, and who seemed to feel that he was performing deeds of military strategy and valor before which such fields as Waterloo would pale to a mere skirmish, halted in his valorous and vigorous pursuit, perhaps to exhort and arrange his forces for the final struggle that was to settle all question of his greatness in the tribe forever. But he was dangerously close to us.

I said to Owens that, as that Indian had treacherously and without cause attacked us and tried to kill us, I thought we ought to return his fire.

"I should like to take a pop at him," said John, "but I am afraid I will miss him."

"Rest your rifle across my saddle," said I, "and I think you can hit him."

He did so and fired. I think he missed the Indian but he must have cut pretty close to him. The Indian began to jump, first to one side and then to the other, as fast as he could. Then, I pulled away at the Indian when he tumbled down and disappeared.

Whether I hit him or whether he dropped to hide himself in the grass when he found the bullets flying uncomfortably close to him, I could not tell. But we could not get sight of him again. The grass was very thick and high and completely concealed him.

By this time the rest of the Indians, who had not yet come as close to us as the one we had shot at, began to shoot their arrows at us, many of which stuck in the ground about us. Our guns were both empty so I told

Owens we would mount our horses and gallop away out of their reach and reload.

Just as I vaulted into the saddle an arrow struck me in the right groin and another struck my horse in the right thigh or muscle just above the hock joint. We rode off as fast as we could for about a quarter of a mile when we dismounted and loaded our rifles, the Indians still coming on, yelling after us. But they had not yet come up on the high flat or table land which we had reached. I told Owens that, if they should come up on this plain, we would charge upon them, which movement I felt confident would take them completely by surprise, and that we could put them to flight in this way, and fire on them with deadly effect as they fled.

But they stopped as soon as we mounted our horses and turned facing them. We then turned and rode leisurely away towards our company; the Indians turned back and did not attempt to pursue us further.

When we reached the wagons, we found that the men who had preceded us had reported that there were about five hundred Indians in pursuit of us and that they supposed Owens and I were killed.[119] The company was so paralyzed with this intelligence that they were standing in bewildered amazement, too much dismayed to make any preparation for defense.

I soon quieted their fears to a great extent by assuring them that we had not seen over fifty warriors and that I did not apprehend any danger of an attack from them. I assured them that my wound was not a dangerous one and I did not think it would give me any inconvenience besides making me a little lame for a while.

My horse recovered from his lameness in about a week and in a few days I suffered no further inconvenience from my wound.

The Indians gave us no more trouble but we never recovered the stolen horse. They would have certainly killed Dan Toole had not Owens and I covered his retreat.

Having left a written note giving an account of our trouble with the Indians attached to the top of a willow stick which we stuck in the ground by the side of the trail where the teamsters would be sure to find it, we proceeded on our way down the valley of the Humboldt.

---

119 This exaggerated estimate of an enemy is a common feature of war stories as well as the assumption, or hope, that the men who were abandoned in the field were killed. The legends of the West include many such stories.

When we reached the point we had fixed upon, we left the California Trail in the morning and camped that night at the Antelope Spring. We reached the Rabbit Holes late in the evening of the next day where we could not get a sufficient supply of water for our stock to warrant us in camping there and it was fully twenty miles, or more, to the hot springs at Black Rock. Our way lay across a level plain of sand and volcanic ashes which must necessarily be a heavy road for our suffering teams, and many of them must surely fall by the way if we attempted to cross with the hot sunbeams streaming down upon us, so we resolved to cross it that night.

We started at sunset and traveled directly towards the great black promontory until it became too dark for us to see it. But, as the stars came out, we took our relative bearings so as to be able to keep our course very closely all night.

The night was pleasantly cool compared with the day time when the scorching sun was blazing down upon the sand. And, after toiling incessantly, the foremost plodding ox-teams came through about daylight the

Black Rock Springs from the peak of the Black Rock. These springs and the meadow that surround them made the Black Rock Desert crossing viable. The Henderson child, Olive, was born here in 1846. *Photo courtesy Stafford Hazelett.*

next morning. But the last wagons in the train did not reach camp before ten o'clock in the forenoon.

By the carelessness of the stock-drivers, some of the loose cattle were allowed to squander away in the desert. Some of these came through to the camp in the course of the day and following night, but some of them were never seen again; they wandered further and further away into the desert and could not be found, although we lay here two days recruiting our teams and trying to recover the missing cattle.

While some of the emigrants were camped near Black Rock, some young ladies found a bottle of laudanum in a pocket attached to the bows of Robert Henderson's wagon and put the vial to their lips to test it in order to find out what it was. Mr. Henderson's little girl, about five or six years old, saw them do this and, when they were gone, got the bottle and proceeded to test it as she had seen them do. But the little child drank so much of the poison that in a short time afterwards she was found in a dying condition. Everything possible under the circumstances was done for her. But she died. And the heart-broken family was compelled to bury their little darling there in the lonely desert.[120]

Robert Henderson settled on the Yamhill River in the Willamette Valley. He had a large and interesting family, and became one of the wealthy farmers of the country. His eldest daughter, Lucy, who was a mere child when they crossed the plains, was afterwards married to Hon. M. P. Deady, who has filled the office of United States District Judge for the District of Oregon, I believe, ever since the admission of the State into the Union. He is the author of the excellent Codes of Civil and Criminal Procedure adopted by Oregon in 1862, and 1864. He is an able judge, and a distinguished man, and has, in various ways made a large figure in the history of Oregon, and especially in the history of its constitution, its legislation, and its jurisprudence.[121]

After leaving the springs near Black Rock, we had about twenty miles of heavy, sandy, sage desert to cross before reaching the next water. Then, after crossing a few miles of low hills, we entered the High Rock canyon. After passing through this remarkable place, which has already been

---

120 Lucy Henderson Deady, age eleven in 1846, related the story in her reminiscence, as well as the fact that her mother gave birth to a new sister, Olive, three days later at Black Rock Spring. Lockley, "Impressions and Observations," Jan. 24, 1923, 6, col. 7.

121 *See* biographies of Judge Matthew Deady in Corning, *Dictionary of Oregon History*, 70-71; and Engeman, *The Oregon Companion*, 114-15.

described, we had about three days hard travel through a broken—sometimes sandy, and sometimes rocky—sage-covered country with only here and there a spring to furnish water for so many people and their stock. At these oases in the desert the best grass was usually crisp and dry and yellow, and, in many places, had been burned off by the Indians, and the waters were dried up to the mere spring or fountain. Where the fires had been, and in many places where there had been no fire, our sole dependence for stock feed was the long, green, hard, round wire-grass, which is something like the tule, or the bulrush, only smaller and tougher. Growing in marshy places, it could not be burned. It is not very nutritious forage and stock will not eat it if they can get any other prairie or desert grass.

On the fourth day, we crossed a broad level plain which had the appearance of having recently been a great lake.[122] It was covered in places with a thick crust of soda, for miles having the appearance of vast fields of snow. In this desert we witnessed some very curious and remarkable mirages. A man walking a few rods in front of you would suddenly seem to grow up to the height of a hundred feet, or more, and would appear like some slender giant striding along the plain. Then, perhaps, you could only see, for a while, his head and shoulders moving along in the clouds, and, again, nothing but his legs measuring the desert like an immense pair of compasses or stilts from fifty to seventy feet high. Then, at times, he would seem to be cut in two in the middle and, while his long legs moved along the earth, his head and shoulders with his hands and arms swinging the ox-whip would move through space perhaps fifty feet, or more, above the highest visible point of the lower extremities. Sometimes, in looking forward or back, the whole line of wagons would appear to have risen from the earth and to move along in the clouds giving a mirage so perfect that the people could be distinctly recognized, and the several wagons and oxen were as easily recognized as at any other time or under the most favorable circumstances. The day we crossed this desert was a little cloudy and the sunlight by no means as glaring and oppressive as usual.

Many of the people gathered large quantities of the white soda or salaratus, as they called it, while crossing this desert which they used instead

---

122 This was Upper Lake, Surprise Valley, California. There are three intermittent lakes in the valley named Upper, Middle, and Lower Lake from north to south.

of yeast powders in making bread. And it answered the purpose about as well as the carbonate of soda usually sold in the grocery stores.

In 1847, the next year, I found this plain a vast lake of water. And it took the wagons several days to pass around the south side of it so as to reach the place at the foot of the mountains on the west side where we camped at night on crossing it in 1846.

The next day after crossing the desert, we traveled north, along the foot of the mountains, and camped at a small branch running down from the mountain side and sinking in the great alkali desert. This we called Plum Creek on account of the dense growth of wild plum bushes along its banks where we camped.[123]

The next day we crossed the only mountain of any consequence which we had yet encountered and this the only one that we must necessarily cross between the Humboldt and the Siskiyou Mountains west of the Klamath Lake. And this, although the descent on the west side was pretty steep, was not a difficult mountain to cross. It was a single ridge and the distance not more than four or five miles and there was no timber on it except some large scattering pines. On this ridge, the emigrants first saw the great sugar pine of southern Oregon and of northern California and Nevada.[124]

We camped that night on a small branch we called Trout Creek near a great plum thicket in a nice valley covered with plenty of grass.[125]

At this place we found B. F. Burch, W. G. Parker, and Charles Putnam, of Captain Applegate's road-working party. Mr. Burch had taken sick here, and was unable to go on with the Captain's party, and the other two men stopped with him, until the wagons should come up.

While they lay here, Putnam walked out one day on the hills above their camp, alone, and entirely unarmed, which was certainly a very thoughtless and dangerous thing to do, but there are many men who lose all thought of sense of danger by being long familiar with it. He was

---

123 Plum Creek is now called Heath Creek according to Richard Silva, "Emigrant Trail Through Photography," *Overland Journal*, 18, no. 2 (Summer 2000) 7.

124 The ridge was first called Lassen Pass, then Fandango Pass, which has become permanent. The explorers and emigrants often thought this mountain range was part of the Sierra Nevada or the Blue Mountains of Oregon. It is not. It is the Warner Mountains.

125 Now Willow Creek.

Traces of the Southern Route to Oregon in Fandango Valley, California, Modoc National Forest, nearing the junction with Lassen's Trail. In the right foreground is a carsonite marker placed by the Oregon-California Trails Association and Modoc National Forest. *Photo courtesy Stafford Hazelett.*

sauntering along, lost in meditation, when he suddenly awoke from his reverie to find himself in the presence of two strapping warriors. They had slyly stolen upon him and were almost near enough to lay their hands on him before he was aware of their presence. On his discovering them, they all three paused.

Putnam had on a large overcoat. He straightened himself up, thrust both hands into the side-pockets of his overcoat, and stood looking steadily and sternly into their eyes for about a minute, neither party speaking nor moving. He then turned coolly away and walked leisurely, and with a firm, self-possessed step, towards his camp.

The Indians walked along, one on either side and within an arm's length of him, till they came in about two hundred yards of the camp, which was concealed from view by the bushes, when they saw Parker, with his rifle in his hand, coming towards them. He called to Charley not to bring those Indians into camp and made signs for them to come no further.

The Indians, who had neither spoken nor made any sign, either friendly or hostile, turned silently away, leaving Putnam to go into camp with a deep sigh of relief and without an escort.

Charley always felt that he owed his life, on this occasion, to his apparent coolness and the mysterious depths of his overcoat pockets.

From this camp, we passed over a stretch of high, rocky country which was covered with large, scattering pines, and made our next camp on the east side of Goose Lake.

The waters of the lake had dried up until a large portion of its bed, at the south end, was exposed, and it had dried out and cracked in great fissures, much like we had found the valley of the Humboldt, so that in passing around the lake we had to keep near the edge of the water to avoid the large cracks in the ground a little further away. The lake was very shallow so that a person could ride far out into it on the south side and some of the boys waded out for half a mile or more shooting ducks.

When Captain Applegate was one day's journey west of Goose Lake, a man of his party by the name of Sevy, who rode a little jenny which traveled very slowly, fell behind, and, when he came to where they had crossed a very rocky place for a long distance, he lost their trail and could not find it, again.[126] After hunting for the trail until he gave up all hope of finding it or of overtaking the Captain's party, and, as it would not be best for him to search through this region alone till he should find some of the natives, he turned back, followed the back track till he came to the Pot-Hole Coulee, and concealed himself there to await the coming of the wagons.

Sevy was entirely destitute of provisions. Game was very scarce and it was dangerous to fire a gun for fear of being discovered by the Indians. Here he lay concealed for a week, during which time he only killed one jack rabbit and a sage hen. He was nearly starved when the wagons came up. He said he had told his jenny that morning that he would have to kill her the next day if the wagons did not come before that time. But

---

126   A "jenny" is a female ass or donkey.

the wagons came in time to save the poor jenny's life and, perhaps, her master's, too.

Poor Sevy was almost speechless with famine and joy when he found himself again with the emigrants. He did not ask for anything to eat, famished as he was, and no one seemed to think of offering him anything until I suggested to Robert Gilliam, with whom I was camping, that some one ought to give the poor fellow something to eat.[127]

The day before, Bennett Osborn had killed a mule deer—a very large species of deer found in this region—and Mrs. Gilliam had some of the venison cooked, which was given to Sevy. After he had eaten some of it, he seemed to be very much refreshed and became quite cheerful. He was very happy that the "Diggers" had not discovered his retreat at the Pot-Holes before we came up.

Two days travel from Goose Lake brought us to Goff's Spring where we lay by two days to recruit our teams and to give me an opportunity to go forward and examine the country and select the best way for a road.

I went forward, alone, and selected the road into Clear Lake Valley. Between Goff's spring and this valley is a very rough, rocky region or lava bed for a distance of five or six miles. After passing this lava bed, we entered the valley and, having crossed its broad and grassy plain, we camped at a fine spring near the lake. This valley was then dry but, when I was here, again, in 1849, I found it all a great swamp.[128]

We were now entirely south of the route I had passed over in going out and the difficulties we had then experienced in this region made me very anxious about our way through here. I took James Robinson with me and we went forward to view out the way ahead of us. The face of

---

127 In Scott's original manuscript, Sevy and Robert Gilliam were not mentioned, nor this incident. There was a "Robert Gilliam" on the 1846 emigration, but he emigrated by the northern route to The Dalles according to his son's biography. "Robert A. Gilliam," in F. A. Shaver, *An Illustrated History of Central Oregon* (Spokane: Western Historical Publishing Co., 1905), 668-69. Robert was a nephew of Gen. Cornelius Gilliam.

128 Collins and Scott described Mammoth Spring, now under the waters of Clear Lake Reservoir. The nearby Steele Swamp was off the path of the road and too far from the historic lake to be the place they camped. Later, Jesse Applegate settled and made a claim for an extensive ranch surrounding the historic Clear Lake. *See* Robert B. Johnston, "Two Jesses and the Modoc War," *The Journal of the Shaw Historical Library* 5, nos. 1 and 2, 1991, 1-43.

the country would appear level and seem to be all one could wish for a road but, possibly before proceeding half a mile, we would come to some impossible gulch or other obstacle which would compel us to make a long and vexatious detour.[129] From the high point of a ridge north of Tule Lake, we could see up the valley of Lost River nearly to the Klamath Lake, and I was pleased to see that this would bring us onto the line of our travels during the summer where I should know the ground better and be able to proceed with more confidence.[130]

On the south side of Clear Lake there appeared to be high bluffs of rock and lava beds stretching away to the south as far as we could see.

From Clear Lake Valley, we traveled about twelve miles and came into a large flat north of Tule Lake, across which we traveled for about twenty miles to "Lost River," or "Fall River," or "Rock Bridge River," as it has been variously called, being the stream between the Klamath and Tule Lakes which we had crossed on the natural bridge.[131]

We camped a few miles below the crossing of this river where we were overtaken by thirty or forty more wagons.[132] During the night the Indians stole four head of oxen, and wounded several others with arrows. One pair of the cattle driven off was a very fine, large yoke of oxen belonging to Washington Crowley, one of the party that had just overtaken us. They were his wheel cattle, and were a very serious loss to him. Several of us

129 These were the sorts of places where a note of direction from Jesse Applegate would have aided the emigrants.
130 The high point was Bryant Mountain.
131 Lost River is located between the Klamath Lakes and Tule Lake, but does not connect them. It begins in Clear Lake, California, courses north into Oregon near Malin, turns west toward Merrill, and then turns south to end in Tule Lake, California.
132 Pringle recorded that his company came up with the lead companies on September 28, two days before the combined companies crossed the Lost River. Pringle also noted it brought the front group to fifty wagons and that they spent the next day chasing cattle stolen by Indians. They "Crossed the Sacramento River on a singular rock" on September 30. Pringle, "Diary," in Morgan, *Overland in 1846*, 183. It is worth noting that Pringle's brother-in-law, Orus Brown with the Robinson company, signed a note for a portion of his toll over the Barlow Road on this same date. Lockley, *Oregon Journal*, August 28, 1928. Jesse Applegate arrived home at Salt Creek on September 26 and Lindsay arrived home a week later. The emigrants still had more than two hundred miles of forests, rivers, and mountains to the southernmost settlements in the Willamette Valley, with no trace of a road ahead of them.

went in pursuit of the stolen cattle, and found them slaughtered in the tules near the Klamath Lake. The Indians fled into the tule marshes along the edge of the lake, and we could do nothing with them.

The emigrants now insisted on electing me Captain and putting the whole command of all the consolidated trains that had come together here into my hands. I refused to assent to this unless they would agree to obey my orders. I told them that the mere title of Captain of the company would put burdens upon me and be of no benefit to them unless I could have some real authority. That I did not think many orders would be necessary and I would not give any except such as I thought ought to be obeyed for the good of the whole company, but if they expected me to take the responsibility of Captain of this large train, they must expect to obey my orders which I feared they would not do just when it might be most important that they should do it.

They still insisted and pledged me that all of my orders should be strictly obeyed. I then consented to accept the sole responsibility of commander of the company, relieving the Captains of the various parties that had joined us of their command. They held a great mass meeting and elected me unanimously. This was in the evening after we had returned from the pursuit of the Indians who had stolen the oxen.

We started again the next morning and, after having crossed on the Rock Bridge in the forenoon, we passed over some low sand hills covered with sage to the Klamath Lake.

Late in the evening, we came to a place where a very steep promontory comes square up to the lake. I knew we could pass over the hills on a reasonably good route by bearing a little to the east but I thought that possibly we might pass along the lake shore under the bluff and, by so doing, save a longer pull over the sandy hills.[133]

So, I directed the teams to be driven slowly, to give me time to ride forward and examine the situation and, if we could not pass under the bluff, I would meet them by the time they should reach a suitable point

---

133 Scott described the hill at the southwest edge of Lower Klamath Lake. The hill is to the west of the lake and the good route is still further west, rather than east. The shoreline route that he scouted is now the Dorris Brownell Road, made possible by the draining and diking of Lower Klamath Lake. The route taken by the emigrants still seems impossible. The emigrant route has been confirmed and marked by Richard Silva and members of Trails West.

to turn into the hills to the left. I went on till I found it impossible to pass near the margin of the Lake but, on turning back, I was astonished to find that the wagons had pressed forward and were now some considerable distance past the point where they could turn to the left.

In front of them was the head-land, perhaps, three hundred feet, or more, high, and apparently too steep for a horse, or an ox to ascend it. On the right hand was the lake, and they would have to retrace their steps for nearly a mile to reach a convenient point at which they could take the sand hills to the left.[134]

It was nearly sunset and it seemed to me that we would be compelled to camp here in rather an inconvenient position, while, if we should attempt to go around to a better camping place which was just a few hundred yards distant on the other side of this high ridge, it would take us till after dark, and I could see no way to reach it without turning back and going over the hills. Such a movement must occasion considerable delay, and would be difficult to explain to the immediate satisfaction of every one, and every one would be sure to insist on a satisfactory demonstration of the necessity of such a retrograde movement.

Some of the men said we could double teams and cross the ridge in less time than it would take to avoid it. I must admit that I did not think it possible, but told them if they thought they could do it, they might make the effort. They began at once to hitch several teams to one wagon, so as to make a line of oxen nearly to the top of the hill, and up they went with one of the light vehicles.

All began industriously to imitate this example and it was not long till the whole side of that steep ridge was covered with ascending wagons and teams for more than half a mile along its almost precipitous northern slope.

The multitude of people, the wagons, the cattle, the horses and mules, the humming murmur of the women and children, the clanking of chains, the clashing of horns, the popping of whips, the noise of the drivers, and the shouting produced a scene there, under the slanting rays of the setting sun, as animated and sublime as the fighting of a great battle.

Isaac Lebo had a large wagon of the Prairie Schooner style with an immense, blue, boat-shaped bed. Just as this wagon reached the summit

---

134 The geographic feature is now called Big Tableland. The first summit is 450 feet above the surface of the neighboring lake.

of the ridge, the king-bolt broke and the hind-wheels started back, down the hill, dragging the bed from the forward axle. The hill below was completely covered with wagons and teams, with men, women and children, and there was a little child in the forward part of the recoiling wreck only just tall enough to look over the top of the wagon bed and laugh at the fun.

Every one who witnessed this fearful accident paused in speechless horror except Mrs. Lebo, the heroic mother of the crowing infant in the wagon. She seized a great stone, seemingly larger than any man of ordinary strength would care to handle, and, staggering in behind the threatening vehicle, deliberately chucked it under one of the wheels before the backward motion had become much accelerated. The other wheel swung round, nearly across the slope of the hill, and the forward part of the heavy bed dragging on the ground brought it to a stand, and, thus, she saved the lives of her child and of the vast multitude below at the imminent risk of her own.

The steep ascent to Big Tableland above Klamath Lake where Isaac Lebo's wagon broke loose with a child inside and emigrants in harm's way below. *Photo courtesy Stafford Hazelett.*

She sprang to the front, snatched her babe from the wagon, and, reeling away a few steps, sank to the ground, clasping it to her bosom.

When the danger was past and the mother had rescued her baby from the grasp of death, the pale men who stood near her broke forth with a shout of grateful admiration. I have frequently thought of this deed of maternal heroism and I have no doubt that many people whose lives were saved by it, never, perhaps, knew of it and, possibly, not half a dozen persons besides the Lebos ever thought of it for ten minutes after it took place.

And thus, in an incredibly short space of time, the whole train was looking down upon the Lake from the top of the cape. The descent on the south side, although rather rocky, was comparatively easy and, a little after dark, the wagons were all in camp at the foot of the hill.[135]

---

135 The descent was on the north side of the Big Tableland and their camping place that night became known as Laird's Landing. Devere Helfrich, "The Applegate Trail," *Klamath Echoes* 9 (Klamath County Historical Society, 1971): 87.

∾

CHAPTER XIII

Trouble: No Road and
Death and Distress

The next morning about daylight, two strangers, one named Kelly and the other Hudson, came into our camp. They stated that they had left the train next behind us and came forward on foot with a view of overtaking us. They had traveled alone for nearly a week and had encountered no trouble till the evening before.

A little after sundown, when they were near the Rock Bridge and not far from our camp where the Indians stole our oxen, one of them shot a sage hen when, almost immediately, about a dozen armed Indians appeared on the opposite bank of the river, not over a hundred yards away, making hostile demonstrations.

By exhibiting their arms, and warning the Indians off with threatening signs, they were permitted to pass without being attacked. But, instead of camping for the night near the crossing, as they had intended, they traveled all night, feeling that their safety depended on reaching our camp as soon as possible, and they felt sure that we were not far in advance of them as they had found some of the small willow faggots still smoking at the camp fires we had left in the morning. They came up with us about daylight in a very hungry and exhausted condition.

Smith Collins, who afterwards settled near the Luckiamute River in Polk County, gave one of the men some breakfast and permitted him to ride in one of his wagons during the day.[136] Someone else provided for the other man and they traveled with us till we reached the great Canyon in the Umpqua Mountains.

One of the men, Kelly, was the first white man ever judicially executed in Oregon. He was hung at Salem for murder in 1850 or 1851. I have

---

136 Smith Collins was the father of James Layton Collins, Scott's collaborator and
    author of this text.

heard that it has been fully demonstrated since his execution that he was innocent of the crime for which he suffered. He asserted his innocence to the last.[137]

The other man, Hudson, was a printer. After reaching the settlements, he worked on the *Oregon Spectator* at Oregon City till the next spring when he joined our overland party and returned to the eastern states.[138]

About the time Hudson and Kelly came in, a rumor went through the camp that one of our men was missing, and that he was probably killed by the Indians. The name of the missing man was David Tanner. He was probably about thirty-five or forty years old. He was a man of rather peculiar and eccentric disposition and was reputed to be a little insane at times. His complexion was rather dark; he would weigh, perhaps, about one hundred and sixty or seventy pounds, was nearly, or quite, six feet high, and a very muscular, powerful man, when in full health and vigor.

Tanner was traveling with the Rev. Abraham Garrison who afterwards settled on the Yamhill River near the town of Amity. He was driving loose stock for Mr. Garrison and he complained of not feeling well. He insisted on riding Mr. Garrison's mare that day but Garrison refused to let him have her and told him to get in the wagon and ride there if he did not feel well. But Tanner refused to ride unless he could have the mare. So he started afoot, as usual, with the rest of the drivers.

---

137 This story appears to have muddled together at least two different stories. The first man judicially executed in Oregon was William Kendall in April 1851. Kendall asserted his innocence to the end. *Oregon Statesman*, "Trial of William Kendall for the Murder of William Hamilton, in Marion County Circuit Court, at March Special Term, 1851," April 18, 1851, 1; and April 25, 1851, 1. Diane L. Goeres-Gardner, *Necktie Parties: Legal Executions in Oregon, 1851-1905* (Caldwell, ID: Caxton Press, 2005), 1-5. No one named "Kelly," or a variant of that spelling, was hanged in Oregon during Levi Scott's life. The man Scott met in 1846 on the trail might have been Nimrod O'Kelly, convicted of killing another man regarding a land claim boundary dispute. However, O'Kelly arrived in Oregon in 1845, his sentence was commuted and reduced to a prison term, and he died in 1864 at age eighty-four of natural causes. Lawrence A. McNary, "Oregon's First Reported Murder Case," *Oregon Historical Quarterly* 36, no. 4 (December 1935): 359-64; and Ronald Lansing, *Nimrod* (Pullman: Washington State University Press, 2005).

138 W. P. Hudson was the printer of the *Oregon Spectator* from May 27 to June 10, 1847. He left Oregon with Scott in 1847, returned in 1848, and left for the California gold fields, thus interrupting its publication for a time. *See* George H. Himes, "History of the Press of Oregon, 1839-1850," *Quarterly of the Oregon Historical Society* 3, no. 4 (December 1902): 346-47.

We got into camp late that night, as has already been stated, all very tired and everything a little in confusion. Tanner did not put in an appearance at Mr. Garrison's tent, but they supposed he had not yet recovered from his fit of indignation and had gone to some other tent to spend the night, and, not thinking it probable that anything was seriously wrong with him, the weary family retired to rest.

As Tanner did not come to breakfast the next morning, Mr. Garrison began to inquire through the camp for him. The last place he had been seen by any of the company was just after crossing the Rock Bridge in the forenoon, at which time he was on foot and with the rest of the stock drivers. The report brought in by Hudson and Kelly concerning armed Indians on the river spread through the camp and the greatest apprehensions were felt for the safety of Tanner.[139]

I directed the company to get ready and move on around the margin of the Lake, while I should take a few well mounted and armed men with me and go back to look for the missing man. Charles B. Graves, David M. Guthrie, Chas. Helms, and a man named Boon, who was generally known by the soubriquet of "Texas," went with me.

We followed our trail back to where he had been last seen, where we found his track. Some of the men who were with me recognized his track by the shape of the boots he wore and from the fact that the heel-tap of one of them was missing.

After we had followed his track for about a mile, we could see by the appearance of it that he had been running. On examination, we found an Indian track on each side of the road running in the same direction. A little further on, we found that Tanner had, apparently, fallen to his knees. We could plainly see the prints of his hands and knees in the sand. But he had risen and run on a little further, when he fell, again, and now the Indian tracks closed in upon him. Here we found evidence of a hard struggle and the ground was spattered with blood.

But, now, all further traces of the conflict and of the parties engaged in it disappeared, and we searched diligently for sometime before we could find any vestige of either. At length, we found where the body had

---

139 In his original manuscript, Scott placed this event on the day following the crossing of the stone bridge at Lost River, timing corroborated by the reminiscence of Tolbert Carter. "Pioneer Days," in *OPAT* 34, 72. *See also* Garrison, "Forty-two Years in Oregon," 32-33.

been partially dragged and partially carried from fifty to a hundred yards from the road where, after stripping him, they had thrown him into a thick patch of sage bushes and had bent and pressed them down over him so as to pretty thoroughly conceal the body. They had stripped him of his boots and every other article of his clothing. We found about half a dozen arrow wounds in his breast, shoulders, and the pit of his stomach. The Indians had evidently flanked him on either side, run him down, and killed him with their arrows. He was entirely unarmed and could make no effectual resistance.

We saw that it would be extremely difficult for us to bear the dead body with us to the train and we had no suitable tools with which to dig a grave. Finally, however, while some held the horses and stood guard, the rest of us went to work with our butcher knives and our hands, and dug and scratched out a narrow trench about three feet deep in the sandy soil, and, having wrapped the dead body in the best blanket we had with us, we laid the poor pilgrim to rest in the lonely desert, far away from the home of his childhood and the friends of his former days. Poor Tanner! I felt that he had come a weary journey to find a lonely grave in a lonesome and unfriendly land.

After having thus disposed of the dead body, we started to overtake the train. While passing near some tules on the margin of the lake, Mr. Guthrie was startled by something suddenly striking against his powder horn. He and another one of the party, who was riding at his side, thought, from the direction the missile came and the sound it made, that it was an arrow shot from the tules. By their exclamation the party was thrown into some momentary confusion and we moved further from the point of danger. None of us, however, saw the arrow, and, as no Indian made his appearance, some began to conclude that there was a mistake about it and that it was not an arrow which had caused the perturbation among us.

A little further on some Indians made their appearance in a canoe upon the lake. One of them appeared to have a shirt upon his person and some of the others, articles of civilized apparel. Some of our men at once jumped to the conclusion that they were dressed in Tanner's clothes but this was mere conjecture as they were too far away for us to recognize any article of clothing so distinctly. Several shots were fired at them and they paddled away out of range of the best rifle and were soon lost to sight in the tules.

We came up with the company late in the evening where they were camped on a small stream running into the south side of the Klamath Lake, and the people gathered around us with sad and solemn countenances to hear our account of the sad fate of poor Tanner.

Early the next morning, James Robinson shot at an Indian whom he found trying to drive off some of the cattle which had fed out furthest from the camp. But it was supposed he missed him, as the Indian fled into the bushes along the creek and made his escape.

We traveled on around the margin of the Lake and camped at night near the head of the Klamath River, where it flows out of the Lower Klamath Lake. The next day, which was about the first day of October, 1846, we crossed the river, traveled down it about eight miles and camped.[140]

Before us lay a stretch of densely timbered country for about thirty miles, part of which was level, but the most of it in the mountains. Through this timber we found the way blazed but very imperfectly opened. As we had no spare hands to send forward to do the work, we were frequently compelled to stop the train till the teamsters could go ahead, open and prepare the road for the passage of wagons, and then return and bring them up.

We had relied upon Captain Applegate and his party of hands to open the road through this timber and they had done but little besides blazing it out. The most bitter murmurs and complaints began to be heard against the Captain, who was regarded as the head of the enterprise of making a new road through here to the Willamette Valley, and who had gone ahead expressly to prepare the way for the wagons. The emigrants expressed themselves without any reserve as to the conduct of the Captain, for he was not present to hear their compliments [sic].[141] And while some of their complaints were just, many of them were ill-natured and

---

140 Pringle recorded that they camped at the outlet of the Klamath River on October 3 and moved on the next day. Pringle, "Diary," 53; Morgan, *Overland in 1846*, 184.

141 Rev. Abraham E. Garrison: "I knew the emigration was terribly enraged, often swearing they would take Applegates life on sight, but I thought no violence would be committed on the person of Mr. Scott." "Forty-two Years in Oregon," 29. *See also*, Thornton, *Oregon and California in 1848*, 1: 176, 187, 212.

unreasonable.[142] Captain Applegate hastened forward and blazed out the road. He left a man in charge of the hands who was to proceed more slowly and to open and put the way in good condition for the passage of the wagons, which he failed to do as it should have been done and, in many of the most difficult places, he neglected to do, altogether.[143]

On account of the delays in working on the road, we were unable to reach water on our first day in the heavy timber, but were compelled to camp at night in the dense woods without supper and without grass or water. The men, after toiling hard all day, had to guard the stock during the night to keep them from wandering away in the forest and being lost. I did everything in my power and made every suggestion that seemed wise to aid them and make their burdens as light as possible. But, the people were cross, sullen, and sour, and, if Captain Applegate had then been in their reach, I fear he would have fared badly if I may judge from their fiercely muttered complaints.

---

142 In the records that developed after 1846, the complaints of J. Quinn Thornton have taken first rank as published in two of his letters to the *Oregon Spectator* and his book, *Oregon and California in 1848.* Thornton publicly withdrew some of his wrath in a speech to the Oregon Pioneer Association on June 14, 1878. Judge J. Quinn Thornton, "Occasional Address," *OPAT* 6 (1878) (Portland, OR: E.M. Waite, 1879): 69; *see also,* Jesse Applegate, letter dated June 23, 1878, to S. A. Clarke, Oregon Historical Society Research Library, Mss 1156, Box 1, Folder 8. "As it regards the enmity of the Hon. J. Q. Thornton and his desire to make my name 'infamous' in the records of the Oregon Pioneer Society I am absolutely indifferent[.] believing him to be a bad man I stood in the way of his ambition and he may think I thwarted him in his most cherished hopes. He once offered to 'make friends' but this I refused unless he withdrew his slanders in as public and permanent a manner as he had uttered them, i.e., by writing a book confessing the falsehood of the one he had published. / As he has not done this he still no doubt looks upon me as an enemy. In this he is mistaken. For tho' my opinion of him remains unchanged, I have long ago ceased to have any personal feeling in the matter." And, yet, seven years later, Applegate wrote to A. G. Walling to complain and correct his version of events on the Southern Route in 1846 which allowed that the fault did not lie entirely with the emigrants nor the elements. Albert G. Walling, *Illustrated History of Lane County, Oregon,* (Portland, OR: Printing House of A. G. Walling, 1884): between pages 196 and 197.

143 Scott repeated this assertion that another man was left in charge to open the road promised by Jesse Applegate, but there is no corroboration from the Applegate family nor any other source.

As soon as it was light enough to see our way the next morning, we started, again, and, after making about four or five miles through the forest, we reached Beaver Creek where we camped until the next morning.

Here, some of the more cheerful began to smile a little, but many of them did not get over that gloomy day and night in the woods, with their wives and children and all they possessed, with all they suffered there for more than a week.

When we camped on Beaver Creek, I stated to the company that I thought we were in danger of depredations from the Indians, and gave orders that a sufficient guard be kept constantly with the stock while they were out grazing. But the people could see no sign of Indians and thought there was no danger from them. The cattle were so exhausted and hungry that they apprehended no danger of them straying away; the men had toiled hard through the timber and kept watch where we bivouacked all through the previous night, so they failed to obey orders and refused to go on guard.

The next morning there was a horse gone. We found Indian tracks near the camp and, after searching for a long time we became satisfied that the Indians had stolen him.

I reminded the people of their promise to obey my orders which they had made scarcely a week before when they elected me their captain. I called them to witness that I had kept every promise faithfully that I had made them and had discharged my duty to them to the best of my ability. I told them that matters had gone very much as I had feared, and, as I had suggested to them, that I now gave up all authority as their Captain, and would not attempt to command or control them any further, but would only act as their pilot or guide as I had originally promised to do.

The people seemed to be very sorry that they had disobeyed me. They did not elect any one else for Captain. And so we went on, they obeying every suggestion from me more carefully than if it had been issued as an order, and I assuming no responsibility nor authority over them, whatever. My unassuming control over them seemed to be more effectual and absolute than it had been when I openly commanded as Captain.

We went down Beaver Creek and camped on it, again. The next day, we crossed over to the northwest side of the summit of the Siskiyou

Mountains and camped at a spring on the mountain side.[144] The next day, we reached the Rogue River Valley and camped on Emigrant Creek, a branch of Bear Creek.

The toil and suffering of the people since we crossed the Klamath River had been very great. Many of them were sick and could not get out of their wagons and, in many places, the jolting of the vehicles over the rough and unbeaten road made the traveling very hard on the sick. In many places it took two, or three, and sometimes more, persons with ropes attached to the wagons to keep them from upsetting. These things, with a multitude of other difficulties, rendered our progress slow and extremely laborious.[145] But, from here on, we had plenty of water and grass most of the time.

We went down Emigrant Creek and camped on it another night. The next day we struck Bear Creek, traveled for some distance down its beautiful and fertile valley, when we crossed the broad prairie and camped at the Willow Springs between this creek and Rogue River. The next night we camped on Rogue River just above the Point of Rocks, a place afterwards rendered famous and a dreaded Thermopylae to travelers during the wars with the treacherous and bloodthirsty Rogue River Indians.

Captain Medders Vanderpool had a fine flock of about fifty head of sheep which he had brought safely through the buffalo wolves and all the other dangers of the long journey thus far, but, one morning while we were eating breakfast at a camp on Rogue River, just below the Point of

---

144 This description suggests they camped at what has become known as Tub Springs, near the Green Springs Summit on Oregon Hwy 66. No spring was identified in Scott's April 1848 waybill. Levi Scott [attributed to Jesse Applegate], "Waybill: From Fort Hall to Willamette Valley," *Oregon Spectator*, April 6, 1848, 1, col. 6, – 2, col 1-2. Jesse Applegate sent a cover letter with Scott's waybill to Provisional Governor Abernethy who had the waybill printed in the newspaper without Applegate's cover letter. Jesse Applegate to George Abernethy, Letter, March 20, 1848, Oregon Historical Society Research Library Mss 929. *See also*, Stafford Hazelett, "Letter," *Oregon Historical Quarterly* 110, no. 2 (Summer 2009): 317-18.

145 Scott and Collins glossed over the considerable difficulties crossing the Cascade summit along the route approximating modern Oregon Highway 66. Pringle's diary reveals it took ten days to find and build the road from the Klamath River to the Rogue River. Pringle, "Diary," in Morgan, *Overland in 1846*, 184-85.

Rocks, they were driven off by the Indians and we were compelled to go on without making an effort to recapture them.

After we had left camp about a quarter of a mile, there was also a cow reported missing. Several of us went back to search for her and found the Indians butchering her near the camp. The Rogues ran off into the bushes and did not show themselves again. So we were compelled to go on leaving the beef with them as well as the mutton.

We traveled down Rogue River about forty or fifty miles and crossed it at a place where the ford was rather deep and rough.[146] It is a swift, turbulent, and rapid stream, and there are not many places where it can be forded with safety, even late in the fall when it is at its lowest stage.

The second day after we crossed Rogue River, we came to a place where the road-cutters had done nothing and it was impossible for us to pass with the wagons. So the train was brought to a halt. I went forward, and after searching for a long time, I found a place where we could pass by cutting through the thick bushes for about a furlong.[147] The place where the horse trail passed was too rough, and could not easily be made passable for wagons. We went to work on the line I had blazed out, and cut our way through the woods, which brought us out near the Tetalum, or Louse, Creek as it is now called by the realistic and unpoetical people who live along its banks.[148]

In two or three days after passing this place, we reached the Jump-Off-Jo, where the road-cutters had, again, done nothing, and we were compelled to stop and cut our way through to the open ground beyond, which occupied us for several hours, working all the available force of the company.

Three days from here we struck the head of a small branch running into Grave Creek, which we followed down to its junction, through heavy timber and thick bushes. The road had been so poorly opened, that the

---

146 Present-day Grants Pass.

147 A furlong is one-eighth of a mile.

148 Scott has mixed up some places along here. Louse Creek is over the first grade going north from Grants Pass and the pass may have been as difficult as he described, but it was only a short haul from the ford. Pringle traveled eight miles the next day, beyond Louse Creek, and thought the road was good. Pringle, "Diary," in Morgan, *Overland in 1846*, 185.

train was frequently compelled to stop and remove obstacles that ought to have been cleared away by the party in advance of us.[149]

As we came down this branch Miss Leland Crowley died. The wagon in which the sick girl lay stopped while she was dying and those behind could not pass. This made a breach in the train as those in front still continued to advance without noticing that those in the rear were delayed.

The circumstance, perhaps, caused the Indians who were constantly skulking in the woods near us to become more bold and to venture upon us more closely. They shot one of the oxen of Virgil K. Pringle, as it stood in the team, with an arrow, wounding it so that the animal soon died. Yet, the savage who aimed the arrow from the thick bushes by the road side was so completely concealed that he was not seen, at all, for it was late in the twilight of the evening.[150]

About the time that Pringle's ox was shot on the right hand side of the road, one of the teamsters noticed that his dog turned up his hair and snuffed towards the thick bushes on the left hand side where the drivers stood. On looking in the direction indicated by the dog, he saw an Indian, about fifteen paces from the road, with a gun resting on top of a large log and pointed towards him. He hissed on the dog, at the same time springing into the wagon to get his rifle. At his bidding, his own dog and two others dashed at the Indian who, finding himself thus suddenly assailed, and by such a formidable and unlooked-for force, fled, precipitately, into the thick forest and instantly disappeared from sight.

But the resolute dogs pressed upon him and soon caught him, for we could distinctly hear what seemed to be a life-and-death struggle between them for a few minutes, about a hundred yards away in the thicket. After the struggle had gone on for five minutes or more, it ceased and the dogs

149 The troubles of the next month, and the confusing use of pronouns and unspecified reference points in Scott's original text, combine to make it appear that Scott's recollection extended the time involved and the difficulties of these days. The terrain north of Grants Pass is still hilly and timbered. It makes sense that Scott had to make some extra effort to find and open a road from the Rogue River to Grave Creek. According to Pringle, the time from crossing the Rogue River to the burial of Miss Crowley on Grave Creek was actually three days, October 16 to 19. Pringle, "Diary," in Morgan, *Overland in 1846*, 185.

150 Pringle's diary does not have an entry to corroborate this incident at this place. The only recording by Pringle of an ox shot by an arrow had occurred on September 19 in Surprise Valley on the day before crossing Fandango Pass. Pringle, "Diary," in Morgan, *Overland in 1846*, 182-83.

came back to us. One of them was severely, but not mortally, wounded with an arrow which was sticking in his side. We supposed that they had either killed the Indian or that he had been succored by some of his comrades. At the very least, he must have been fearfully mangled by the dogs.

When Miss Crowley was dead, the rear part of the train moved on, again, and came into its place in the camp after dark.

The next morning we moved up a little and crossed the main creek where we stopped to bury the dead girl. Mrs. Tabitha Brown, a generous and noble-hearted widow lady, who afterwards founded the College at Forest Grove, in the Tualatin Plains, gave the upper side-boards of her wagon to make a coffin.[151] We dug the grave in the middle of the correlle, or circle of the camp, and, after depositing the remains, we filled it up level with the surface of the ground, replacing the sod which had first been carefully removed, so as to give it the appearance of the natural, unbroken ground as much as possible; we then corralled all the stock so that they should tread over the grave and, when we got ready to start, drove all the wagons one after another over it in the hope of so obliterating all traces of it as to prevent the Indians from finding or disturbing it.

But after all our pains, they found the grave, dug up the corpse, robbed it of the burial clothes, and left it a prey to the wolves. I suppose the savages were watching us from the hills all the time we were at this place and saw everything we did. They probably thought we were making a *cache*, or deposit, of valuables which we could carry no further and for which we intended to return at some future time as the trappers sometimes did with their furs and supplies.

Travelers afterwards found the bones and hair of the dead girl scattered upon the ground where the Indians and wolves had left them,

---

151 The death of Martha Leland Crowley made a strong impression on the emigrants. There are multiple stories of her death, burial, and the subsequent disturbances of her grave. The nearby creek was named originally for the location of her grave, the first of many close by its banks. *See* Corning, "Grave Creek Affair," *Dictionary of Oregon History*, 102. Tabitha Brown was mother-in-law to Virgil Pringle. She was a founder of Pacific University. Her own recollection and the Pringle diary do not corroborate this instance of her characteristic generosity. For biographies of Tabitha Brown, *See* Corning, *Dictionary of Oregon History*, 36; Engeman, *The Oregon Companion*, 57-58. David Guthrie built the coffin and was reputed to have felt affection for the girl. Fred Lockley, "In Earlier Days [David Guthire]," *Oregon Journal*, January 23, 1914, 6, col. 8.

which they gathered up and reburied. Ever since, this creek has been called Grave Creek.[152]

The next morning, two of the men, who had been delayed a little, had a flight of arrows shot at them just before reaching camp. The Indians were concealed in the bushes not more than two hundred yards from our camp and could not be seen on account of the thicket. The men escaped unhurt although the arrows whizzed close about them and stuck in the ground all around them.

The Indians seemed to be hanging about us now constantly and they were growing bolder and harassing us continually.

It was not necessary now for me to be called *Captain* or to assume any authority to be obeyed. The people listened to every suggestion I made and did all they could to follow every hint I gave them as to what they should do and how they should do it.

At my suggestion, they put out a strong guard over the stock and the camp. I told them to fire several guns into the thicket where those arrows came from, and to fire off a gun at least once every fifteen minutes during the night, that the Indians might know that we were under arms and on the watch. When our men commenced firing their fire was returned from the hills above the camp. But the Indians seemed to be retiring. We passed the night in great suspense under arms but we were not again molested by our savage tormentors.

It was about twenty-five miles to Cow Creek but the road lay through very rough timbered hills and it took us three days of hard labor to reach that creek.[153] If the Indians had continued to pursue us and had attacked us in these hills, we should certainly have suffered much more severely than we did. However, we felt compelled to exercise nearly as much vigilance as if they had been howling around and shooting arrows at us all

---

152 Collins expanded on Scott's original reminiscence of this event with information from published letters by James W. Nesmith, "Southern Oregon History," *Oregonian*, November 23, 1883, 2, col. 2, and Charles P. Fullerton, "Miss Crowley's Grave," *Oregonian*, November 23, 1883, 2, col. 2. Fullerton was Tabitha Brown's hired driver and nephew of Virgil Pringle. Their correspondence provoked a letter from Judge Matthew Deady, "Southern Oregon Names," *Oregonian*, December 5, 1883, 1, col. 7. *See also* McArthur, *Oregon Geographic Names*, 424-25 (Grave Creek) and 571 (Leland).

153 From Grave Creek to the last camp on Cow Creek, near Azalea, is seventeen highway miles. Pringle recorded six miles in one day's travel from Grave Creek to this camp: October 20. Pringle, "Diary," in Morgan, *Overland in 1846*, 185.

the time and by the time we reached Cow Creek the men were pretty well exhausted.

The next day we moved up the creek only about eight miles and camped to give the cattle a chance to graze and the men an opportunity to rest a little.

The next morning, when we were about ready to start, Jack Jones and Tom Smith, of Oregon City, came into our camp. Jones had gone into the Willamette Valley with Captain Applegate and, now, in company with Smith, had returned to meet us with a few beef cattle.[154] They came to our camp just as we were about ready to start. The people were anxious to hear anything from the place of their destination and about the condition of the road they must travel. So, they gathered around the two men and began to pour in volleys of questions from every side.

Smith had interests at Oregon City and was very much opposed to a southern route into the Willamette Valley as it was generally supposed by the people at the Falls of the Willamette that such a road would have a tendency to damage the property and importance of that place which, it was thought, would be the great commercial and manufacturing center of the Northwest and those who had settled in the village feared that a rival might spring up further south.[155] He told the emigrants that they could only go about six miles further when they must stop; that it would be impossible for them ever to go through the Umpqua Canyon with wagons.[156]

Smith depicted the insurmountable difficulties before them in such graphic terms that the people seemed to be stunned with amazement bordering on despair. With my utmost exertions, and the most encouraging arguments I could employ, it was three o'clock in the afternoon before I could induce them to move from this camp and then they would go only about two miles when they camped, again. The next day, I could only prevail on them to advance about three miles. A great many of them,

---

154 Rev. Abraham E. Garrison: "He sent provision to meet the emigrants which he sold to them at a very high price." "Forty-two Years in Oregon," 28.

155 Other than the Applegate and Scott reminiscences, there is no evidence of anticipated harm to the commercial interests of the settlers in and around Oregon City.

156 Jones's and Smith's assessment of the situation repeated what the road explorers had thought three months earlier on first encounter with the canyon. Jones and Smith now had the advantage of viewing the path immediately before the emigrants, even after the alleged improvements by the road-clearing party.

especially of the children, were sick and the whole company seemed to be stupefied and almost overwhelmed with despair.[157]

I induced them to move, again, a short distance when we came to the dreaded, and I must say *dreadful*, Canyon where we really could go no further without first having made a road through this formidable gorge. I spent two days in a fruitless endeavor to get a party to go with me on foot through the Canyon. No one would go. Finally I emphatically called the company to attention and told them that I was going through the next morning. If some of them would go with me, we would see what must be done on the road to put it in a condition to admit of the passage of wagons. When we should have ascertained what work was necessary, I would come back and we would raise all the force we could to go and do it so as to get the train through if it were possible. If no one would go with me, nor make any effort to get through the mountains, I should go home, I said:

> I will not stay, idly, here, and see you all perish because you will not put forth an effort to help yourselves. You all know, just as well as I do, that nothing can be done without trying to do it. You all know, as well as I do, that if you lie, idly, here, winter will soon be upon you. Your provisions are now nearly exhausted and yourselves, with your wives and children, must starve to death and be buried under the snows of the winter. Now, you can do as you please. I mean just what I say. I shall start into this canyon early in the morning. Will you go with me? Will you help me to make a way for the deliverance of these helpless woman and children? If you will, I will stay with you and work with you to the last. And I have reason to hope that we may succeed. If you will not, then, I must leave you to your fate and seek the settlements as soon as possible. Settle with yourselves tonight what you will do.

Early the next morning, I was ready to start into the canyon but there were only four men ready to go with me. We struggled through the worst ten miles for a road I ever saw. On careful examination, we concluded that with a few days work, employing the whole available force of the

---

157 Scott's memory extended this time period by several days when compared with the Pringle diary. Clearly, the party struggled with exhaustion and hunger, and worn-down draft animals. The emigrants who had continued down the traditional Oregon Trail were already in the settlements.

company, the canyon might be put in a condition that the train could pass through it.[158]

We returned to camp and made our report, giving it as encouraging a turn as we truthfully could. The next day, every able-bodied man that could be spared from the camp went resolutely to the task. They had been resting, now, for several days and, when they roused themselves up and went to work, they did it with an earnestness and energy that produced very satisfactory results.

We worked through the canyon in four days and concluded that it would now be possible for us to get the wagons through on the road we had made.[159] There was a swift, rocky creek running through the canyon which was a serious difficulty that we could neither remedy nor avoid. In many places it was shut in between high, perpendicular walls of rock, where there was no other possible place for the road except in the channel of the stream sometimes for a distance of fifty yards to a furlong in a place. The bed of the creek was, in many of these places, a slick, smooth rock, pitching down at a steep angle or with an equally steep dip to one side over which the wagons must be steadied and let down with ropes.[160]

There were several short bends in these narrow places which were very difficult to get through and, in some of them, large boulders blocked up the channel where the strait was narrow and bluffs abrupt so that a

---

158 Scott also gave no indication that he observed evidence of road improvements since his passage through the canyon in July 1846. Yet, we know from two letters that a considerable effort was made by about a dozen men over a period of about two weeks. M, *Oregon Statesman*, September 25, 1852, 2, col. 4; Emigrant of '46, *Oregonian*, March 12, 1879.

159 Pringle seems to corroborate Scott's reminiscence on the amount of time to open the route down the canyon, which may perhaps be explained in part by the presence of a transcription of Pringle's diary in the Collins records. Pringle, "Diary," in Morgan, *Overland in 1846*, 185. Rev. A. E. Garrison recalled that his brother, Joseph, met the party at the canyon and helped work on the road there and that his nephew, Jeptha, son of brother Enoch, joined the party at the north end of the canyon to help get them along. "Forty-two Years in Oregon," 38, 40.

160 The rigors of travel in Canyon Creek Canyon were legendary. *See* S. A. Clarke, "Overland to California in 1851," *The West Shore* 5, no. 8 (August 1879): 226-27. "Climbing the Umpqua mountains consisted of wading through Canyon creek over a hundred times, at crossings, and marching up against the current for a goodly distance, with an occasional abrupt climb of one to four feet of rocky ledge, where the wagons and their loads had to be lifted bodily over the obstructions."

wagon could not by any means pass around them. We had not the time nor the means to blast them out of the way and, in some places, it would have taken us weeks to have removed them in this way if we had been possessed of the necessary drills and fuse for the purpose. In such places we were compelled to throw in logs and brush with earth and stones to fill up and bridge over the boulders. And, by the same means, we were sometimes compelled to level up the dip of the bed-rock in the bottom of the stream.[161]

There was not much water in the channel of the creek now but it would take only a few hours rain to raise it to the swimming stage when it must necessarily be impassable and such a flood would be certain to disarrange and wash away much of our temporary bridging and filling. The winter rains were now beginning with little showers which soon increase to steady rain of a week or more without intermission and continue from the latter part of October till the last of March. There were a few places where the creek was pretty deep at low water but its general course was so swift that it soon ran down when the storm ceased and, as yet, there had been nothing more than sprinkling showers.[162] We could see that delays were dangerous.

---

161 The improvement of this segment of the trail by strong men with appropriate tools was first undertaken by the Gold Rush company of Peter Burnett in 1848 on their way south to California. The next major improvements were funded by the U.S. government to build a military road under the direction of Major Benjamin Alvord. Alvord's subordinate, Joseph Hooker, who would gain fame in the Civil War, was in charge of the work. William Colvig, "Annual Address," *OPAT* 44 (1916), (Portland, OR: Chausse-Prudhomme Co., Printers, 1919): 342-43. Kendall, *Pacific Trail Camp-Fires*, 179. The road was built in 1853-54. It was cut into the banks of the hills and the creek bed was filled with debris, thus obliterating all traces of the original emigrant trail. Tolbert Carter, "Pioneer Days," *OPAT* 34, 80. A series of subsequent improvements were attempted, but it remained a steep and muddy mess until the Pacific Highway, US 99, came through and finally removed almost all traces of the original emigrant trail in southern Oregon.

162 Scott carefully noticed that it would not take much rain to make the creek nearly impassable. Despite the legends of heavy rain that fell on the emigrants in fall 1846, there is no evidence to support a conclusion that an unusual amount or timing of rain caught the emigrants. *See* Mark McLaughlin, *The Donner Party: Weathering the Storm*, 3rd ed. (Carnelian Bay, CA: MicMac Publishing, 2008). Alfred Franklin Davidson Papers, Oregon Historical Society Research Library,

We were compelled to stop and fix many places as we came to them. When a wagon stopped, all behind it were compelled to stop for it was impossible for one wagon to pass another. Some of the rear wagons were as much as a week in getting through to the Umpqua Valley. Some of the teams could get a little browse in places in the canyon, and some of the men brought their teams out to grass in the evening and returned to their wagons in the canyon the next morning.

A young man, the son of Alonzo Wood, died and was buried in the canyon. Just after the young man died, the wagon containing the corpse was upset in a deep hole of water. A hive of bees, which the old gentleman had successfully brought thus far on the long journey in the rear end of this wagon, was submerged and all the bees drowned.[163]

At one place, some thoughtless person set fire to a dead fir tree by the road side. The flames ran up the tree for more than a hundred feet and continued to burn and to drop coals and fire-brands upon those who came behind. A coal from this burning tree fell upon the neck of a sick child of Isaac Zumwalt, a boy four or five years old, when no one happened to be present. The child was too weak to remove the fire and, when the mother returned to the wagon, she found her child badly burned on the face and neck with the fire still roasting the flesh. The child recovered but he was badly scarred. But, what was most singular about it, a blistering, eruptive disease seemed to be settled in his face which would frequently break out and from which he never could be wholly relieved by the best medical skill.

It would not, perhaps, be interesting to enter into a detailed account of the sufferings of the people and their misfortunes and adventures in

---

Mss 386. Claiborne Walker and William B. Walker, "Letter Home," *Northwest Trails: Newsletter of the Northwest Chapter of the Oregon-California Trails Association* 20, No. 8 (Nov/Dec 2005): 3. Jesse Applegate, "Umpqua Agriculture, 1851," *Oregon Historical Quarterly* 32, No. 2 (June 1931): 137. Bryant, *What I Saw in California*, 342-49. Pringle, "Diary," in Morgan, *Overland in 1846*, 1:185. Daniel H. Good Letters, April 11, 1847, Oregon Historical Society Research Library, Mss 173. Charles Henry Carey, ed., "Diary of Rev. George Gary," *Oregon Historical Quarterly* 24, No. 3 (September 1923): 328.
163 Tolbert Carter confirmed the story and recalled that Mr. Wood had an offer for $500 for his hive if it had arrived in the Willamette Valley. "Pioneer Days," *OPAT* 34, 79.

passing this canyon. But there was a company, or two, behind us, who suffered, here, much more severely than we did.[164]

---

164 Scott's vantage point at the very front of the emigration perhaps helped ease his conscience about the events that would occur on this segment of the new route. Emigrant accounts tell the rest of their stories of distress. At times Collins was more faithful to Scott's original in this chapter than elsewhere, while in other places he exercised more editorial license. Notable was Collins's amelioration of Scott's concluding comment: "now thare was another train came through this place after us that sufered much worse than we did X thay abandoned thare wagons and lost most of thare teams and starved very near to death themselves." *See* Scott reminiscence in Appendix 1.

CHAPTER XIV

෴

More Trouble in 1846, and the 1847 Emigration

When I left the Canyon with about ten wagons, we went about six miles down the South Umpqua, where we camped till I could look out a way for five or six miles across a high, rocky ridge on the north side of the river.

The next day, with great labor and difficulty, we crossed this ridge, and camped on the Umpqua River again, just below the confluence of Cow Creek, which latter stream, by a long sweep, comes through the Umpqua Mountain west of the Canyon, and is one of the principal tributaries of the South Fork of the Umpqua.[165]

We traveled down the South Umpqua till we reached the mouth of Deer Creek, where the city of Roseburg is now situated, when we crossed it and passed over to the North Fork of the Umpqua which stream we crossed a little below where the Winchester Ferry now is.[166]

As soon as were started into the Canyon, the company, as a company, seemed to be dissolved. It just went to pieces. And everyone appeared to think that, henceforth, his progress and his safety depended only upon himself.[167]

As the emigrants emerged from that terrible place, they acted like a broken army of fugitives, each one striving to find a place of refuge for

---

165 Nineteenth century references to the canyon as the "Umpqua Canyon" have misled many to believe the emigrants came down the canyon of the South Umpqua. McArthur makes it clear that "Umpqua Canyon" was a pioneer-era reference to the defile of Canyon Creek. McArthur, *Oregon Geographic Names*, 158. Today's Interstate 5 uses the same canyon, except that it has been blasted with dynamite to clear and straighten it.

166 Actually, the primary ford was impassable at the time and the emigrants were forced to backtrack and drive to the lower ford, as will be clarified shortly.

167 Confirmed by Tabitha Brown, "A Brimfield Heroine," 53: "The word was *Fly*, everyone who can, from starvation…"

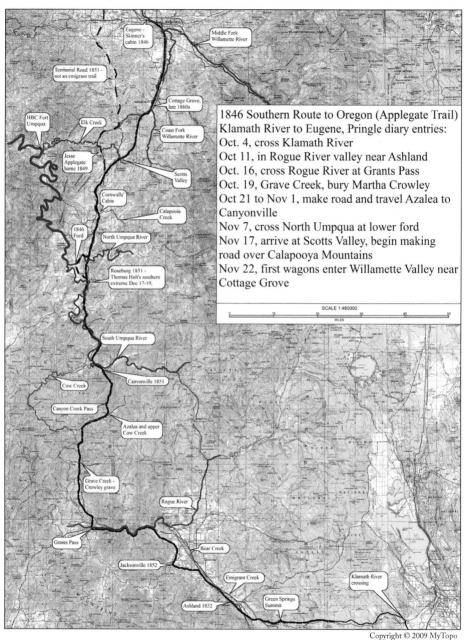

Within the map image:

Eugene - Skinner's cabin 1846

Middle Fork Willamette River

Territorial Road 1851 - not an emigrant trail

Cottage Grove, late 1860s

HBC Fort Umpqua

Elk Creek

Coast Fork Willamette River

Jesse Applegate home 1849

Scotts Valley

Cornwalls' Cabin

Calapooia Creek

1846 Ford

North Umpqua River

Roseburg 1851 - Thomas Holt's southern extreme Dec 17-19,

1846 Southern Route to Oregon (Applegate Trail) Klamath River to Eugene, Pringle diary entries:
Oct. 4, cross Klamath River
Oct 11, in Rogue River valley near Ashland
Oct. 16, cross Rogue River at Grants Pass
Oct. 19, Grave Creek, bury Martha Crowley
Oct 21 to Nov 1, make road and travel Azalea to Canyonville
Nov 7, cross North Umpqua at lower ford
Nov 17, arrive at Scotts Valley, begin making road over Calapooya Mountains
Nov 22, first wagons enter Willamette Valley near Cottage Grove

SCALE 1:480000

MILES

South Umpqua River

Cow Creek

Canyonville 1851

Canyon Creek Pass

Azalea and upper Cow Creek

Grave Creek - Crowley grave

Rogue River

Grants Pass

Bear Creek

Jacksonville 1852

Emigrant Creek

Klamath River crossing

Ashland 1852

Green Springs Summit

Map of the 1846 Trail, Klamath River to Skinner's Cabin. *Annotation by Stafford Hazelett.*

himself, and they did not seem to expect either aid or sympathy from each other. So, they went on in squads of three or four wagons and, frequently, one wagon traveled alone. Some had broken their wagons in the Canyon and left them and some had lost so much of their teams that they were compelled to abandon their wagons. Some packed their provisions and beds on a horse, some on an ox; some who had neither horse, mule, nor ox packed all they had upon a cow; while a few, who had no animal left, took a pack upon their shoulders and trudged on as best they could towards the settlements.[168]

John Newton, who had lost his wagon and the most of his team, had a mare left on which his wife rode while he, with his brother, Thomas, and an orphan boy who was with them, packed the tent, bedding, and what little provisions they had left upon the oxen which they had succeeded in getting through the canyon. When they reached Deer Creek, John Newton was sick and their provisions were exhausted. Thomas Newton went back to meet some friends who were behind them, to see if he could get some provisions and medicine for his brother.

While he lay here, sick, in his tent, two Indians came to the camp in the evening just before sundown. Newton gave them to understand, by signs, that was out of provisions, and would be glad to traffic with them for something to eat. They signified to him that, if he would let them have his gun, they would go and kill a deer, and bring it to his camp. He loaded his rifle and gave it to them and they went off to hunt for a deer, as they pretended.

A little after dark they returned to the camp without any venison. They shot Newton with his own gun as he lay in bed and struck him with an ax, nearly severing one of his legs, when taking his mare and the gun with them, they disappeared in the darkness.[169]

---

168 Harris, Nesmith (writing for Goff), and Applegate insisted there were no such losses. Harris, *Oregon Spectator*, Nov. 26, 1846; Goff [Nesmith], *Oregon Spectator*, April 29, 1847; Applegate, *Oregon Spectator*, March 18, 1847. *See also*, Hazelett, "'To the World!!!': The Story Behind the Vitriol."

169 Newton's story is corroborated in many other places. Thomas Holt, "Diary of Thomas Holt," *Oregon Spectator*, March 4, 1847, 4; reprint in Morgan, *Overland in 1846*, 191-98, citations to Morgan; Levi Scott [attributed to Jesse Applegate], "Waybill: From Fort Hall to Willamette Valley"; Thornton, *Oregon and California in 1848*, 1:238. Collins adjusted Scott's original draft to conform to the standard narrative.

Mrs. Newton and the boy, I think his name was Sutton Caldwell, spent a most wretched night with her wounded husband who died of his wounds the next morning.

At daybreak, the boy started and ran alone some five or six miles to where some emigrants were camped to solicit aid from them, leaving the wretched woman with her dead husband, in dread every moment that his murderers return to sack their camp and, perhaps, to stain their hands with more blood. But, it seems that the mare and the gun were all that the savages coveted, or had courage to take, and with them they were content to escape.

Newton's mare and gun were recovered from the Indians the next summer. The chief of their tribe gave them up on demand of a party of white men to save his camp from a hostile attack. But he represented that the murderers were a couple of renegades of the Umpqua Indians whom he would gladly deliver up for punishment if he could catch them. He said that he had taken the property from them to restore it to its owner, and that the murderers had fled to the Klamath Indians for fear that he would either punish them himself or give them up to the white people to be punished by them. He said that they were bad young men, and that he would catch them and deliver them up if he could. But they were never given up.[170]

When the small party that was with me in advance of all others reached the North Umpqua, that stream was up so that we could not ford it and we had no other means of crossing it.[171] I had crossed it in summer about three or four miles below, so we went down to that place which was very deep and rocky. We hired a canoe from the Indians who were camped along the stream, in which we ferried over the women and

---

170 Mrs. Newton remarried two years later to Truman Powers. *Oregon Spectator*, "Married [Newton-Powers]," Sept. 2, 1847, 3. Powers was an emigrant who became a road worker. After getting safely into the settlements, he returned to help rescue emigrants after Thornton's plea was published in the *Oregon Spectator*. "The Emigrants—Southern Route," December 10, 1847, 1, col. 1.

171 Scott and the 1846 emigrants were the first to try this ford with wagons in the month of November. The summer ford was usually upstream near the present town of Winchester, but it was too high around July 1 when the explorers tried it. Scott did not seem to think the river had risen much, if any, since he crossed it before the rains. Pringle, "Diary [Nov. 6-8]," in Morgan, *Overland in 1846*, 186.

children with the baggage, and then managed to cross the teams with the empty wagons at the ford.[172]

It was now about fifteen miles to the foot of the Calapooya Mountains with an open country and reasonably good ground for a road, but with our jaded teams it took us two days to reach that point.[173] Here we found our progress barred by a heavily timbered mountain, fifteen miles across, and the way over it had not even been blazed out.

Between the crossing of the North Umpqua and the Calapooya Mountains, the wife of John B. Bounds died. She was buried on the north side of the creek, not more than about a half mile above the crossing at the present town of Oakland.[174]

The wagon of Richard Linville upset in a little creek just before we reached the foot of the mountains, not far from Yoncalla, and his wife, who was quite an old lady, was drowned before she could be rescued from beneath the overturned wagon and its contents.

Now, here we were, at the foot of this densely wooded mountain, a mere handful of the first stragglers of a broken and disorganized company of exhausted emigrants who had traveled more than two thousand miles through burning deserts, dust, and storms, and treacherous foes, with exhausted teams and disheartened men, out of provisions, and it was a hundred and fifty miles, yet, beyond this pile of mountains to

---

172 Pringle noted that the ford was impassable and that they had to backtrack and go to the lower ford. Pringle, "Diary," in Morgan, *Overland in 1846*, 186. The crossing was near where Garden Valley Road now crosses the North Umpqua River, about seven river miles below Winchester.

173 Scott's estimate is short and he forgot Rice Hill. The pass is at 723 feet after clearing the trees and improving the terrain with dynamite for the modern highway. The distance was at least twenty-three miles. Scott estimated it at twenty-five miles for the waybill, from the crossing of the Umpqua River to Scott's Farm in Scott's Valley. Scott, "Waybill from Fort Hall to Willamette Valley." Pringle recorded crossing the North Umpqua River on November 7, traveled fifteen miles in four days, laid by three days to rest the draft animals and obtain food for the people, then fourteen miles more in three days to the foot of the "Callipoa Mountains." Pringle remained near the front of the emigration. Pringle, "Diary," in Morgan, *Overland in 1846*, 186-87.

174 Scott described the death and burial of Mrs. Bounds on November 14 at about the same location as Pringle recorded. Pringle, "Diary," in Morgan, *Overland in 1846*, 187. Since this was not in Scott's original manuscript, it may have been prompted by Collins's access to Pringle's diary. This was the fifth of six deaths in that family in less than two months.

where anything could be had for us to subsist upon during the winter. The
dreary winter rains were drizzling down upon us almost constantly, day
and night. Without the hard discipline which had exercised every one of
us, we could not have looked this mountain in the face with any degree
of resolution or hope. If such difficulties had been at the beginning of the
journey, it would never have been attempted.[175]

I knew the general course we must go, but knew little in detail of the
ground we must travel over and of the difficulties we should encounter in
making a road across the mountain. But, from the general observations
I had made on our way out, I was confident that a reasonably good road
could be made for wagons to cross. But there had not yet been a stick cut
nor a blaze made.[176]

I rallied a small force of hands, a forlorn hope, and attacked the apparently impenetrable forest. We sent forward a small party by the Indian
trail to the settlements for provisions and assistance. But, I think that
Enoch Garrison, from the Yamhill who had met us at the Canyon, and
myself were the only men besides emigrants who worked any upon the
road from the entrance of the Canyon to the Willamette Valley.[177]

---

175   Scott again sympathized with the difficulties of the emigrants and graphically
described their condition. Scott's estimate of the distance was also very close.
Professor Richard Rieck has calculated the total distance from Independence,
Missouri, by way of the Southern Route to Oregon at Dallas at 2,175 miles.
Richard L. Rieck, "Geography of the Oregon Trail West of Fort Hall: A Plethora
of Options," *Overland Journal* 17, no. 2 (Summer 1999): 9-23. Oregon City was
roughly sixty miles beyond Dallas by any route.

176   Scott expressed his frustration concerning the failure of the road clearing party to
leave even a trace of its passage across this obstacle. The Applegates' reminiscence
dismissed the Calapooya Mountain crossing as insignificant: "Road working,
hunting, and guard duty had taxed our strength greatly, and on our arrival in the
Umpqua valley, knowing that the greatest difficulties in the way of immigrants
had been removed, we decided to proceed at once to our home in the Willamette."
Applegate, "Notes and Reminiscences, etc.," 40-41. The route over the Calapooya
Mountain was sufficiently strenuous that the Oregon Territorial Government
made opening the Territorial Road by way of Yoncalla, where the Applegates
settled, its highest road priority. The bypass was open for pack trains in 1851. There
was still agitation for a better route. Army engineers Abbott and Williamson
mentioned construction of a new road was in progress on the Pass Creek route in
1855, today's route for Interstate 5. R. W. Sawyer, "Abbott Railroad Surveys, 1855,"
Oregon Historical Quarterly 33, no. 2 (June 1932): 125.

177   Scott again expressed frustration about the failure of the road-clearing company to
leave any trace of their passing. This was all the more remarkable knowing his two

I would go forward, view out and blaze the way for a considerable distance, and then return to the working party, and help them to cut up as far as I had blazed. Then, I would blaze ahead, again. In this manner we finally got a rude way opened and, by doubling teams at the steep places, we managed to get nearly all of the wagons over that had now reached the mountain.[178]

When we reached the head of the Willamette Valley, on the north side of the mountain, we were met by a few wagons from the settlements laden with provisions.[179] This was a joyful meeting for the starving emigrants and it seemed to remove a great weight from my heart. I felt that my task was accomplished, although with infinite pain, toil, and anxiety. I had kept my engagement, I had performed the duty I had assumed, and had led the immigration into the Great Valley at the head of the Willamette River and, most likely, by the best way for a road that could be found. I felt sure that a little time and labor would make this a good road and the principal route of travel to the Willamette.

The track made by the wagons that met us could be followed into the settlements by the immigrants and I felt that my task was ended. Yet the troubles of the poor immigrants were not over. The winter rains had raised the streams and rendered it impossible to ford many of them,

---

sons, with whom he spent much of his life, were on that crew. Rev. A. E. Garrison recalled that his brothers, Joseph and Enoch, along with Enoch's son, Jeptha, helped cut the trail across the Calapooya Mountains. Garrison, "Forty-two Years in Oregon," 38, 40, 42.

178 Pringle recorded his arrival at the foot of the Calapooya Mountains on November 17. He crossed one ridge the next day, making two miles. He crossed another ridge the next day, making three miles. He climbed to the top of the mountain the next day, making four miles, and camped with the lead company, again. He recorded two more days of two miles each helping the road workers to finish the final leg to the bottom of the mountain and the entry into the Willamette Valley. Thus it took Pringle five days building road to cover the thirteen miles over the Calapooya Mountains. "My wagons and one other the first that entered the valley." Pringle, "Diary," in Morgan, *Overland in 1846*, 187. Here Morgan made one of his few bad guesses about the route, believing the Pringles traveled the present route of Interstate 5 in the valley of Pass Creek. Morgan, *Overland in 1846*, 1:396n97.

179 Scott and Collins did not identify anyone associated with this relief party. Pringle did not record any relief from the north side of the Calapooya Mountains until December 6, when Orus Brown, his brother-in-law, arrived north of the Long Tom River. Pringle, "Diary," in Morgan, *Overland in 1846*, 187-88. Thomas Holt, diarist and leader of the most thorough relief party, arrived at the Long Tom River the next day and at Eugene on December 9. Holt, "Diary," in Morgan, *Overland in 1846*, 192.

which must be ferried over on the rude rafts hastily constructed by the travelers. And the ground, which had never been trodden into a solid road anywhere, was soft and miry, and the rain was almost constantly drizzling down, day and night.

The Rev. Joseph A. Cornwall, a minister of the Presbyterian Church, with his family, and Ezekial Kennedy, with his wife and a little grandson, wintered on a little branch near Oakland in the Umpqua Valley because they had lost their teams and could get on no further. Several wintered near the head of the Willamette Valley but most of the immigrants reached the settlements in some way by a little after Christmas.[180]

Herman Buckingham, whose team had failed so that he could advance no further with his wagon, built a raft near the junction of the Middle and Coast Forks of the Willamette and, going upon it with his family, attempted to reach the settlements by water. Before he had proceeded ten miles, his raft upset and it was with the greatest difficulty that he himself and family escaped a watery grave. They lost everything they had in the raft, and suffered the most extreme privation before reaching the settlements.

I went on from the Calapooya Mountains with the foremost wagons. When we came to the Long Tom River, we found that it had been very much swollen by the recent rains and in many places its broad, low bottoms were overflowed. It could not be forded anywhere. So we were compelled to dig out a canoe for a ferry boat. In this we ferried the woman and children over with the baggage. We compelled the stock to swim over and then we took the wagons to pieces, floated the beds across, and then, balancing the running gear of each wagon upon the canoe with the wheels in the water on either side, we finally got everything safely over.

A man by the name of Lloyd had settled during the summer of 1846, near the head of a tributary of Mary's River, called Muddy, some ten or twelve miles west of where we crossed the Long Tom, and J. C. Avery had taken a claim at the mouth of Mary's River, about twenty miles

180 On December 14, Holt was near the site of today's Oakland where he encountered the Kennedys, Halls, Croisans, and Lovlen on the "north fork of Elk Creek," now known as Cabin Creek, and the next day he found the Cornwalls and Dunbars near Calpooia Creek. Holt, "Diary," in Morgan, *Overland in 1846*, 193-94.

further down the valley. So we began to feel now that we were getting into the settlements.[181]

I went about forty miles further to the Prather settlement near the mouth of the Luckiamute River where I stopped for a while.[182] I then went on to Captain Applegate's place and helped him for a time in a mill he was building near the head of Salt Creek.

Now I had spent pretty much the whole of the year 1846 in the exploration and in helping the immigrants through for which I got nothing except the curses and abuse of some who came this way and of some of the most selfish of the settlers in the north end of the valley who feared that a southern route might have a tendency to retard the settlement of their immediate neighborhood.[183] But I have the satisfaction to believe that, so far at least as I was, myself, concerned, both of these classes of grumblers were few and confined to those whose opinions were of little weight and of no permanent disadvantage to me.[184]

I afterwards noticed that those who had said they would shoot Captain Applegate on sight seemed to change their minds when they reached

181 John Lloyd and Joseph Avery were emigrants of 1845 by the Meek Cutoff. Avery is considered the first settler of Corvallis. Corning, *Dictionary of Oregon History*, 15, 64; Engeman, *The Oregon Companion*, 101; McArthur, *Oregon Geographic Names*, 254.

182 The William Prather Donation Land Claim, No. 1197, was located on the west bank of the Willamette River just below its confluence with the Luckiamute River. The Buena Vista Ferry crossing is slightly north of the land claim.

183 Rev. Abraham E. Garrison claimed to have paid Scott $21 and a letter writer claimed that someone paid $14. Garrison, "Forty-two Years in Oregon," 29; One of the Road Hunters, *Oregon Spectator*, April 15, 1847.

184 The contentious public discussion in the *Oregon Spectator* provided fair warning to anyone who questioned the new route. Only J. Quinn Thornton spoke up in public. *See* Hazelett, "'To The World!!' The Story Behind the Vitriol." Seven years later, Tabitha Brown summarized the emigrants' version of Scott's assessment: Applegate "decoyed [us] off...and left us to the depredations of Indians, wild beasts, and starvation" and Scott "proved to be an excellent man; otherwise we never would have seen Oregon." Tabitha Brown, "A Brimfield Heroine," 52. Letters home were safer than confronting the road-hunters. Scott suspected "hundreds of letters...cautioning them not to travel the southern route." *See* Appendix 3. One of those letters-writers was John Luce, although 19th century handwriting being what it was, and spelling a rather flexible concept, his name has been rendered as "Long" and "Lose" and "Loose" in addition to the land patent records with the spelling "Luce." He was a single man in 1846 who finally packed into the settlements. His letter describing his experience on the Southern Route to Oregon appears in Appendix 4.

the settlements where they could get plenty to eat, and had rested a little from the fatigues of their toilsome journey, and had heard the settlers relate their experience on the route down Snake River and the Columbia. And they generally met the Captain with a show of the respect he certainly deserved, notwithstanding he may have made some very natural, and in most instances, unavoidable mistakes.[185]

In 1845, a party of emigrants had attempted to come in by the head of the Malheur, John Day's, and Deschutes Rivers, intending to cross the Cascade Mountains near Mount Jefferson and enter the valley at the head of the Middle Fork or of the McKenzie's Fork of the Willamette. The very statement of this scheme shows the mistaken ignorance of their guide, as neither of these streams head was near Mount Jefferson. After very great suffering and the loss of most of their property, they were compelled to abandon their design, to turn north along the eastern base of the mountains, and reach the Columbia River at the Dalles.[186]

---

185 With a figurative wave of his hand, Scott dismissed his own comments about the Applegates' failures to recruit enough road workers and to make a road. Scott and Collins make it seem as if everything had been forgiven and forgotten. However, oral traditions and reminiscences, many coming to light decades later, indicate that the bitterness lingered. "Taken all in all this was the most deeply shadowed page in the history of Oregon immigration, and has left a heritage of more acrimonious and bitter discussions and heart burnings to the historian of Oregon." Rev. H.K. Hines, *An Illustrated History of the State of Oregon* (Chicago: The Lewis Pub. Co., 1893), 131–32; Karen Bassett, Jim Renner, and Joyce White, *Oregon Historic Trails Report* (Salem, OR: Oregon Trails Coordinating Council, 1998) 50.

186 In 1845, several wagon companies led by Stephen Meek attempted to find a route across central Oregon to The Dalles, never intending to cross the Cascades. Solomon Tetherow, "For the Oregon Spectator," *Oregon Spectator*, March 18, 1847, 3, col. 2-3. Scott conflates Meek's 1845 party with the later efforts, notably by Elliott in 1853 and Macy in 1854, that culminated in the Free Emigrant Road which did cross over the Cascades near the head of the Middle Fork of the Willamette River at Emigrant Pass, south of Willamette Pass on Oregon Highway 58. For a more complete description of the emigration of 1845 with Stephen Meek, *see* Keith Clark and Lowell Tiller, *Terrible Trail: The Meek Cutoff, 1845* (Caldwell, ID: The Caxton Printers, 1967) and James H. Hambleton and Theona J. Hambleton, *Wood, Water & Grass: Meek Cutoff of 1845* (Caldwell, ID: Caxton Press, 2014). The best source of information about the developments of 1853 and 1854 is a series of six articles by Leah Menefee and Lowell Tiller. "Cutoff Fever, I-VI," *Oregon Historical Quarterly*, 77, no. 4 (December 1976) to 79, no. 1 (Spring 1978). Scott approved a plan to improve the Free Emigrant Road while serving in the territorial legislature. William M. Macy, et al., "The New Emigrant Road," *Oregon Statesman*, March 19, 1853, 2, col. 1-2.

During the same season, a party had made an effort to cross the mountains near Mount Hood on a route viewed out by William Barlow of Oregon City but they were compelled to abandon their wagons in the mountains and get into the settlements the best way they could after having suffered the greatest hardships. Many of them thought that they never could get their wagons through.[187] These and other difficulties and embarrassments led to our explorations and search for a southern pass in 1846.

During the summer, while we were engaged in our southern road enterprise, those who had left their wagons in the mountains on the Barlow route went to work on the road and brought them through. They put this road in such a condition that many of the immigrants crossed the mountains that way in the fall. Now there were two ways by which it was possible to get into the Willamette Valley with wagons; one at the head and the other at the mouth of the river. These were regarded as achievements of untold value to the country.

In 1847, I was employed by some of the settlers to meet the immigration and lead them through by the southern route; at least, all who wished to come in that way. For this service I received a very small compensation. I am almost ashamed to say that I only got a hundred bushels of wheat for it. But as I had worked a great deal harder and encountered more danger the year before, and got nothing for it, I thought this would do pretty well as it would, at least, give me something to eat.

The Hon. Felix Scott raised the subscription for me and gave thirty bushels of the wheat himself.[188] He was an intelligent, energetic, and enterprising gentleman who had come to this country from St. Charles County, Missouri, which county, I believe, he had represented in the legislature of that state at an early day after its admission into the Union.

Several years after this, Mr. Scott went east and purchased a lot of fine stock. While returning to Oregon, it is supposed that he was attacked by

---

187 This was a very brief summary of the attempt to open the Barlow Road. Collins and Scott persisted in their confusion between Samuel Barlow, the explorer of the new road, and his son, William. Its history has considerably more reminiscences to tell its stories and is far less controversial. Two good histories are William Barlow, "Reminiscences of Seventy Years," *Quarterly of the Oregon Historical Society* 13, no. 3 (September 1912): 261-68, 274-76, 280-81; and Joel Palmer, *Journal of Travels Over the Rocky Mountains* (Cincinnati: J.A. & U.P. James, 1847); reprint Ye Galleon Press, Fairfield, WA, 1966.
188 This was Felix Scott Sr.

the Indians near Goose Lake and himself and all his party massacred. It was several years before any definite information could be obtained concerning his fate and then only the meager stories told by the Indians. No trace of his stock was ever found except that one of his finest stallions was seen and recognized at Salt Lake City sometime afterwards.[189]

There was a party of about thirty young men going back to the states, some of whom expected to meet friends coming to Oregon in which case they would return with them, otherwise they would go on to their old homes in the east.

I believe that B. F. Burch was the only one of the party who returned to Oregon with me. He met his father and a good many of his kindred in company with Hezekiah Davidson (whose eldest daughter Mr. Burch afterwards married) on their way to the Willamette Valley and he returned with them.[190]

This party of young men proposed at the start to elect me Captain of their company, which responsibility I refused to assume unless they would agree to obey all of my directions. To this they consented and I took command of the expedition.

We got along without any difficult or serious embarrassment till we reached a small branch of Bear Creek in Rogue River Valley, near where the town of Phoenix now is, where we were attacked by the Indians. They hung upon our flanks all day and we could frequently hear the warwhoop upon the hills. For fear of an attack during the night, we pitched our camp on the prairie about sixty yards from the nearest timber. We picketed our horses close around the camp and mounted a strong guard.

Sometime in the night, the guard noticed a commotion among the horses and, on examination, we found a mule shot with an arrow. In a little while, the arrows began to whiz into our camp. One stuck in the ground by the head of one of the men before he got out of his blankets and several went through the tent. We fired a volley into the nearest bushes. Then a man, whom we called Little Osborne, mounted a horse

---

189 An excellent biography of Captain Felix Scott Sr. is on the Lane County history site: www.orgenweb.org/lane/hisscott.htm (accessed March 2015). Felix Scott originally emigrated overland to California in 1845 with his family. The next year, they traveled overland to Oregon in the company of Eugene Skinner and two other families and arrived at the Dallas area by June 1846.

190 Caroline F. Burch, "The Burch Family," in DAR, *Polk County Pioneer Sketches*, 2:5-8.

and galloped all around the camp to see if any of the Indians were concealed in the long grass.

The next morning, we found the mule had been shot in the hip and a horse in the muscle of the hind leg, just above the hock joint. The mule was not seriously injured but the horse was quite lame. The arrow had broken off in his leg. We caught him and, after considerable trouble, we got the piece of arrow out.

After breakfast, we started on and went about a quarter of a mile when a detachment of five men returned towards the camp to see if there were any Indians entering it, which we supposed they would do as soon as we were out of sight. They rode back over the hill as fast as they could and found several of the Indians already in the camp, one of whom was on horseback. The boys charged and fired upon them. The Indians on foot immediately fled into the bushes. The one on horseback ran to the creek but could not get across with his horse, when he leaped off and fled into the woods afoot.

The horse proved to be one that had been stolen the year before, from a young man by the name of Miller, who was one of our party, and was very glad, thus, unexpectedly, to recover his property. The horse had been stolen the fall before, a little further down the Rogue River Valley, from the pioneers, or road-working party, of which Miller was one.[191]

This bold dash from a handful of us, with the loss of their horse and their narrow escape from our bullets if, indeed, they did entirely escape from them, gave the Rogues such a taste of the mettle of our company that they let us alone and we did not see another Indian, nor hear a whisper of the war-whoop, again, while we were in the Rogue River Valley.

We pursued our journey following the trail of 1846 without anything further happening beyond the ordinary incidents of camp life till we got through High Rock Canyon where I wished to see if we could make a cut-off, crossing the Black Rock ridge north of the Boiling Springs, and reaching the Humboldt River further up that stream than the point where we had left it the year before.

---

191 Miller was identified by Scott in his original manuscript as a member of the road-clearing party. He may also have been the writer of the letter from "M," a member of the road-clearing party in 1846, about Truman Powers published in the *Oregon Statesman*, Sept. 25, 1852, 2, col. 4. This story of Miller's horse is similar to one told by Joseph Watt, a member of the 1847 eastbound emigration, to Samuel A. Clarke. "Pioneer Days, Article XXIII," *Sunday Oregonian*, Sept. 27, 1885, 2, col. 1-2.

We crossed a spur of the Black Rock Mountain and, about twelve or fourteen miles on the east side of it, camped on a small lake in the edge of a sage plain which was from fifteen to twenty miles across which seemed to be level in the direction of the Humboldt. Here the company became very much discouraged with the appearance of things to the eastward and Black Harris strongly opposed trying to find a road in that direction. So, we finally concluded to turn more to the south and strike the Humboldt as soon as possible.[192]

We camped the next night at a small spring branch three or four miles from the river. The next morning we struck the Humboldt some distance above where we had left it the year before. The waters were so high that we could not cross, so we traveled up the stream all day and camped at night on a small branch running into it. We went up the river the next day till we found a place where we could cross it when we struck the trail of 1846, again, and followed it till we reached Fort Hall.

I went on with the company past the Fort to Smith River, a tributary of Bear River, about half way between the Soda Springs and Fort Bridger. Here we found a camp of some old mountaineers. Pegleg Smith, an American, Anderson, an Englishman, and a Frenchman, whose name

---

192 Scott's description of trying a new route avoiding the terrible crossing of the
Black Rock Desert between Rabbit Hole Springs and Black Rock Spring was
also corroborated by Joseph Watt. Clarke, "Pioneer Days, Article XXIII." It seems
likely that Scott brought the company nearly to the Black Rock where there is a
low pass across the range about two miles north of Black Rock Spring. There they
could have turned east, crossed the low ridge where a road now runs, crossed the
sage plain that is the east arm of the Black Rock Desert, and reached the area of
occasional small ponds at about the point he described. From there they could
see the pass where the railroad and Humboldt County Road 55 (Jungo Road),
presently cross between the Jackson Mountains and the Kamma Mountains. This
route would have brought them near the town site of Jungo from which, to the
east, they would have seen their way blocked by the Eugene Mountains. If they
had continued slightly north of true east, they would have crossed a nearly level
plain for about twenty miles to the Humboldt River and arrived at the California
Trail near Little Tabletop Mountain about fifteen miles west of present day
Winnemucca. As described by Scott, they turned more to the south. The direction
suggests that they turned to avoid the Eugene Mountains and skirted them
coming out on the Humboldt River near Imlay, "some distance above where the
original trail left it," as he wrote in his original manuscript.

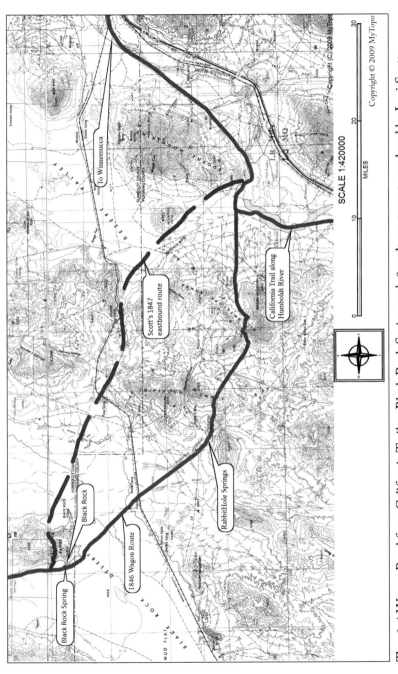

The 1846 Wagon Road from California Trail to Black Rock Spring and 1847 alternate route explored by Levi Scott. *Annotation by Stafford Hazelett.*

I have forgotten, were camped here with their squaws and children. I stopped with them for about two weeks.[193]

Pegleg Smith, for whom this river was named, had lost a leg in some of his Indian battles in the mountains and took his singular prenomen from the peg of wood which supplied its place. He was one of the most famous and daring men of the mountains and an overbearing, tyrannical bully, withal. He was a dead shot and could hold an argument with firearms that I soon learned was much more convincing than satisfactory. His squaw was a woman of the Flathead tribe, down on the Columbia River, and they had a little boy of some five or six months old, of whom Smith was very fond. One day, in the heat of one of their domestic disputes, Mrs. Smith pettishly allowed the child to roll from her lap to the ground when Pegleg instantly whipped out a pistol and fired, neatly cutting out a wisp of the lady's scalp-lock, just barely blistering the crown of her head. Without offering any response to this cutting, conjugal argument, she meekly took up the child and dropped the subject.

Anderson was a man of good education and had evidently been brought up in refined society. His squaw was a Ute and they had no children. The Frenchman was a Canadian, I think, and his family consisted of his Shoshone squaw and three children.

While I was here, one of these men killed an old doe that was big with young. When I saw that he was very careful about saving the fetus, I inquired what he intended to do with it. He said he was saving it for their squaws who considered it a great dainty. He took it to camp where the women boiled it in a pot till it was reduced to a mass of jelly which they ate with evident relish. I felt that I should not like to enjoy very intimate relations with beings who had sunk to such a filthy degree of degradation.

One day, while I was at this camp, a strong party of Indians came in sight and seemed to be approaching our camp. There was at once a great flutter of excitement and apparent anxiety among my mountaineer neighbors. My comrades did not seem to be quite sure whether it was a

---

193 Smith's trading post, often identified as "Smith's Fort" or "Big Timbers," was not a fixed place, but was always along the Bear River somewhere north of Fort Bridger. John Unruh, *The Plains Across* (Urbana, IL: University of Illinois Press, 1979), 248. John Howell, traveling east by way of the Barlow Road and Oregon Trail, was at Fort Hall on June 26 and at Smith's on July 4, noting that Scott's company arrived at Smith's on or about June 24. "Diary of John E. Howell," *Washington Historical Quarterly* 1, no. 3 (April 1907): 157. When Lester Hulin, diarist of the 1847 Oskaloosa, Iowa, company, passed by Smith's on August 12, Scott had already left.

party of friends or enemies. So, the men, armed to the teeth, mounted their horses and went out to meet them.

They proved to be a party of friendly Crow Indians who had come to Bear River to trade with a party of Snake Indians whom they expected to arrive in a few days. Along with the white men, they rode into our camp with great pomp and ceremony and pitched their camp along with us.

As soon as they had dismounted, they took out the Great Pipe of Peace and we all arranged ourselves in a circle and smoked it, passing it around from one to another. After this very grave and solemn ceremony, we found ourselves on terms of easy affability with each other as if we had been brought up together from childhood and had all graduated from the same University.

In coming out here, I had made some valuable observations which enabled me to shorten and improve the road in many respects and at many of the most difficult places.[194]

When the emigrants came up, about two weeks after I reached Smith River, they made a great deal of inquiry about the different roads. I gave them plainly and impartially all the information I could respecting the two routes. I told them that I had come out on the southern road and for what purpose I had come, and that I was going back the same way with all who wished to go that route, and that it would be my sole business and study to aid them all I could. Moreover, I told them that I would not solicit nor advise anyone to go one way nor the other, each must settle that matter for himself without my advice; but all who should see fit to go the way I did would find me ready to assist them as much as I could.[195]

194   Scott otherwise left us no information which might have identified these "improvements" other than the new path through what became the Bear Valley National Wildlife Refuge west of Worden, Oregon.

195   Governor Abernethy had printed a circular warning people to stay with the old road in April 1847 (published in *Oregon Spectator*, January 20, 1848, 3, col. 4). (*See* Appendix 2.) Some of the men who returned east by way of the old Oregon Trail passed Smith's fort and warned emigrants not to take the Southern Route and showed them the circular. One of those men, John Howell, had performed service with a relief party for the 1846 emigrants and did not need the circular to warn people. Upon returning to the Oregon settlements following the 1847 migration, Scott wrote a letter to the *Oregon Spectator* in which he described meeting people who had been warned not to take the Southern Route to Oregon. He saw a copy of Abernethy's circular and heard that other men heading east had recommended that the emigrants should inflict serious harm on anyone who proposed to lead them off the old Oregon Trail. *Oregon Spectator*, November 11, 1847, p. 3, c. 1-2. (*See* Appendix 3).

When we came to the forks of the road, the most of those who were with me and had talked with me concerning the relative merits of the two roads took the southern route with me.[196]

Soon after we reached the Humboldt, a bright, intelligent, goodlooking, young Indian fell in with us. He seemed to be very much pleased with our society and tried to help drive stock and made himself as useful as possible in every way he could. He appeared to enjoy the bread, and other good things we gave him to eat, immensely.

Some of the boys took a great liking to him and concluded that they would take him to Oregon with them and have an Indian of their own. He agreed to go with them, apparently with the greatest pleasure. And they dressed the naked child of the desert in pants, and shirt, and vest, with a good pair of shoes, and a hat, making quite a good-looking man of him. He was extremely proud of his outfit and his pale friends were vain of what they had done towards civilizing and christianizing this untutored child of the wilderness.

I suggested to the boys that they had better not be too liberal and charitable on such short acquaintance, that this young brother had not been brought up in the Sunday Schools with them, and that he was, undoubtedly, an *Indian*. Nay, but they would make a civilized man and a christian of him. They had faith in him. He would come out all right. Alas, for misplaced confidence in our brother man! He did come out all right from his point of view but not from theirs. About the third or fourth night, he stole three blankets and a lot of clothing and went in search of "the girl he left behind him." And I feel confident that his snobbish outfit and the treasures for the wardrobe and the bridal bed which he was able to lay at her feet must have called forth a gushing benediction from her when they met, again, in the drawing room of her paternal villa.

His liberal young friends felt that they had, indeed, met an Indian who was proof against the benign influence of civilization and christianity.

---

196 Levi Scott may have explained the advantages and disadvantages of each route, but few were persuaded to join him. Unruh estimated four thousand overland emigrants to Oregon. Unruh, *The Plains Across*, 119. Fewer than three hundred took the Southern Route, and not all of those with Scott. Bancroft documented forty-five wagons altogether. Helfrich thought there might have been another train of seventeen wagons. A common estimate of people to wagons is 5:1. Helfrich, "Applegate Trail," 5, 8-9.

༜

CHAPTER XV

Emigrant Adventures and the Whitman Incident

After we had traveled down the Humboldt for several days, the Indians stole six head of our oxen. We found their trail when fifteen of us mounted our horses and went in pursuit of them. When we came within about a mile of where they had stopped with the cattle, we saw an Indian coming directly from where the stolen cattle were. He was running across a level plain about half a mile from us. Three of the boys gave chase and soon caught him.

When they brought the captive to where we were, he asserted his innocence by signs most vehemently. But he showed us exactly where the cattle were and then desired us to let him go as a reward of merit.

We took him along with us to where he said the cattle were and found everything just as he had represented. He assured us that other Indians had done it; showed us which way they had gone, and proposed to help us track them up. But it was useless for us to follow them. We knew, as well as he did, that we could do nothing with them, and that further pursuit could result in nothing unless it might be that we should fall into an ambuscade and some of us be killed. We declined his generous offer to help us track them up. He was ready to say or do anything to prove his innocence, but we were satisfied that he was guilty and that all of his actions and protestations were part of a ruse to aid his comrades as well as himself in escaping our vengeance.

We found two of the oxen butchered and the meat all cut and prepared, ready for jerking or drying. Two others were just dying and two were but slightly wounded.

We were now in a quandary as to what we ought to do with this Indian. Two of the men were determined to shoot him; nothing else would do;

they had their guns cocked and presented while others were begging for him. As a spectator of the tragedy, I looked on and said nothing.

After a while someone proposed to leave it to me and they said they would do as I should decide. All agreed to this. The Indian was standing by the pile of beef which had been cut up and stacked in a pile by the thieves. I said, "Shoot him, and leave him on the pile of meat. It will be a warning to others."

I turned and walked away. The gentlemen who, a moment before, could scarcely be restrained from shedding his blood, failed to execute the judgment they had so loudly called for. They did not shoot. No one would shoot him. They seemed to expect me to do it. I told them that I would not shoot him any more than they would, but we would take him to camp and give him up to the owners of the cattle that had been stolen and see what they would do with him.

We had fifteen miles to go to reach camp and it was now nearly sundown. Our way lay over an open level plain. The Indian was afraid to run from us, so we drove him along before us with the two wounded oxen till it began to be dark when we tied him. I requested Robinson to tie him but he was unable to do it. I dismounted and threw him down on the ground. When I put the loop over his head he squealed, caught it in his teeth, and fought like a very devil, till I got it down about his waist and tied it there. Then, after I tied his hands behind him, he ceased to struggle and quieted down.

I took charge of the prisoner and thought I would drive him on ahead of me but he did not drive well. As it grew dark, he would turn first one way and then another and would blunder and fall and make all the trouble and delay he possibly could, till, finally, getting out of patience with the rascal, I went ahead and thought I would lead him. But he was stubborn and would not lead any better than he would drive. Then I began to be provoked with his obstinacy and concluded I would break the young colt to lead, anyhow. So, I took a turn around the horn of my saddle with the end of the larriette and, the first blunder he made, I spurred my horse into a trot which jerked the Indian down when I dragged him a little and then paused to let him get up. But I had to repeat this operation with him. When I let him up, again, I started my horse in a trot and kept that gait right along, the Indians trotting behind me.

I had no more trouble with my charge till we reached the Humboldt River when he made signs that he wanted to drink. We let him lie down by the margin of the water to drink. He made several ineffectual attempts to reach the water. He pretended that he could not reach it with his lips unless we would unbind him.

When we became satisfied that he was just maneuvering to get himself released from the rope so that he might have a good opportunity to escape in the darkness among the willows, one of the boys caught him by the breech-clout and heaved him, neck and heels, into the river. The water was shallow but deep enough to give him a good ducking and ample opportunity to get a drink.

I got him to camp without any further trouble. We kept him bound till morning, when the owners of the cattle said: "Let him go. He may be innocent."

I told them, I thought it would be best for us to lynch him. I turned to Jake Martin, who had said nothing about the matter, one way nor the other, and asked: "Will you whip him?"

"Yes," said he, "I would be glad to do it."

So he got five or six of the best willow sprouts he could find. We unbound him while six or eight men stood around with guns, ready to shoot him if he should attempt to run.

After Martin had given him as much of the willow wand as I thought he could stand without seriously impairing his health, I made signs to him that he might go.

He started promptly but very slowly, looking back with a doubtful glance, first over one shoulder and then over the other, at every step as though he expected to be shot down. The further he got away, the faster he moved and, as far as we could see him, his speed seemed rather to increase than to slacken. I feel sure that the next time he went for beef he was more cautious about how be obtained it.

After we had passed High Rock Canyon two days, we camped at a spring about which was a flat that was covered with a dense growth of wire-grass which formed a thick, strong, sod, and grew from a foot-and-a-half to two feet high. The swamp grass is evergreen and during the autumn is about the only green thing to be found in many parts of this country.

At this camp the wife of Wesley Burch died. In order to prevent the Indians from rifling the grave, we dug it in the wire-grass, near the camp, on this flat. We cut out the sod carefully and laid it aside, and after the grave was filled up, and the loose earth all well packed down, and what was not needed removed to a distant place, we replaced the sod, so as to leave the surface of the ground as though it had never been disturbed.[197]

From this camp, we were compelled to make a detour to the south for two days to get around a lake of water which covered the plain between here and Plum Creek, which plain we had crossed the year before where we saw the singular mirages mentioned in our account of that expedition.

When we camped at Plum Creek, we saw a small body of Indians on the hills near the camp. We kept out a strong guard and, by exercising the utmost vigilance, and employing means to let them know that we were ready to give them a warm reception if they should attempt to molest us, we convinced them that they would do well to let us alone and so they let us pass without any attempt to injure us.

But, when the next company behind us camped at this place, the Indians shot several head of their cattle. It was a trick of the red rascals all the way from the Humboldt River to the Umpqua Valley to shoot the cattle of the emigrants whenever they had a favorable opportunity, by which means they were sure to get the meat and the hides after the company had gone on and left the dead or wounded animals.

But, after a while, when they became too bold and troublesome in their practice of this method of getting beef, the emigrants put a check to it and brought wailing into some of their most distinguished families by putting strychnine into the carcasses of the animals the Indians killed.

The next night, when this company whose cattle were shot at Plum Creek had crossed the mountains and camped by a plum thicket near the head of Trout Creek Valley, while they were occupied around their campfires after dark, the Indians fired into their camp.[198] Several persons were slightly wounded, and a young lady by the name of Davis received a very severe wound from an arrow. It was thought for several days that Miss Davis would die, but she finally rallied and recovered.[199]

---

197 Based on the next part of the narrative, the burial of Mrs. Burch took place in Surprise Valley on the east side of Upper Alkali Lake, perhaps in the area of Leonard's Hot Springs.

198 Trout Creek is now called Willow Creek.

199 Hannah Ann Davis. Charles Davis, a descendant of the 1847 emigration Davis clan, collected versions of the story including one that she was killed. *The South*

When the camp was attacked, the lights were immediately extinguished and their flights of arrows so vigorously returned with rifle balls and buckshot that the assailants soon retired without having done much further damage after their first onset.[200]

We reached the Canyon earlier in the season than the emigration of the year before.[201] The teams were in good order, and the men in fine spirits. With a little well-directed effort, the road was put in a passable condition. But when we started into the Canyon with the train, we met with so many difficulties and hindrances, that we only got two wagons through the first day. The next day we brought them all through, except one.[202]

The wagon that did not get through the second day belonged to a man who had a small family and plenty of provisions. He was not popular in the company. He had an extra barrel of pork, and several persons who were out of meat, had applied to him to purchase some of his pork,

---

Road, 162-63; and *The Oskaloosa Company*, 116-18. Scott's facts were corroborated by Lester Hulin's diary entry for September 29, 1847. "Day-Book or Journal of Lester Hulin," monograph at the Lane County Pioneer-Historical Society, 1959; reproduction copy at Oregon Historical Society Research Library, Call Number 917.91 L24H, 1959; reprint Devere Helfrich, "The Applegate Trail Part II: West of the Cascades," *Klamath Echoes* 14. Klamath County Historical Society, 1976, 63.

200 Scott was not with the Davis party on September 29. He was with the lead party and arrived in the Willamette Valley on September 26, according to Jesse Applegate, "Immigrants arriving via the Southern Route," *Oregon Spectator*, October 14, 1847, 2, col. 3.

201 Pringle arrived at the pass on October 21, 1846, but then had to work for four or five days to clear a road. In 1847 Scott was more than a month ahead of Hulin, who reached the pass on October 22 and entered it the next day. Hulin, "Day Book," in Helfrich, "The Applegate Trail Part II," 40. Helfrich, quoting freely from Hulin's diary, erroneously changed Hulin's dates from October to September but made the correction for the last entry of October. Helfrich did not, however, catch the duplicate date of "October 11" in the original which makes Helfrich's dates off by one day after the second "September" 11. Consequently, Helfrich indicated that Hulin was at the Canyon on "September 21" and entered the Canyon on "September 22." It should have been October 22 and 23.

202 Lester Hulin's account of coming through the canyon a month or so after Scott was not as carefree as Scott's account suggested. Hulin's party, coming along after Scott's improvements, took four days to get through and recover some of their wreckage before camping on the bank of the South Umpqua River. Hulin, "Day-Book," in Helfrich, "The Applegate Trail Part II," 40. "In both passings through this canyon [in February 1848] the wreckage of the immigrants of 1846 was plentiful." John Minto Papers, "Capt Levi Scotts Company in the Cayuse War," Oregon Historical Society Reearch Library, Mss 752.

before we reached the Canyon. He refused to let them have any. He said he would need it during the winter, after he got into the settlements.

His wagon broke down in the Canyon, and it was said that his barrel of pork sat over the wheel that went to pieces. He got through all right with the wagon in which his family rode, and it was his provision wagon that remained behind. He went to some of the men who had tried to buy provisions from him, and told them, if they would stay with him till he could repair his wagon, and get it out of the Canyon, he would let them have all the pork they wanted. They said to him: "No! You would not let us have any pork when we wanted you to sell it to us, to save our lives, now, we will not take any of it, to save yours."

So they drove off and left him. No one stayed with him, except his father-in-law, and he only on account of his daughter and her children. They repaired up the wagon and came on again in about two days.[203]

Grass and water were much more abundant this year than they were the year before and we reached the Willamette Valley early in the fall with the stock in fair condition and the people in good spirits. Most of them settled in the upper part of the valley.

The excellence of the southern route was now established beyond a doubt and much excellent country had been examined and brought into notice which in a few years was filled with settlers. I may add that, in less than five years, Oregon was settled clear through to the California line.[204]

I came through in fine health and I felt pleased with the thought that my two years hard work would be of great value to the country, although, I was left as poor as when I started into the enterprise. I felt that two years of my life, at least, had been spent *pro bono publico*. And I suppose I was just as happy as if I had made a fortune out of it.[205]

---

203 Scott put the Barker story with the 1846 emigration, no doubt because of the reference to starving emigrants, but the Barker family emigrated in 1847. Collins must have verified the information with his neighbors and moved the story to its chronological place.

204 Scott's assessment was correct regarding the amount of settlement, but he failed to mention the impact of the gold discoveries in California (1848) and southern Oregon (1851) as primary contributors to settlement.

205 Scott composed a letter dated October 25, 1847, to the *Oregon Spectator* on his return (*See* Appendix 3). His later recollection softened his expression of feeling in that letter. Levi Scott, "Letter," *Oregon Spectator*, November 11, 1847, 2, col. 1-2.

I stopped for the winter in the Applegate settlement at the head of Salt Creek Valley.[206]

Once, while I lived on Salt Creek, I went to Oregon City in company with Wm. Wilson, Bob Smith, and my son John.[207] We started on foot and went about twenty miles to where Dayton now is situated on the Yamhill River a few miles above its junction with the Willamette. Here we expected to get a small boat and go the rest of the way by water. Another party had gone down the river with the boat, which was only a large skiff or bateau, and was expected to return at any moment.

It was about thirty miles or more from here to Oregon City, and we did not like to walk and carry our blankets if we could get a boat to float down in.

Everybody who traveled had to carry his bed, or lodge without any. And travelers, usually, must carry their provisions, also, or go without anything to eat. We had our beds on our backs but had neglected to provide ourselves with the staff of life as we had expected to reach the city before night, which we could have done had we not been delayed by our failure to get the boat, and we knew that in the city, which was but a little village, we could be sure of getting plenty of salmon with bread and Sandwich Island molasses.

There was a Frenchman by the name of La Bonte living with a squaw at the point where we were waiting for the boat.[208] Bob Smith was acquainted with La Bonte and, when we had waited till late in the

---

206 During this period the Oregon Provisional Government authorized improvement of the Southern Route, appointed Levi Scott as commissioner of the road, and authorized Scott to charge tolls. "AN ACT to improve the Southern Route to Oregon [Dec. 23, 1847]," *Oregon Spectator*, January 6, 1848, 4, col. 3-4. Scott declined the appointment with a letter to the *Oregon Spectator*. Levi Scott, "To His Excellency, George Abernethy," March 23, 1848, 2, col. 6. He offered to guide a proposed exodus east and meet new emigrants if the sum of $300 were raised and paid. It was not, and Scott retired from leading wagon companies.

207 These four men participated in the May 1846 exploration. It is unclear what year this adventure took place, but it had to be before 1848 when Scott moved to the Umpqua River valley.

208 This was probably Louis LaBonte Sr., a French-Canadian member of the overland party of Astor's Pacific Fur Company led by Wilson Price Hunt in 1810-11. LaBonte Sr. lived with his Indian wife along the Yamhill River near Dayton from 1836 to 1860 except for a period in the California gold fields. Corning, *Dictionary of Oregon History*, 138.

evening, and the boat did not come, and we were about as hungry as we thought we ought to suffer ourselves to become, Bob went to La Bonte's cabin to see if we could get something to eat. When he was asked if we could get supper with him, the kind-hearted and affable Frenchman responded, "Very good! All de same Monsieur Schmit! I got no bread; I got no meat. Fe I got plentee provisions, you eat wiv me; fe I got none, I believe, by God, you can't have some. I tink it bes for youl go on my jardin, dig some small potatoes, make leetle fire, on rosee. Youl very welcome, Monsieur Schmit! Youl very welcome!"

So we went to the garden where we found the potatoes not larger than hen's eggs, for the hospitable Frenchman had not cultivated them very energetically and his potato crop was anything but a success. But the little potatoes were very good. So we camped there and lived on small potatoes till noon the next day when the boat not having yet returned, we started to finish the journey on foot.

We went to the Willamette, near the mouth of the Yamhill River, where there was another Frenchman by the name of Le Five, who also had a squaw for a wife. We called here, expecting to get something to eat. They lived in a cabin without any floor and with fir poles laid loosely overhead for a ceiling. This ceiling was covered with fishes in almost every stage of drying and there was a fire in the middle of the cabin below to smoke and dry them. The house was filled with smoke and the fish stunk so badly that our appetites would not endorse our courage to ask for something to eat. We only asked to be set across the Willamette River.

Le Five put us over and we concluded to go down the river about four or five miles to the town of Champoeg where Bob Newell, an American, lived, with whom we were all acquainted.[209] Newell was the proprietor of the town-site and, of course, the most important and affluent man in the city. We felt sure we could get dinner with him. But he was not at home and, when we asked his squaw if we could get some dinner, she answered us, shortly and angrily: "No! The white people is all the time coming here for something to eat. I won't give you any!"

---

209 Robert "Doc" Newell was one of the best known fur trappers who settled in the Willamette Valley. T. C. Elliott, "'Doctor' Robert Newell: Pioneer," *Quarterly of the Oregon Historical Society* 9, no. 2 (June 1908), 103-26. Corning, *Dictionary of Oregon History*, 175.

Champoeg was called a town but there were only two cabins in the city.[210] The other cabin was the residence of a Frenchman, his squaw, half-breed children, and his dogs. But he was keeping tavern. As Mrs. Newell unfeelingly turned us away empty, we resolved to go to this public house and indulge in a square meal at the hotel. We got it, sure enough.

We called for dinner. The landlord, with pompous ceremony, said: "Yes. *Oui, Messieurs, oui.*"

He made up a fire, immediately, in the great wide adobe fireplace. The old squaw began preparations to make tea and a half-breed girl, about sixteen or seventeen years old, commenced making batter in a large pan which she picked up by the door. The old squaw sat flat down on the clay hearth at one side of the fire and gave her undivided attention to the tea kettle.

When the young lady had whipped up the batter sufficiently to suit her ideas of the eternal fitness of things, she took up an old frying pan from a corner near the fireplace, set it on the fire with some kind of grease in it. She then set her pan of batter near the fire and, with a fork in one hand and a spoon in the other, she sat down flat on the hearth on the side opposite the old lady and began to fry fritters.

There were several gaunt and hungry looking dogs lying around the fire watching this cooking operation apparently with as much solicitude as we were. As the aroma of the *cuisine* rolled out and filled the shanty, these hitherto-lazy and dejected looking hunters assumed a more absorbed expression. They rose and sat up, snuffing towards the fireplace.

The young lady had set an empty pan on the hearth into which she now threw the fritters as they were fried. As the cooking went on, each dog began to quiver with a sort of covetous anxiety. They seemed to be seized with a sudden attachment for the young lady and began to crowd close to her. Now and then a dog would dart his head forward and snap at a fritter as it passed from the frying pan to the receiving pan, when he was always met in time by a blow on the nose with the batter-spoon, in which case he would back off with a mixed look of gratitude and reproach as he licked the batter from his nose. Sometimes the vigilant young lady would prod him in the nose with the fork she used to turn and lift the fritters, which usually elicited a whine and sometimes the wounded cur

---

210 For Champoeg, McArthur, *Oregon Geographic Names*, 187-88; Corning, *Dictionary of Oregon History*, 50-51; Engeman, *The Oregon Companion*, 75.

would viciously snap at her. But the damsel proved herself equal to every emergency; she fought it out on that line and never lost a fritter.

The land-lord set the table which was a bench six feet long and one foot wide and assumed the double purpose of a table and a sofa. There was a knife and fork, a tin plate, and a tin cup for each of us.

A pan of fritters was set in the middle of the table with a tin cup full of Sandwich Island molasses, not the most refined article in that time, either, and, when all things were ready, the old squaw looked towards us and pointed to the bench at the same time giving us the invitation: "Chaco, muccamuck!" That is to say: "Come to dinner!"[211]

We took up the three legged stools on which we had been sitting and advanced towards the board; but we were checked with a momentary suspense as we witnessed the fierce struggle among the dogs for precedence in licking the vessels in which our repast had been prepared.

But we, like the dogs, were too hungry to be long restrained by trifles. We took our tin plates on our knees; the old squaw filled our tin cups with tea and set them on the bench with a nod and a grunt which signified: "Now, you may fall to, as quick as you please."

We soon demolished the greater part of what was set before us and, after we had settled the reckoning, a bateau came along bound for Oregon City when we secured a passage on it and went on our way rejoicing.

Early in December 1847, the startling intelligence reached the settlements in the Willamette Valley that Dr. Marcus Whitman and his wife, with a number of men, women, and children who were with them at the Waiilatpu Missionary Station on the Walla Walla River, had been massacred by the Indians on the 29th of November. That the Indians east of the Cascade Mountains were in arms and threatening to proceed to the Willamette Valley and exterminate every American settler in the country.[212]

211 According to George Gibbs, *Dictionary of Chinook* (Smithsonian Institution, 1863): "Chah´-ko, *v.* Nootka, Clayoquot, CHAKO; Tokwaht, TCHOKWA. *To come; to become.* Muck´-a-muck, *n., v.* The word has been regarded as an invented one, but is probably Ojibwa, as it is said to be in use at the Sault St. Mary. *Food; to eat, to bite.*"
212 Collins greatly elaborated on Scott's brief note. He related the exaggerated beliefs and fears of the American settlers at the time. For a more complete and balanced review, *see* Erwin N. Thompson, *Shallow Grave at Waiilatpu* 2nd ed. (Portland, OR: Oregon Historical Society Press, 1985); Clifford M. Drury, *Marcus and Narcissa*

There had been a diplomatic struggle going on for several years between the United States and Great Britain for supremacy in the valley of the Columbia and throughout the Northwest which had been settled by treaty the year before to the satisfaction of the settlers and the people of the United States, but to the chagrin of the Hudson's Bay Company which had established Posts and monopolized nearly all the business that was carried on throughout this region of the country.

The treaty had fixed the end of the prosperous monopoly of this company in Oregon. The settlers knew that its officers and attaches were sullen and dissatisfied; that they had great influence with the Indians, and had, possibly, determined to stir them up against the settlers who, they seemed to think, had been chiefly instrumental in crowding them out of this part of the country.

There had, also, been a religious struggle going on for several years between the Protestants and Catholics for the ascendancy in influence and power among the Indians.

This attack had been made upon a Protestant Mission, yet, the Priests of the Catholic Church seemed to be on the best of terms with, and free to come and go at will among, the hostile Indians.

The American settlers were nearly all Protestants, the foreigners nearly all Catholics. And there were very many intelligent persons who seemed to be well informed about the matter who openly charged the Catholic Priests and the employees of the Hudson's Bay Company, who were mostly Canadian French Catholics, with being the instigators of the trouble.[213]

Whatever may have been the causes of the uprising and slaughter, the people were thoroughly alarmed for the safety of the settlements and the greatest consternation prevailed in every quarter.

At two o'clock in the afternoon of December the 8th, 1847, the Legislature, then in session at Oregon City, received a communication from Governor Abernethy, informing its members of the tragedy, and asking

---

Whitman, and the Opening of Old Oregon (Glendale, CA: Arthur H. Clark Co., 1973); and Theodore Stern, *Chiefs & Change in the Oregon Country* (Corvallis: Oregon State University Press, 1996).

213 Hudson's Bay Company employees actually took the lead in paying the ransom and conducting the rescue of the hostages. The accusations of Catholic complicity in the event were reviewed and refuted. Malcolm Clark Jr. "The Bigot Disclosed: 90 Years of Nativism," *Oregon Historical Quarterly* 75, no. 2 (June 1974): 112-18.

them to take prompt action to rescue the survivors of the massacre and punish the Indians.

Someone offered a motion to refer the Governor's message with the accompanying letters from Governor Douglas of Fort Vancouver and Captain McBean of Fort Walla Walla to a committee, when the Hon. J. W. Nesmith, representative from Polk County, sprang to his feet and, in the most vigorous language, asserting that the women and children held as prisoners by the savage perpetrators of the bloody outrage must be rescued, and those who had not yet fallen into their hands protected, and that the circumstances would admit of no delay, offered the following:

"*Resolved*; That the Governor be and he is hereby authorized and required to raise, arm, and equip a company of riflemen, not to exceed fifty men, with their Captain and subaltern officers, and dispatch them forthwith, to occupy the Mission Station at the Dalles, on the Columbia River, and hold possession until reinforcements can arrive at that point, or other means be taken, as the government may think advisable."[214]

This motion was put to the vote and carried unanimously and in less than twenty-four hours a company of forty-one volunteers, under the command of Captain H. A. G. Lee, was on the march for the Dalles.

In view of the temper and threats of the Indians and the situation of the settlements, it was thought to be unwise to let the matter rest till spring and give the Indians time to organize a raid upon the settlers; but, it was the general impression that the people must show a bold front and carry the war into the enemy's country at once; that they might be occupied in defending their own homes instead of preparing to invade ours.

Governor Abernethy and all the officers of the Provisional Government of Oregon were active, energetic, and determined men who were not to be checked nor intimidated by a war-whoop nor by having the bloody scalp of a friend shaken in their faces. After the first shock of the calamity had gone through their nerves, they rose with indignant and redoubled energy to prepare for the struggle. While a deep gloom hung over every home in the Willamette Valley, the utmost activity prevailed in every department of the resolute little Republic which had not yet been superseded by any action of Congress.

---

214 *Oregon Spectator*, December 10, 1847, p. 2.

On the 11th of December, Cornelius Gilliam was elected by the Legislature to command the forces to be sent against the Indians.

Mr. Nesmith introduced the following resolution which passed the Legislature Assembly by a unanimous vote:

"Resolved: That the executive as commander-in-chief, has full power to adopt all means necessary for the prosecution of the existing war, and that it is the opinion of this House, that it is expedient for the executive to issue orders for five hundred men, and trust to the patriotism of the citizens of Oregon for their support in the field."

In a few days, Col. Gilliam with two or three companies of volunteers followed Captain Lee and, taking command of all the forces that could be put into the field, pushed a vigorous campaign during the winter against the hostile Indians.[215]

---

215 The events at the Whitman mission have generated volumes of historical interpretation. One of the earliest manuscripts was a letter by Columbia Lancaster written December 22, 1847, to U.S. Senator Alpheus Felch of Michigan. Mentor L. Williams, "A Columbia Lancaster Letter about Oregon in 1847," *Oregon Historical Quarterly* 50, no. 1 (March 1949): 41-44. The tenor of the times and most of the events as understood in the Willamette Valley were briefly described, as well as the perceived necessity that the federal government take action. The Indian viewpoint was unknown to the settlers in the Willamette Valley. Stern, *Chiefs & Change in the Oregon Country*, 168-225, provides some balance.

ᢙ

Levi Scott's Life After 1847

T HE KILLINGS AT WHITMAN MISSION in the Walla Walla Valley cre-
eated an uproar in the Willamette Valley settlements to the west,
and Provisional Governor Abernethy reached out to the leading settlers,
including Levi Scott, for aid.[1] As noted in chapter fifteen of the Collins
account of Levi Scott's life, the territorial government authorized the
raising of a militia, and troops were dispatched up the Columbia. Governor Abernethy also sought help from California, sending Jesse Applegate
as his agent and Levi Scott as captain of an escort company of fifteen
men, south through the Siskiyou Mountains with a plea for assistance.
Deep snow impeded progress with the horses, so the party split. Jesse
Applegate and half the men crafted snowshoes to attempt to cross the
mountains, while Scott and the balance of volunteers and horses started
back toward home. Incidental conflict with local Indians along the Rogue
River created additional apprehension among the men, and they lost
several horses and mules from fatigue and starvation. Applegate's party
floundered and turned back, rejoining Scott's band along the Umpqua
"in a very forlorn condition."[2] Scott drafted his waybill for the Southern

---

1   This postscript summarizes chapters sixteen through twenty of the Collins text,
and the matching portions of the Scott reminiscence. The full manuscripts of Levi
Scott and James Layton Collins are housed at the Knight Library, University of
Oregon, Eugene.

2   Collins manuscript, chapter 16. Scott filed a public report of the expedition, with
a roster of the volunteers. Levi Scott, "To His Excellency, George Abernethy,
Governor of Oregon," *Oregon Spectator,* March 9, 1848, 2, col. 5-6. John Minto
wrote an article with the same list, found in "Pioneer History, A Struggle On
Snowshoes in Southern Oregon 50 Years Ago," *Oregonian,* December 30, 1894,
11, col. 5-6, also, John Minto Papers, Oregon Historical Society Research Library,
Mss 752. The muster roll compiled by the Provisional Government listed nineteen
men in addition to Applegate, including all of the ones on Scott's list. Frances
Fuller Victor, *The Early Indian Wars of Oregon* (Salem, OR: 1894), 504-20. Jesse
Applegate's version of the expedition is found on pages 141-51 of Victor's book.

Route based on his journeys of the past two years and submitted it to Jesse Applegate who passed it along in March to Governor Abernethy, who published it in the *Oregon Spectator* on April 6.[3]

While Scott, Applegate, and their party struggled in the mountains, a watershed event took place in the Sierra foothills east of Sacramento, California. On January 24, 1848, James W. Marshall and his work team, including Scott's 1844 companion, Charles Bennett, found gold in the tailrace of the sawmill they were building on the South Fork of the American River at Coloma. As news of the discovery spread, Levi Scott and his sons returned to their claims in the Umpqua Valley, planting crops and tending stock.

Gold fever infected much of the Oregon population in 1848. Scott's sons were anxious to sell out their claims and improvements and head for the mines, but their father advised them to let him care for their holdings while they prospected in California. Despite the economic dislocation of the rush south, Argonauts returning to Oregon in the following months brought with them increased wealth that proved a boon to the young territory.

Not all Oregon settlers were immediately drawn to California. Jesse Applegate, Rev. Glen O. Burnett, and several others formed a cooperative association they called the Klamath Commonwealth with the intent of founding a settlement on one of the southern Oregon rivers, building a fort for their protection, developing farms, raising stock, and digging gold.[4] Scott's home was on their route, and in vain they tried to recruit him to their enterprise. Despite high expectations, the community soon disintegrated, and Applegate moved his family to the west side of the Scott family claims in the Yoncalla Valley.

---

3   Jesse Applegate to George Abernethy, letter, March 20, 1848, Oregon Historical Society Research Library Mss 929.

4   Kendall, *Pacific Trail Camp-Fires*, 178-81 (gold rush) and 187-94 (Klamath Commonwealth). The story of the Klamath Commonwealth has been obscured by the passage of time. There are sporadic references to it without much detail except in the reminiscences of Scott and Elisha Applegate. In addition to the reference in Kendall, *Pacific Trail Camp-Fires*, *see* Julia Veazie Glen, "John Lyle and Lyle Farm," *Oregon Historical Quarterly* 26, no. 2 (June 1925): 143; and F. A. Shaver, *An Illustrated History of Central Oregon* (Spokane: Western Historical Publishing Co., 1905), 927-28.

In August 1848 Congress created Oregon Territory. Mexican War General Joseph Lane was appointed governor and arrived March 2, 1849, to announce Oregon's new status. In summer 1849 the first U.S. troops were sent west to be stationed along the Oregon Trail. The American Rifle Regiment, or Mounted Riflemen, marched west from Jefferson Barracks in Missouri. Scott was employed by Lieutenant Hawkins at Oregon City to help guide a supply party to meet the incoming regiment at Fort Hall with provisions.[5] Following the Southern Route, they encountered large parties of emigrants coming west near High Rock Canyon who regaled the supply party with stories and rumors of the rich California mines. Soon the troops, who were being paid seven dollars a month, began deserting.

From Mud Meadows, between High Rock Canyon and Black Rock Spring, Scott took three companions to explore for a new route beyond the Black Rock, hoping to avoid the worst part of the Black Rock Desert crossing of the emigrant trail.[6] During that exploration Scott had an altercation with a small party of Indians during which a Mr. Garrison was killed and Scott wounded. Scott killed one of the Indians. Scott returned to the Army escort with Garrison's body, and received treatment for his arrow wound.[7]

---

5   For the official report of the supply officer of this regiment, *see* Col. Osborne Cross, *March of the Regiment of the Mounted Riflemen in 1849* (Washington, D.C.: C. Alexander, Printer, 1851); reprint, Raymond W. Settle, ed., *The March of the Mounted Riflemen* (Glendale, CA: The Arthur H. Clark Co., 1940); reprint, *March of the Regiment of Mounted Riflemen to Oregon in 1849* (Fairfield, WA: Ye Galleon Press, 1967). *See also* Robert Carlton Clark, "The Military History of Oregon 1849-59," *Oregon Historical Quarterly* 36, no. 1 (March 1935): 14-59; *Dictionary of Oregon History*, 7 (American Rifle Regiment).

6   Several '49er diarists noted the Army contingent and some mentioned Scott. Among the first, on August 23 at the Nevada-California border, was Alonzo Delano. *See* Delano, *Life on the Plains and Among the Diggings* (Auburn, NY: Miller, Orton & Mulligan, 1854), 198. The party was also mentioned in J. Goldsborough Bruff's journal on September 8 on the Humboldt River near Gravelly Ford. Georgia Willis Read and Ruth Gaines, ed., *Gold Rush: The Journals, Drawings, and Other Papers of J. Goldsborough Bruff*, 2 vols. (New York: Columbia University Press, 1944), 1:290-93.

7   Garrison's death and Scott's injury were located and dated by contemporaneous diary accounts. Garrison's death occurred on the evening of August 25 and his burial the next day. Jonas Hittle, "Diary," Illinois State Historical Library, Springfield, Illinois; and other sources cited in Richard K. Brock, ed., *A Guide to the Applegate Trail, The South Road to Oregon, Second Edition* (Reno: Trails West, 2005), 160-61; Richard K. Brock and Donald E. Buck, *A Guide to the Applegate Trail from Lassen Meadows to Goose Lake, Third Edition* (Reno: Trails West, 2010), 156-58; and Will Bagley, *With Golden Visions Bright Before Them* (Norman: University of Oklahoma Press, 2012), 223.

After joining the California Trail the provisioning party met the massive gold rush migration pushing down the Humboldt River. They were repeatedly questioned about what lay to the west, despite the party's demurring response that they had come from Oregon, not California. Arriving at Fort Hall they found that the main party of Mounted Riflemen had already passed, using the original trail to Fort Boise, over the Blue Mountains, and down to the Columbia. Two hundred men had been left to winter at Fort Hall, and Scott was employed to carry messages to their commander in Oregon City. With four others, Scott set a fast pace, arriving at Oregon City in twenty days, an average of over thirty-five miles per day.

Oregon Territory was growing, despite the rush to California, and Scott saw opportunity. In 1850 he explored routes down the Umpqua River from his claim at Scotts Valley looking for a likely place for a seaport. He found a favorable location, marked out a claim at the head of tidewater, then traveled to Vancouver to hire a vessel to explore the river entrance. Scott returned to the Umpqua River to see if an ocean-going ship could navigate up to his new claim. The ship that appeared was not the ship he engaged, but the captain confirmed the river was navigable for the twenty-five miles up to his site, so Scott laid out the town of Scottsburg. He filed his claim for a Donation Land Act patent which was granted in 1874.[8]

Philip Kearny, then a major in the U.S. Army, was assigned to the West Coast following the Mexican War, and in spring 1851 he met Levi Scott in the Yoncalla Valley while escorting a regiment of dragoons from Fort Vancouver to California. He hired Scott as a guide to help find the best routes for his wagons through the rugged mountains south of the Willamette Valley. As they neared the Rogue River, they ran headlong into another skirmish in the long running but occasional incidents between the local Indians and the settlers and miners who had started arriving in 1851. Scott mentioned this incident. The conflicts ended in 1856

8   For the history of Scottsburg, *see Oregon Geographic Names*, 856-57; *Dictionary of Oregon History*, 219; *The Oregon Companion*, 335; Beckham, *Land of the Umpqua*, 140-41; Minter, *Umpqua County, Oregon, and Its Pioneers*, 84-106; Jerry Winterbotham, *Umpqua: The Lost County of Oregon* (Brownsville, OR: Jerry Winterbotham, 1994). The record of Scott's DLC patent can be found at www.glorecords.blm.gov/search/default.aspx#. Accessed July 21, 2015.

with the removal of the Indians of southwestern Oregon to the Grande Ronde reservation west of Salem.

Kearny left his wagons on the South Umpqua and, following the road opened by Scott and others, traveled to the relief of the settlers. Though the conflict involved only a few small skirmishes, and lots of chasing, there were casualties. Captain James Stuart was killed in a fight near Table Rock on the north side of the Rogue.[9] Kearny established Camp Stuart nearby. According to Scott, nine of the Indian dead were left on the field. Scott advised Kearny regarding the local Indians while they parlayed, advising against risk in the face of unfavorable odds.

In a few days supplies ran low, and Kearny sent Scott to Camp Stuart for replenishment. There he found about a hundred settlers and travelers from Oregon and California, amongst whom was former territorial governor and Mexican War General Joseph Lane. Lane had served with Kearny in the Mexican War, and quickly volunteered his services and those of his compatriots. Their action amounted to little more than chasing a few Indian bands across the hills. Kearny proceeded on to California, the volunteers dispersed, and Scott returned to Scottsburg.

In early 1852 Scott joined with James and Richard Robinson in the cattle business in the Rogue River Valley, intending to drive the herd to northern California for sale that spring. However, gold had just been discovered nearby at Jackson Creek, creating a new opportunity for the cattlemen.[10] Over the course of the summer they realized a high price for the beef in and around the new town of Jacksonville.

Summer 1852 brought Scott the surprising news that he had been nominated by the Whig Party of Umpqua County to the Territorial Legislature. He was elected to the Council (or Senate) that year, and again in 1853 and 1854, before deciding that he preferred herding cattle

9   Stuart had served in the Mexican War, receiving recognition for gallantry in the battles of Contreras and Churubusco, and at Chapultepec. Francis B. Heitman, *Historical Register and Dictionary of the United States Army* (Urbana: University of Illinois Press, 1965), 933.

10 The gold discovery was made in December 1851. Earlier in 1851 gold was found nearby on the Illinois River, a tributary of the Rogue River. *See Oregon Geographic Names*, 506 (Jacksonville); *Dictionary of Oregon History*, 101 (Gold Mining, Southern Oregon); and 127 (Jacksonville).

to wrangling legislation.[11] Additionally, he was one of the few Whigs in a legislature and territory dominated by Democrats. As he noted in his reminiscence, "a bitter partisen should not hold office, no difference what party he belongs to. in transacting publick buisaness, men should act in union indipendant of politicks, advocateing political only when the proper time comes. difference of opineon will rise between men honestly on proper polices [policies] for the benafit and good of the whole people. this is all rite and every man has a wright to his opinion and should stick to it if he has good grounds for it...a man [should] think for himself, indipendant of friend or foe."

After a few years in the cattle business on the South Umpqua and Rogue Rivers, Scott's bucolic career was sidetracked once again by politics. With Jesse Applegate, he was elected to represent Umpqua County in the third constitutional convention in preparation for Oregon's admission to statehood. Both men were staunch Whigs in an overwhelmingly Democratic political world, muffling their voices and concerns. Applegate was considered the leader of the Whigs in Oregon, and the Democrat delegates frustrated his motions and dismissed his concerns to such a degree that he left and went home.[12] Scott stayed the course, though in the end he opposed the constitution on the grounds that the territory had neither the population nor resources to support statehood. Despite his reservations, Oregon was admitted to the Union February 14, 1859.

In 1861 Scott returned to Scottsburg with the intention to build up his sawmill business and the town. However, storms in November and

11   As a member of the Council in 1853, Scott endorsed William M. Macy's plan for a new road from Fort Boise to Eugene, which became the Free Emigrant Road. *Oregon Statesman*, March 19, 1853, 2, col. 2. Macy's attempt to open the road across the Cascades was not successful in 1853, but it was opened in 1854. Leah Collins Menefee and Lowell Tiller, "Cutoff Fever, I-VI."

12   Applegate had allegedly announced ahead of time that he would quit the convention if it did not adopt anti-slavery measures that he proposed. Douglas, "Deer Creek, Douglas Co.," *Oregon Statesman*, June 23, 1857, 2. After his resolutions were defeated, Applegate sought a resolution allowing him to withdraw from the convention on three occasions, all of which were denied by a vote of 6 for and 46 against. Charles Henry Carey, ed., *The Oregon Constitution and Proceedings and Debates of the Constitutional Convention of 1857* (Salem, OR: State Printing Department, 1926; reprint, Portland, OR: Press of the Oregon Historical Society, 1984), 203 (Aug. 28, 1857), 208-10. Applegate did leave and his departure was noticed and confirmed. John R. McBride, "Annual Address," *OPAT* 25 (1897) (Portland, OR: Geo. H. Himes & Co. Printers, 1898), 50.

December 1861 brought heavy flooding to the Umpqua River, and on December 8 almost the entire town, including Scott's sawmill, were washed away. In Scott's inimitable prose, "a freshet come, made a clean sweep of everything belonging to the concern and washed away most buisaness houses in town. this brought me down about even with the world."[13]

With the gold strikes in eastern Oregon and Idaho, Scott then went into the sheep business, moving his flocks to the Grande Ronde and Powder River valleys. He moved to Idaho, opened a grocery and boarding house, and started a cattle ranch. His timing was good as mines in Idaho and northeast Oregon created boomtowns that brought wealth to storekeepers, merchants, and ranchers. Scott spent two of those years on the Payette River in Idaho.

Returning to Oregon in 1864 at age sixty-seven, he dabbled at the poultry business, tended sheep, and engaged in various other occupations. In 1876 he served as the first janitor and groundskeeper at the new University of Oregon.[14] But time and age finally wore him down, and he turned to his children and grandchildren for support. At the end of his reminiscence he took stock of his abilities: "I am now in my eightyeighth yeare of age and not able to do hard work any more and not more than half as much of anything els I use to do, but still keep trying to do a little every day. but I am not working for money or for fortune any more now, but for pass time alone so I acomplish my desire every day."

He drafted his reminiscence in 1885 and engaged Judge Collins's help. He reviewed Collins's draft in spring 1889, then moved to live with his son John in far eastern Oregon. There on the North Fork Malheur River near Beulah north of Juntura, Levi Scott planted his last garden.

---

13   Cyrus Hedden's store, built in 1851, survived. Hedden's store is still present and was reopened in 2013. It is listed on the National Register of Historic Places. Winterbotham, *Umpqua, The Lost County of Oregon*, 130-31; Minter, *Umpqua Valley, Oregon, and Its Pioneers*, 90-91, 93; Beckham, *Land of the Umpqua*, 141; *Oregon Geographic Names*, 856-57; *Dictionary of Oregon History*, 219; *The Oregon Companion*, 335.

14   This employment was a subject of embarrassment to his children. "First Student Says Loan Saved Oregon University," *Sunday Oregonian*, October 24, 1926, 10. Fred Lockley, "Impressions and Observations of the Journal Man [W. W. Scott, son of Wm. J. J. Scott]," *Oregon Journal*, November 26, 1926, 14, col 6-7.

On April 21, 1890, Levi Scott died in his sleep. His granddaughter, Bettie Shelton, notified Collins of his passing.

> Baker City, May 3rd, '90 / Mr. J.L. Collins, / Sir, /
> I have just received a letter from father's folks at the Malheur Agency, Malheur Co., telling of the death of our Dear Grand father at their house, Levi Scott, he passed from this earth April 21st 1890, 25 minutes of 2 o'clock, P.M., buried 22nd. he had only been complaining a week. he just complained of being weak and just kept on geting weaker till he died. he never complained of having any pain atall but could not help him self atall for several days. brother Dick stayed rite by him all the time and lifted and turned him, sayed he could not hardly bear to be moved. was ancious for his time to come for him to go. Sayed he had lived his time out and was just wore out. was not afraid to die atall. he was in his right mind all the time. he died very easy, just seamed to go to sleep. he was buried at the Agency. I thought as you knew his history better then anyone else, perhaps you would write a sketch of his life and have printed. he had put in quite a garden this Spring but did not live to see it grow. he has been so healthy & well since he has been at fathers and raised a fine garden their last summer.[15] he raised as fine water melons as I ever saw grow. he was always in good Spirits and loved to tell over things of the past that had happened to him. I have made up a piece of poetry about him and I will put it in this letter and if you think it worth having printed, I would be glad but use your own pleasure. I thought perhaps you could have it put in the Itemizer as he was known their so well.[16] I guess I have wrote enough. our best respects to yourself and family, yours respectfully,
> Bettie Shelton / Baker City
> ps Grandfather was 93 last Feb the 8th.

Levi Scott's unassuming nature has, in part, obscured his role in the history of the Pacific Northwest. The route from the Humboldt River to the Willamette Valley that he helped explore, open, and over which he led many emigrants, eventually bore the name of the Applegates, his neighbors. His account of his life, and Judge Collins's expansion of that account, lay hidden in the papers of the Collins family for a century.

---

15   "Father" was John M. Scott, overland emigrant to Oregon with father Levi in 1844.

16   *The Itemizer* was a Dallas, Oregon, newspaper. A search of its files did not reveal an obituary for Scott.

But greater recognition of his role in the settlement of Oregon, and in overland emigration, is slowly growing. On May 12, 2001, the Oregon-California Trails Association installed an interpretive marker at Levi Scott's grave on a hill between the two forks of the Malheur River above the Beulah Reservoir in eastern Oregon. Among those in attendance were two of his great-granddaughters.

Dedication of marker at Levi Scott's grave, May 12, 2001. Left to right: Stafford Hazelett, Mildred Arriola, Mona Mendiola, and Arlie Holt. Holt, whose role in preserving the Scott and Collins manuscripts is discussed in the introduction to this work, spoke at the dedication of the marker. Stafford Hazelett is the editor of this book. Mildred and Mona are sisters and great-granddaughters of Levi Scott. *Photo courtesy Stafford Hazelett.*

Levi Scott's Reminiscence

1844–1847

The words are as Scott spelled them. I have included his own corrections as they were crossed out in the original. Where it didn't seem obvious to me, I have inserted a probable word according to standard spelling inside brackets. Occasionally I have interpolated a place name in brackets. An insertion with the initials "JLC" indicates a textual addition or correction by James Layton Collins to Scott's original. The numbers between slashes, e.g. /48/, reflect the page numbers of the original text. Chapter numbers in brackets indicate sectional divisions found in the Collins manuscript. An "X" in the text indicates the actual mark made by Scott on his original manuscript, often to indicate some sort of sentence or paragraph structure which the document otherwise lacks. Scott did not arrange his reminiscence in sentences and paragraphs, and there is no punctuation. All of those formatting decisions and virtually all punctuation are the editor's.

[Chapter 5]

That was about the time I left Iowa but I had worked along from 1834 up to this time in Iowa. In 42 I lost my wife and three children, discouraged, and broke me up. I nocked round the best I could a copple of years and then concluded to go to oregon to look at the country.

I now I commenced prepareing. a man, Charles Bennett, that had no one but a wife wished to join the outfit which he wished me to prepare the whole of, another yong man, Abe Tatriger ["*Absalom F. Hedges*" - JLC] in the neighood joined.

I had wagon and we got 4 yoak of oxen, then laid in store of provisheons but was late starting. the roads was bad on acount of much rain so we traveled very /22/ slow and pasing through mosouria we purched 8 cows. when we arived at mosouria river, we couldant cross on acount of high wind. we was detained two days during which time we lost our cows, and had to go on with them.

About six miles from Indipendance, mosouria, we met with another party of five men, germans, with one wagon was like us behind times. we traveled a weak, then overtook on the Waukiroussia [Wakarusa] a party of several from Indiana. thay informed us that the mane body of imigrants was but a little ways ahead waiting for all to git together.

we soon got to whare thay was on the Kansas river, regerly orgaised for the journey. Soposeing it to be a difficult rout to find, thay hired a pilot, an old mountainman called Black Harris, at $2.50 cts per head. another man was trying to get wages as interpriter named Adams, and safeguard amonst the indians, but he failed to do so and returned.

this guide, Harris, received pay from all that had fell in before us. thay met him at Indipendance whare he was considereble involved and thay had to advance foure or five hundred dollares to git his serveses. He turned out to be one of those men that amagoned he knew as muche or more than anybody else and knowed naughthing but to talk. By the time we fell in to the croud, some that had paid him had become disgusted with his big stories and thought he would be of no service on the trip atall.

now when the Germans that we first met had never saw or heard of each other before meeting on this trip but we had formed slite acquaintans by this time but neither of us acquainted with any other person in the whole crowd and had agread to stick together and help each other whenever it was nessasery through the whole trip. now some was adviseing us to not pay the guide, he would be of no service.

But the captain, Nathaniel Ford, came to us to collect fees for the guide, who he said we cold [could] not posably do without /23/ we told the captain we knowed naughthing about this guide nor the rout we had to travle, but we doubted the nesesaty of a pilot, but if he was of any service we would pay when we got through. Still we wished to travel with the company. he said it would be very unfare unles we paid the bill, but we did not pay.

The next morning, we ferried across the Kansas river without accident. we fel in the rear of the line of wagons, traveled until 3 o'clok in the afternoon, heare we came to a stream caled knife creek. camped before crossing.

in the night, thare came up a heavy raine and rained all night. was not raining the next morning, but the stream was impassable for our bagges tho we could swim our stalk over. thare apeard to be no positive orders from the cap but several plans spoken of for crosing the stream.

I had made my wagon box in the shape of a small boat to meet such amergencies. I proposed takeing that cork [caulk] it, crosing in it. One man fell in with my plan but then watter began to subside and he changed his mind, said he would wait and ford the stream but we went on preparing the craft.

of stalk we had only our teame, 4 yoke, two cows, and one mule. The Germans had 2 yoke, 2 cows + 3 ponies. Thare was 8 men, one woman, and a hardy boy of sixteen, my son John M. Scott, of us, swam our stalk over, lanched our boat, and commenced frateing bagage over and stack it up on a small noal [knoll] of dry ground neare the bank.

it commenced raining again, raised the watter over all the dry land we had to stand on. we had to drive stakes in the ground and build a scaffle [scaffold] to put our goods on.

now it was about night. we had to shift the best we could untel morning. I found a large piece of bark that had been pealed off a tree or log, seven or eight feet long, cusped up in shape of a howlo log. I raped a blanket round me and layed down in this bark.

the next morning when I got off the bark, it raised and /24/ floated like a boat, now we had but very little dry ground to stand on whare we was and surounded by swimming watter and the watter still riseing. it was half a mile to dry high ground in the direction we wished to go, the watter from two to eight feet the whole distance. half a mile further to a place we could have a comfortable camp. at we took the running gear of my wagon to the edge of the watter on the other side, about half a mile away, and drove our stalk out, yoaked up one pare of oxen then commenced boating our bagage, and set one man to hauling it on the running gear of the wagon from the boat landing to the campground. we worked hard all day and got our bagage all in and aranged for camping about sundown. sometimes we could wade, sometimes we had to swim and tow our craft.

now the remainder of the crowd was on high dry ground on the oposit bank of the creek and was hallowing, laughing, and makeing jest of us all day; but the joke turned on them at last, for it was eight days before thay got across that stream and thay had to make a raft to cross on.

Thay went above whare we crosed and had dry banks on both sides of the stream. thay commenced crosing in the morning, by noon thay had thare stalk and part of thare wagons over.

the pilet and foure or five other men came by our camp going on to look out a camping place for the night. we had got tired laying in camp, gathered our horses and followed them. thay came to prety good place for camping and stoped. we came to whare thay stoped, ast if thay was going to camp thare, thay said yes, then we turned loose our teames and prepared for camping for the night.

in about an hour, the captain came rideing past our camp. "What," said he, "are you going to camp heare?" yes, we said, we had stoped for that purpose and thought thay was all going to camp heare. he said thay was not going to stop thare. thay would go on about two or three miles further, and passed on without saying any more.

This we thought /25/ prity cool but consulted each other about it that night and concluded to fall in with them the next morning and travel with them and abide by and comply with the rules thay had established. The next morning we harnesed up our teams early and drove up to thare camp before thay was redy to start and stoped near whare thay was driveing thare wagons in to line.

one of our young men, Absalom Hedges [several words indecipherable] was walking along near thare lines when the captain come rideing along, pointing to our wagons and, speaking to the pilot, says, "major, I wish you would convey them wagons off into them hills whare thay never can git out again." he hapend to be rite by this young mans side who spoke very quick and short, "you cant do it, sir, we are not so green as you think."

after passing a few hard words with the captain, he came to our wagons and we started on passed them, following a trail that thay was on, traveled until noon through open prairia. we could see them all the way comeing on behind us, we thought so small a party as ours might not be safe traveling amongst the indians and consulted each other.

Finaly took a vote on the question whether we should travel alone or fall in with the croud. 10 of us voting, 8 for and 2, Mrs Bennett and myself, against traveling with them. so we wated until thay passed us then fell in the rear, travled on, camping with thare rules and regulations, everything going on peaceably and friendly, the captain giving us a frown ocationly but this soon wore off, and we was aparently about on an equil footing with the croud.

In traveling up plat river, two other men and myself concluded to take a buffalow hunt in the morning. we started, we went off the road through the hills, keeping in site of the train but got 6 or 8 miles away in the afternoon. a band of buffalow come dashing past us, two of us fired at one of them /26/ we both hit it. it run two or three jumps and fell, it was a cow and thare was a large bull run up to it and stoped. the band was some out of sight but the bull stud his ground, scrapted and pawed, would loll out his tong acting as tho he would come at us. we about fifty steps from him, and loded and fired foure shots each without bringing him down. but at last he siconed [sickened] and went off about a quarter of a mile and lay down. we then skined and cut off all we could carry with us.

by this time it was near sundown and us 12 or 15 miles from the train. now when we started for the trane, we had sawn it stop and could keep our corse even in the hight, one mans boots hurt his feet, so he declared he could not travel any further, so we camped for the night. all the fire we could make was a few bufelow chips and few partickles of vegatation to start it with.

this part of the country is all a region of sand hills with heare and thare a patch of grass, no timber or brush except on the watter corses and that quite limated. now our location was anything but plesant but we was very tiard and slept very sound. the wolves was plenty heare. thay stole our meat from within a foot of our heads while we slept.

next morning we found ourselves about five miles from the train. we went into camp without any buffalow meat or anything to show for it, only what we could tell. X

now we found thare was another party of two men out bufalow hunting the same day and thay had worse luck than us. thay saw a band of bufalow feeding some distance away. thay dismounted, tided thare horses head and foot with thare bridles, crept up to the bufalows, fired at them and kiled one, then one butcherd it while the other brought the horses. he went back but could not find them. the other butchered the bufalow, got it redy for packing, then thay /27/ both hunted for the horses until thay had barely time to git to camp that night but failed to find them.

[Chapter 6]

The train had came to the crossing of South plat river, laid by one day to look out a ford, I went with these men to take another look for thare horses. we was late starting but got in what thay thought the vecinaty of whare thay left them, kiled a bufalow, and campt for the night, hunted the next day til noon but found no horses nor no sign of horses or whare the men had been the day previous. we then went back to the train.

got thare just as the last wagons was crosing the river, by this time allmost every person in the trane was more or less dissatisfied. some complaind of the captain, some of one man and some of another. when we would lay by, the children fall out. some of the wimmen would disagree when we was traveling. the men was finding fault first with one thing then another til it apeard like the devel or something else had got into the whole croud. thay had all fel out with the pilot, even the captain refused to board or have anything to do with him, said he had no use for him any more.

we traveled on a few days and came to fort Laramy. layed by a copel of days heare.

The trane split, one half stuck to the captain, the remainder traveled one day without then organised. I was now elected captain. we traveld on now but growling, scarcely any two agreeing; every now and then a party brakeing off untel we came to fort Bridger, heare the company had got redused to 14 wagons.

now thare was one man very sick with a seveare fevor on account of which we lay by 3 or 4 days. it was giting late and we fearful of being caught with snow in the mountains. I purposed the famlies should go on, having no famly myself nor no famly with the wagon the sick belonged /28/ to, I would stay with them untel the sick got better or died, which every hour was expected. we lay thare two days and the sick man died. the third day we buried him and started on our jorney near three days in the reare of all the others on the road. X

we then came next to bear river. heare we camped and saw a number of indian lodges in the vally. a few came to our camp in the evening and the next morning. when we was hitching up to start on our jorney, a young indian rode up to us and spok to me. he taked plain english, he ast me if thare ware any more whites coming. I said, yes, thare was a grate many more coming. he say, what are you going to give the indians for traveling through thare country? thay always expect something from the whites when thay travel through this country. I said I had noughthing to give them, I was only traveling, had no more with me than I need myself and I wasant going to give them anything. he said the indians may play hell with you if you dont give them something. I says, boys, git youre guns out of the wagon now, says I, you leave heare or I will play hell with you pretty quick, now I would have been fraid to molest him atall, thare was hundreds of indians in sight but I thought he ment to scare me, and thought I would turn the joke on him which I believe I did, for he looked right at me for a moment then rode off without saying a word more. X

we campted another night and not another indian came near us but the same day we met a white man with indian principles who was of the loist [lowest] and worst grade. this was a white man who had been living with the indians several years, he plaid a dirty but funy trick on us, he said his name was Stags [*Staggs* - JLC], some of our croud was ancious to git ourselves some fresh meat and /29/ ast him if he had any. he said "no, but I shot an elk just back heare a little ways. I keard but little for it and did not fowlow it but I am shore I kiled it and can soon find it and will meet you at your camp tonight."

then he directed us whare we should camp. this camp was at the sody springs on beare river. we went on and camped at this place. after we had been in camp a short time, we saw him coming but a long ways off. then about sundown he was on foot leading his horse, we had our supper prepared and eat before he got to camp.

he was driving a cow and calf which he said he had baught from the imagrants and had been with a band of indians that had started this morning to salt lake. he told them to drive this cow with them, but thay failed to do so, and he was going to take hur himself.

we helped to hang his meat up in a ceder tree that we campted under, give him his supper which we had redy cooked for him. it was now dark and he said he must go and look after his cow, the wolves would eat the calf if he did not have it close to camp. he went out, was gone half an hour, came back, said he didant find hur, but must find hur, then went and sadeled his horse, which was picketed not far away, was gone several hours, said he had not found them and soposed the wolves would eat them up before morning; but thay didant for thay was not fare from whare thay was last saw at dark.

yet in the morning hourse we left bare river and had a long drive to make to the next watter. so we got up early, got our breakfast, by daylight we was redy to gather our stalk, stags ast an anormus price for his elk meat and we did not take any of it, but turned out all hands after our teames, got them up, but we had two poneis which was missing but we geared up and started out teams.

these men I had stoped with /30/ was all germens but as good a party as I ever fell in with. one of them, Charles Zummordie, and myself concluded to stay and hunt for these ponies a while. we had but little provishion cooked and didant keep any thinking we might overtake the wagons by noon but we did not.

I went to whare the horses was turned out with the view of tracking them. The dutchman took the road and went back to our camp the night before. I found the trackes redaly and could trck them prity handily. thare was a stick of timber tied to the end of one of the ropes thay was draging but I only trailed them 3 or 4 hundred yards til I found the stick of wood and the rope had been cut from it. Staggs left me before I found the stick of wood. then I was satisfied thay had been run of by some one, I thought by stags, for he had been with me pretending to help trail them. he kept before me sigsaging, makeing his horse make all the tracks he could. I spoke very short to him, told him to ride behind, he was doing more harm than good and he left and was gone till noon.

I trailed on near two miles when I came to a smooth, partly level rock, two hundred yards or more each way between two pretty high and very steep butes, I found redaly whare thay went onto this rock but went round it three or foure times before I found whare thay left it. now thay went strait up one of these butes, the soil heare was loose with some loos rock and very steep, I could fowl-low the trail heare as fast as I could travel, it was about a mile to the top, when I got to the top, I went on about two hundred yards, came to a sink or flat basin. heare was the poneys tide to a cedar tree.

now about 10 o'clock I took them to camp, wattered and hobled them out to graze, tel the dutchman would come, and I thought Stags might come back. I almost made up my mind to shoot him if he did, but he did come, but I didant shoot him. about twelve o'clock he came /31/ rideing up to camp whare I was seting with my rifle on my lap. he says, whare in the world did you find youre horses. I said I found them on top of the moutain whare thay was tied. he said no more. neither did I for a space of twenty minutes. he then said, "I must be going for I have a long ride to make this afternoon."

I wished him to stay untel my comrade would come, and I told him when he come he would buy some of his elk meat which still hung thare. he had lit from his horse and set down. he now got up, stood a few minutes, set down again, set about 15 minutes without either of us speaking a word. then raised to his feet, picked up his gun, mounted his horse and spured him sudantly into a long lope. kept that gate [gait] as far as I coud see him.

by this time I was giting pretty hungre. I thought I would rost some of this elk meat. it had good marrow bones in it when I come to examon it, and I cut foure bones out of it with a goodly quanaty of meat, as much as I thought two could eat, put them down to roast against the dutchman would come.

it got thoughorly dun and no dutchman yet. I then divided the rost and eat half of it, kept the other half for my comerade. he came about 2 o'clock, hungry as a wolfe. I told him the circumstances and give the rost and bones to him. he trimed the bones, craked them, and eat the marrow the same as I had done. he said, "I didant tink elk meat vus so cud [good]. I bleve it is peter [better] as [than] buflow." I joined him in giving the meat a good recommend.

we now got our ponys and perpareing to start, the dutchman says, "I vil take some of dis elk meat vid me" and cut off 40 or 50 pounds. I told him that was tu much, we had 20 miles to ride that night on small and pore poneys. I cut off 10 or 12 pounds, tied it to-gether, he took it and tide it to his saddle. we then mounted and started on our jorney.

[Chapter 7]

we traveled about two miles and saw a lot of crows, ravens and buzards rase and fly from something we could see a little ways from the road. we rode out to see what it was. we found the bones and hide of a three year old steere which we soposed had died thare but had been skined and from every appearances the elk meat we had been eating had been taken off from it. we could see this as plain as tho we had butchered and cut it off ourselves.

the dutchman took a searous [serious] look at the scileton then looked round at me, says "cot tam hell nation, I carries dis meat no furder," untide it, and dashed it down as tho he was mad. we now began to laugh at ourselves for being so badly fooled. we rode on and came up to our teems about twelve o'clock at night, roused up the other boys and had quite a laugh over the joke that had been plaid on us X

The next morning, quite a band of indians rode up to camp. thay had sarvis berries to trade us for anything we might offer them. these are very nice berries and we was ancious to buy them, and thare was red hawes in abundance in that country. the bears was very fond of those hawes and eate them by whole sale, I sopose from appearances, for we had seen in a number places the ground was literly covered with thare discharges which had settled down into flat cakes and dried. looked like pure hawes dried.

I will now go back to the sarvis berries. we got several small lots of very nice berries from the indians X as we was about to start, heare come a squaw with about a bushel in an old buckskin shirt. she had sewed the tail and filled it. this was more than we expected to buy. we hesatated, thought we didant need them, but when we come to see into the burden of her shirt, these looked to be nicer than any we had got, so we bought them, give her a pocket comb for the lot.

we got something to emty them in. she caut hold of the old shirt, made signs for us to put /33/ it in the wagon and she didant want it. we picked it up and set it in our wagon and drove off at noon. we didant like the look of this old shirt that had our nice berries in it. we got a sack and pored them out in to it. thare was about a quart of the nicest thay could find spred over the top and the rest was all bear cakes such as we had saw plenty of laying round whare the bears resorted, now we found ourselves badly sold again, but we threwed away our suply of bear cakes and went on. X

Two days later, we come to snake river a short distance above fort hall. the next day we drove to fort hall and layed by until the day fowllowing. this was a tradeing post of the hudson bay company, an english firm in the fir [fur] trade.

it kept by a man by the name of grant, a very furmilure free-spoken gentleman. he give us a good deal of light on the subject of oregon and the road and distance we had to travel to git to our place of destination. he was tradeing horses, flour, or anything he had to spare that thay wanted to emagrants as thay passed, for cattle. we perposed to trade our cattle for horses and pack riging. he got his horses up and I found I could trad with him but the germen and him couldant trade and I didant wish to leave them so we moved on with our teams to the american falls on snake river.

heare our cattle got scaterd and hid in the willowes and detaind us one day, we now concluded to go back and trade with grant if he would give the germens the same show he offered me and take our teams. whare we was now camped, some of the germen and myself went back on foot twentyfive miles to the fort.

when we got there, we inquired for our cattle we said was mising. after a short time talking we got into a trade. the horses was gathered and we traded, gathered our horses and outfit. now grant, three frenchmen, and ourselves, mounted our poneys about sunset and started for our camp 25 miles awa. I could git naughthing better than a string for a bridle and pack saddle to ride on

/34/ the stile of traveling hear on horse back was allmost full speed. grant and his men took the lead and of corse I had to keep up. to avoid the misery it was to ride this gate on such a saddle I was sometimes leaning to one side and sometimes to the other, then foured and then back. we traveled 25 miles in 3 hours. this was the severest jolting I ever had in my life.

we got to camp and took a nap before day the next morning. now we got up our cattle and delivered them. now when I first talked of trading with grant, I had a steer which was lame by being tender footd. I had sold this steer to grant for a sack of flour but when we made the final trade nither of us menchened this first trade, but when he looked over and counted the cattle, he says, "whare is the other steer?" I says, "didant you git him for the flour?" "Yes, but I paid for him" "why didant you name that before we traded," said I, "it is two late now we have traded and changed stalk. all I could do was to give you all I had and them you have got." "well, well," said he, "I thought I was giting 6 head but I have only 5 but I sopose it must go so under the circumstances." we just had to abandon our wagons.

now none of us knew anything about packing but we went to work, packed up, and traveled 4 miles that day, camped, got our baggage in a little better shape for the next day. we packed our anamels and got redy to start before the germen party was quite redy. We started on and traveled slowly with the view of thare overtakeing us, but soon after we started thare horses stampeded.

we nooned early and till 2 o'clock thay was not yet in sight. we thought we would go on to the next watter and whare we soposed thay would certainly overtake us, but we traveled until 10 o'clock at night before we came to watter. heare we overtook our old party with wagons. next morning we went on and didant see our germen friends any more /35/ until I met them in oregon citty.

They came in with their wagons several days after I had arrived there. they came to the city.

we traveled on, passing emogrant wagons allmost every day all the way through. we came to the crosing of snake river. heare we came up with some wagons who had hired an indian to pilot them across, it was little more than wast deep to this indian, all the dress he had on to hide his nakedness was a strip of cloth about an inch wide which went over one sholder down between his legs, the ends tied together before, we thought it a little comical to see him wade the river with that string on, but he acted as indipendant and proud as ever I saw anyone in any shape, he got .25 cts for his services, which to him quite anitom

the indians heare was bringing to us at every camp or stoping place salmmon to trade us. we traded for and eat it. We thought it very nice.

now the salmon was floting and runing down the streams all run down, pore, and a grate many did this. we knew naughthing about.

we came to boysey river. I rode along the bank taking items and came to a trap made for catching fish, it was a log across on the banks, pols set on the upper side of the log slanting upstream about two inches apart, clear acros the stream. this caught all the fish that come down that stream. I sopose thare was 3 or 4 wagon loads piled in on that rack, some ded, some could just wiggle a little, and others flounceing round quite lively. after this we baught no more fish from the indians.

we went on to fort boysea, heare we got some dried salmon skins of the man who had charg at this fort. we got these on an order we got from grant in our trade. this was a hutson bay trading post.

heare we crosed snake river again, traveled down it 2 days, camped on the Malheur and then next struck Burnt river. traveled up it one day, next day came to powder river, then 1 day to grand round vally.

heare we kiled a small elk, the first we ever seen except the meat got of stags at sody springs. we lay by one day and barbacuded this elk meat. /36/ Then went on, crosed the bleue mountain and in two days came to umatila river.

heare we found plenty of indians, thay came to our camp with potatos to trade. one of them took from under his blacket a small lode of very small potatoes, not more than one man could eat. we baught them. after seting a few minutes, he puld out a sack of nice large potatoes, of course we wold buy them, thay looked inticeing. it seamed to tickle him to see we baught the small one not knowing he had any better.

we next day came to columbia river along the mouth of the Umatilla River, went down this, had to cross John days, then deshutes rivers which was a rough rapid stream and a dangerous ford, and we got an indian to pilot us across.

Then we got within foure miles of the dallsX camped heare, we eat the last provicion we had on hand,

[Chapter 8]

then went to the dalls. heare thay had provisions to sell but no bread. we got fresh beef and wheat and potatoes. the wheat we ground on a hand mill then eat it bran and all together for thay had no bolt or sive. the beef was fat and nice. the bread went prittye well too when we got use to it.

the first night heare, the indians stole one of our horses. I hunted all day and didant find him. next day I didant find him, but found another one of our horses tide in the brush a mile or two from camp. now I was inraged anough to go to kiling indians, but dare not do so. this was wensday.

I hunted until Sunday morning. thare was a misheon establish heare. 2 men, A.F. Waller and Brewer, had charge of it. I thought I would inform these misheonarys and give them the discription of my horses. I rode up near the door, thay was both seting in the house, I spoke to them and one of them, Waller, stepted out. I told him my buisnass, I was going to hunt that day, then leave without the horse if I didant find him. he says, "wy, hunting youre horse on Sunday, I would not be serprised if you never find him." I says, "neither would I be serprised if you stole my horse." I said no more but rode off in disgust.

serched all day. when I came to camp, the boys, Hedges and my son John, had the horse. an indian drove a band of horses in or near our camp, my horse was with them. the boys saw him, and caught him. but his tail was shaved and his legs badly cut /37/ with habels [hobbles].

I then started acros the cascade mountain to willam valy. I took an old trail which had not been traveled only [by] indians. a party a few days ahead of me with a few famlies and a hundred and fifty head of stalk which thay lost the half of before thay got out of the mountain.

we was all alone three of us tel we overtook this party on the forth day on Sandy river, west side of the mountain. thay had come to grase thare anamels and layed by to recrute. thay had lost so meny of thare anamels thay scarce could git thare bagage along. many of them on foot, one man, Elijah Bunton, had a wife and two small children, he had lost all of his stalk but one ox and one poney. he packed the ox and pony with his goods and provishion and him and wife had to walk and each carrie a child. he came to me to git some of his goods packed, so his wife could ride his poney. not having much to pack, I let him have a horse. he then got a long better.

now we had three days travle to wallamet vally. Oregon citty appeard to be headquarters for all the emogrants, we got heare on the 8th of November 1844. we met but one man heare we was acquainted with, a Mr. Straight from Ills [Illinois].

Oregon citty was a new town, the only one in the vally and everyone who had property in it was trying to improve it, making work for all that wished to work, but no money. we had to take goods or provisheon X thare was wheat but no flour or mills. to make it, the bread was boild wheat or peas, no potatos. parched wheat or peas for coffee. salt salmon for meat mostly. one dollar fifty cts was a days wages for common labor.

goods was high and not very good except the goods of the hutson bay company, but thay have money for thare goods. very few had money to pay for anyting, allmost every person had to board themselves and furnish his own bed, at home or travelingX

now 3 of us joind together and bult a temparey shanty made shingles and got out hewed timber, then got some jobs of carpiter work, bought a lot, bilt a temprary house on it. by this time, the winter was near over X

I branched out to look at the country. I first went /38/ down to astory [Astoria] by watter, with a view of burning lime but found the limestone very good, but very limited quantity, not sufficient to pay me in starting the business, little pebbles only.

then up the vally 50 miles to the Rickreal on foot. by this time the watters were down so thay could be foreded. I prepared myself with a horse and riging so fare [fair] as the settlement extended. I rode alone. I had come purposly to look at the country, didant wish to take up land.

about the middle of may, I found three men, Heck, Hovias and Zummordie, who wished to explore. I fell in with them, got an outfit and set out to explore. we went as far outside of the settlement as we thaught was safe on acount of indians to the Butte above Marys River. thay was wild and thaught dangerous. we kiled all the wild meat we wanted as far as we explored. we found plenty of good land, spring water, and watter power for mashenery.

the more I romed, the more I wished to, but I was now giting short of means and took a job of building a house for Lindsay Applegate. got this done, then got out some timber and coopered a short time at the Applegates in fall and winter of 1845-46. X

[The outline of the story of being cheated out of wages was transposed for this chapter from page 58, as Scott numbered it, and page 66 by counting pages.]

I had a proof of this. when I came to oregon, I inquired, in talking to a man I met one day, I [asked] if he knew whare I could git a job of work. "No," he said, but I will enquire and let you know if I find any." a few days after this [I] met him again. he told me whare I could git a job. I went to the man who he said wanted the work and got a job. after this a short time, I done a job of work for the man I first inquired of. when we settled, he had a bill against me of three dollars for contracting. I thought this prity ruff, but it was in his own hands and he kept it.

[Chapter 9]

Now in the spring of 46, thare was no road across the cascade mountain which had to be crossed to git into wallammette vally. no way to git wagons in, only down collumba by watter. emogrants from eastwards had to abandon thare thare wagons at the dalls, a hundred miles from the velly. the navegateing vecilityes [facilities] very pore and dangerous, being no government and very little individual meanes in the country to use in making roads.

in the spring of 1846, the people called for volunteers to look out and locate an imogrant road. thare was a company of fifteen men raised which I joind. we set out the 15th of may, southward soposeing we could cross the mountain from the head of willammett river. we traveled about one hundred miles up the vally on the west side then crossed to the east. in crosing the vally we passed a high bute situated near the senter of the vally, campt on the side of it, went on top of it to take a view of the country. we had a handsom view as far ast the eye could see.

we called it Spencers bute, it still retains that name, Gen. Cornel. Gilliam named it in honor of a man of that name and gave his reasons then for desiring to honor that name, but I have forgotten what those reasons were. this bute is 3 miles south of and in plain view from Eugene citty now, but was then a wild wild wilderness.

our party was not property organised, had no gide nor /39/ leder which are very nessary in any company for any purpose. not having no succes heare, we concluded to go further south.

heare one of the explorers, Gen. Gilliam, got discouraged and left for home, but we continued on southerly, crost the calapoey [Calapooya] moutain, a spur of the cascades moun[tains] betwen willammett and umpqua watters. heare we was devided in opineon. some thought we was still on willammett, others umqua.

here we struck Elk Creek near the head which runs into Umpqua. now thare were too men, Sol Tetherow and [*Wilson* - per JLC], ancious to brak up and go home but was afraid to go, but still kept advocating the idea until noon. we then came to a small brook with very steep banks.

one man, Bob Smith, who was rideing a very small mule, going down the bank his cruper [crupper, the belt holding the saddle on the mule] broke and away went saddel, man, gun, and all, over the mules head, liteing in the watter about ne [knee] deep. this was sport for all but the man who got the ducking. he was allmost fiting mad and swore he would go home with the other two.

we noond heare. when we started the three discouraged men took the back track. it was cloudy, no sun to be seen all this afternoon. when we campted at night, the question came up about the corse of north and south. evry one had his corse pointed out, no two agreeing. I had a pocket compes, took it out, and set it. every man was more or les lost. a man we called our guide, Black Harris, had north for south. we went on two days later, then turned for home. we was now a hundred and fifty miles from home.

we went to whare I had selected a place to locate and settle on 25 miles from the settlement at the Cahoon place in Benton County. Tom Reed jumped my claim, I sold to him for about $20.00. heare I stopted.

we thought likely thare could be a new company raised and try the expodiseon further. I told them in case thay did so, I would join them as I had my outfit all thare ready for the tramp. thay went home.

now jesse appelgate took it in hand and raised fifteen men came by whare I was. I fell in with them and set out again X

went prety nearly the same route we traveled before into umpcaw vally. applegate had obtained a map made by ogden, a member of the hudson bay company who had traveled /40/ through a portion of the country we expected to go through. this map was made by observation whare ever ogden traveled, otherwise gest at, and so long as we was on or near his rout of travel, we found it very correct and of grate benafit, but in other places it was worse than none.

However, we went on very well until we got into the siskau [Siskiyou] mountain. heare come into hevy body of timber to avoid which we bore too much south over worse ground and mutch more circuitous rout, but we kept on until we struck clamoth river. we then turnd up this stream which was more in the direction we wished to go, went on until we came to an impasable canion. we now concluded to go down the river and look for a ford and try the other side but all agread it was going out of our corse. after we came to an understanding, one man started on afoot down the river, after we got a half mile on our retreat, we cam to a good looking place to turn off from the river on the bench land.

I went to Jess Applegate, suggested the idea of stoping a day to rest our horses, which thay very much needed, and 3 or 4 of us would go on foot through this timber that we had turned south to avoid. that was our corse anyhow. the idea took well with appelgate but some of the others kicked at it. consiquently, in acorance with a rule we had established, the croud was caled together and a vout taken on it. all voted to stop, but two those two, Jack Jones and L. Applegate, was put out so badly thay thretend to leave and go home. but we stoped, found a nice place to camp, foure of us started in the direction we wanted to go.

6 or 8 miles from our camp we found a high bute which seamed to rise clear above the timber. we went to the top of it. from heare we could see out into an open country and from our camp to this point was good ground for a road. we now thaught we would succede in our dezine without further trouble, but we found before we got through we knew naughthing about it atall.

/41/ we now went back to camp in gloing spirets and reported our succes. the day fowllowing, moved on through this timberd regeon. at twelve aclock we found ourselves on the clamoth river, eight miles below the little or lower clamoth Lake. heare we nooned then went up this stream to near whare it comes out of the lake, crosed it, and camped X

now we was in an open country, could keep our corse only having to sigzag round bad ground. we had to beare to south heare some to git round the lake. got round to the east side and camped.

from heare we struck northeasterly, came to tooly lake. found wild indians on this. as we came down from the hills to lake, we saw them runing in every direction. some run into the hiding places in the high grass and tooly, others got into canoes, run them out in the lake. we rode to a wigwam, thay had all left but one old squaw. she came runing at us with a stick of dride fish in her hand, presenting the fish to us as a presant, trimbleing and shakeing as tho she was fritened allmost to death. we took the fish, looked at it, handed it back to hur, and rode off X

we then went round the lake on the northerly a short distance. from heare, we saw two indians, one on horseback, the other on foot, leading a pack horse, coming directly meeting us. we saw thim stop, apearantly viewing us, then come on a short distance, then stoped, took another look, then sudantly dashed off from the road or trail into the high vegitation and each throad down a pack, then mounted thare horses, took thare back track in full speed as far as we could se them. we went on to whare thay had shed thare packs. on examoning the packs the indians left, we found it to be roots and seeds such as thay use for food. we did not molest their property. X [Mike Barber interpolated a note from the reverse of "page 35," presumably in Collins's handwriting: "In a short time after they went out of sight we saw a dense smoke arising in the direction they had gone.]

[Chapter 10]

[Continuation of Mike Barber's interpolation from the reverse of "page 35" of the original]: "and in a little while we saw other smokes arising in various directions. This was intended to give intelligence, by a kind of telegraph of the presence of a foe in the country. The different tribes often at war with each other. this rendered it more easy to settle the country. The burning of different fuels, —a black smoke signifies one thing—a light smoke another, etc. etc."]

we went on beareing more easterly round the lake tel we come to a stream leading into the lake with steap banks and deep watter. we turned up this stream. in going along the bank, we sudantly came onto a family of indians. takeing them by surprise, thay was on the opposite side of the stream from us but we had /42/ got so close to them undiscovered thay was afeard to run but the buck came towards us making all the signs of friendship he knew. we by signes gave him to understand we wished to cross the stream. he quickly shoed us by going up the river, we could cross and shoed the debth on his leg.

we went a mile further and found his information correct X heare we found the watter runing over a flat smoth rock not over six inches deep. we nooned heare.

now we was in an extensive level plane, direckly in the direction we wished to go. we could see a green looking clump at the foothills. we consulted about the matter and all agreed this green patch should be our next camp, soposing it five miles off, but when we come to travel it, found it at least ten and was dark before we got to this green spot. It was a clump of junaper treas on dry sand land, no appearance of watter atall.

we turned sutherly along the foothills, traveld three or foure miles and camped in a dry gulch without watter. now thare was meny complants in camp against the captain for giting us into this fix. this junaper was a new thing to any of us. it grows on dry sandy land but we sopposed it willows and grass which we all knew indicated watter. still many of the boys complaind biterly of the captain.

next morning we moved on early, went two miles, came to a splendid spring. heare we stoped, got breakfast, stayed tel ten oclock, all well pleased and cheared up except the captain. he had been so badly complained of without reason for it, he could not forgive it. after we had eate breakfest, the captain say, "boys, now I want you to chuse another leder if you want any, for I will have no more to do with the controle of this croud." now thay all, to a man, insisted that he should continue in leadership of the croud, but he would not agree to it. I perposed to him that he should choose two of the company as his councilers or staff and go on as captain himself, and he choose another man, David Goff, and myself as councilars. this apeard to be satisfactory to all.

/43/ now we had got off from the rout traveled by Ogden in making our map and it was ~~but little~~ of no use to us ~~a stream~~ but we done the best we could without any map. we went from heare easterly round on the south side of a mountain, partly level but rocky. we got to a pavement of rock, then ableaked [obliqued] to the south a few miles, found better ground and camped at a spring we called Goff's spring.

then took our coarse easterly. we next came to the bed of a branch with ocationly a hole of watter and bunches of willows [Fletcher Creek].

In going round one of those clumps of willows, we met an indian. we was within a few steps of him before he discovered us, he come runing up to us holding out and presenting us a ground hog and shivering with fear. we took his ground hog, look at it, handed it to him along with a little piece of tobacco to quiet him, and made signs for him to leave. he started sloly, looking back, the further he went, the faster he run, got out of site as soon as posable.

from heare, we crost a very rocky flat ridge and come to goos lake, this is an extensive flat with a large shallow lake in it. This Lake we give the name it bares yet – goos Lake. we saw some geese and found a grate meny goos quills on the beach.

from heare we traveled over broken land a few miles then across a ridge into another flat now known as Surprise Valley. campt on Plum Creek, then easterly to a canion, High Rock. went through this caneon about 10 or 12 miles. at the east end we went over some broken land a few miles and come into a flat with a nice small brook of watter runing through it. heare we traveled more sutherly to git round a mountain.

twenty miles from heare, we came to black rock. hear is a hot spring tho by cooling we could use it.

now we had bin about two weeks expecting every day to find a stream laid and called maryes river on the map we had been traveling by. we all thought this was south of us but we wished to go east, but if we could strike that as it was laid down on the map to run east and west, it would lead us the corse we wished to go.

now we was in an extensive desert and very dry country. I think this was an extremely dry season, a drouth in this dry country, /44/ and we was fearful we might suffer for watter.

so we took a vote of the whole croud which way we should stear from hear. we voted to go south but jesse applegate, he had not voted, but ast the privelage of taking all that would volinteer to go with him and go southeast toward what appeared to be a gap in the mts. [*Rabbit Holes* - JLC].

when we found this river we had been looking for so long, meet again on it. this we all agreed to and six five men volenteered to go with him.

now we seperated, 7 6 of them and 8 9 of us. we went south twelve miles, come to the hills which surounded the desart, found watter, not very good, but we could use it, noond heare, then kep on south between high mountains and over low sandy hills. we traveled 6 or seven miles. we stoped and left two men with our pack anamels.

all the rest struck out along the foot of these mountains in serch of watter to camp at. myself and two others, Jack Jones and B.F. Burch, was not very far apart when we came to a flat hollow or gulch in the mountainside. we saw a gean [green ?] bunch of low willows, all three steard for the same place about a hundred yards. below this bunch of willows, come near anuf to begin to talk to each other X

as soon as we commenced talking, an indian raised from behind the willows and look at us and broke up the mountain as lite as he could run. we holowd at him, tried to get him to stop, but the more we hollowed the faster he run. we went up to the place he run from, found a nice spring of good watter, a badger skind, the meat fleased [flensed] off of the bones, lying on the hide a small fire of willow sticks, the bones laing round the fire roasting.

we went back to our horses, all got together, and went to this place. campt thare and fared somtious [sumptuous]. The next morning, we turned more easterly in order to keep betwean the clumps of mountains that permeate all over this regeon of country. traveled about twelve miles, found a small branch of spring watter.

we had now got into a sandy desert without the least appearance of watter /45/ in any direction except whare we was. so the next morning we prepared ourselves for a dry days travel by takeing breakfast without meat, on coffee, bread and watter. we had naughthing with us to carry a drop of watter in.

we went south through a sandy plain. this was as hot a day as I ever expearanced. the sand would allmost burn a mans feet through his shoes X

we traveled tel about 3 oclock in the afternoon without any appearance of watter, then struck a fresh trale of indans whare thy walked through the sand. the track looked as plane as tho it was loose snow. we soposed thay would certainly go to watter and took thare track about east stearing directly towards a gulch in the side of a mountain.

thare we expected to find watter but lo it was as dry as any place we had seen and the indians had scraped a bason in the sand and lay thare, I sopose all night, for thare prints showed plain in the sand like a wild hog bed. from heare thay had went acros a mountain. we could only track them a short ways up the mountain-side, it was too rocky and hard but we could see occasionl signs of an old foot trale al the way over the mountain.

we got to the top of the mountain just before sunset, the sun shining brightly on an extensive level plane east of us in which we could plainly see shore [sure] indecations of watter. this was cheering to all of us tho it was thought 6 or 8 miles off, too far to reach it with our pack anamels before dark, so we selected two of the best horses and sent two men, Jack Jones and John Scott, ahead to make a light for us to stear to. by the time thay got to the foot of the mountain, it was dark and thay wated thare until we came to them.

being fearfull of runing into some difficulty in the dark we stopted, unpacked our anamels, tide our horses to sage brush or greeswood, spred our blankets on the ground, and lay down, horses and men allmost famished for watter and had not eat anything since early in the morning. but eating we did not feel the want of after laying a few minutes, our blood giting cool /46/ and settld.

we felt much better and comfordable, slept tel morning X one man by the name of jones had two loos horses. one of them he refuse to tie over night. in the morn-ing, his loos hors was gon. he started on track of his horse, the rest of us took our corse for the soposed watter.

it was cool now and we got along chearfuly, passing over a level plane, part of which was sometimes inundated and bore a tremdeous groth of vegatation. the winter fluds washed the sand and loom over this tel it had filed and rased from one to three feet deep all over the land.

this a very dry season, it was on fire, leaving from 2 to 6 inches of loos sand and ashes. this was like traveling through snow only it was dry.

we at about 9 7 oclock found plenty of watter. it was a deep slugish stream with perpandiculer banks, 40 or 50 feet wide, and bank full, but not a stick of wood of any kind [Humboldt River]. plenty of gras for our anamels. we had plenty of bread baked and raw bacon for our dinner. staid hear tel 12 oclock.

[Chapter 11]

[This next section is the same time period as the preceding chapter of James Layton Collins's redraft of Scott's original manuscript.]

now I will go back & bring the other party up that I said had seperated from us at black rock. thay traveled southeast 10 miles, came to a place, the rabetholes [Rabbit Hole Springs]. heare was a little watter in holes in the [ground] 6 or 8 inches across, watter in them 4 or 5 inches below the serfice of the ground, not very good and run in very slow when diped out. from hear thay turned south over a high mountain, found a very scant suply of watter. the 3rd day early in the morning thay came in sight of our camp, saw us leave, but we did not discover them. thay came to our camp we had left and out of sight or hearing, thay got heare about ten oclock, turned thare anamels out to graze, and cooked a harty meal of fresh meat which thay had kiled. staid tel 12 oclock, then followed our trail to the foot of the mountain whare the indians slept in the sand.

now it was night. thay had to camp without watter. thay could track us /48/ no further but took acros the moutain. thay toped the mountain in the morning looking in direction we found watter, the sun shined rite in thare faces and thay could see naughthing and thay had become so discouraged thay didant agree on anything only that thay must all perish. X

no timber heare but some small shelter thay could have from the hot sun. one man, Bob Smith, said he could go no furthur, lit from his horse, and layed down in the shade of a rock to die. thay tied his horse to the rock and left him, all appearently distracted, some going one way and some another. X

the party I was with had left the watter thay found and, comeing back toward the foot of the mountain, discovered them, directed our corse to them. when thay saw us, two of men came, meeting us, and reported a man left to die. one of our men had emted a tea canister, and filed with watter, had it with him, he went /49/ with the two of the other party who had met us as fast as thay could ride to the relief of the [*man, Bob Smith* - JLC] which had been left to die. but he didant die, thay met him comeing on. after he had cooled off and his blood and mind got settled, he felt much better and upon reflection he didant want to die nohow.

before we met any others of the party, jones who had fowllowed his loos horse met some of them and started to watter. his [*horse had* - JLC] led him to [blank], we all went with them and got together at a pretty good camp for watter and grass. [*Interpolation in Collins's handwriting: They were a sadly dejected party. Applegate spread his blankets on sage brush & lay down, proposed to thank God, etc. Applegate himself wanted to stop and would have lain down to die, but Bogus & Sportsman cursed him and blustered around till they got him to go on. Applegate usually must work in the lead or he became discontented and sullen.* - JLC] by next morning we was all cheard up, in better spirits. we traveled up humbolt river 60 miles, it being the corse we wished to go, tho we didant know the name of this stream at that time.

now we aimed to view out and make a road to fort hall or in that vecinity. by wagon tracks we found runing in that direction, we knew it was a rout traveled by emogrants to calaforna. we knew we had got too far south for a road to oregon and thought this a /50/ proper place to leave this stream [*60 miles from where we struck it* - JLC] and go west [*to Black Rock* - JLC]. X

now we was giting short of provisheon, and we made an estomate of the amount of work it would take to open this road to the willammette vally [*of which men had taken notes all along as we came out* - JLC] and thaught it would take thirty hands to open the road as fast as wagons would travel. we agreed two that the emogrants should furnish thirty hands with a sutable outfit to go ahead and open the road, otherwise we would not assist in convaying them in on this rout atall and I was apointed [*by the vote of our party* - JLC] to convay or guide them through.

jesse appelgate with three other men went on to fort hall to git a supli of pro-visheons for us to go home on X my self and Wm parker set out to view a rout from hear to black rock, about 60 miles, we only went 40 miles [to Rabbit Hole Springs], the balance a level plane we could see across but did not travel it X ~~and returned to camp and~~ moved on in the direction of fort hall very sloly, recruiting our horses, which thay very much kneeded.

/51/ on our return to camp, we saw an antelope some distance from us, feeding. parker got into a rivene, craled up near it, and shot it, and kiled it. I went to him while he was butchering it. we devided it, took it on our horses to carry it to camp.

in looking round near this place, we found a spring of good water [formerly called Antelope Spring but now called Willow Spring]. stoped to refresh and let our horses grase.

this spring was in a level flat and dry looking place very little sign of watter untel you got rite on it. it only run forty or fifty feet til it sunk or wasted away in the sand.

the indians had dug a channel about a foot wide and the same debth and had cramed it full of sage brush so naughthing could git watter out of it except about a foot square at the head of it. about ten feet from this hole of water thay had dug a place about six feet square, 18 inches deep, covered it with poles and brush, and then earth on top, made a hole in one side large anuf for a man to crall into it, and a port hole next to the watter /52/

this is a very dry regeon of country, only a few weake springs in it and the indians waylay them to kill anamels for food, this we found we called antalope spring.

now we started for camp, got thare about 10 oclock at night. the next day we /53/ work our way on about 60 miles and two of the men who we sent after prov-isheon met us with 14 emogrant wagons. one of these men, an old mounearer [mountaineer] [*Black Harris - JLC*] wished to bring himself into notice, he told these emogrants thay could drive rite along into oregon without any troubel atall on this rout and induced them to take it as I had agreed to go as gide. [*Medders Vanderpool was captain of this company. He had 14 wagons. He turned them up Goose Creek. He -Black Harris - was acquainted with Vanderpool and heard that he was going down Snake River, he went down Goose Creek and met him at the mouth of it and turned him up it. -* JLC interlineation]

I went to them, ast if thay understud the condisheons we had agreed to convay emogrants through on this route. "No," says thay. I told them what the terms was. thay snufed at this ~~thought~~. I told them it was imposable for them to git through without more help than was now on hand. if no more assistance came, thay must go back and take the other road or perish.

thay stopet untel the next day, then 7 more wagons came. thay had a note to me from applegate stating that he thought he would git the required number of hands to open the road and I had better go on with what had come to whare I was. in two days he would overtake us with /54/ them.

he did overtake us but only had 5 or 6 hands in place of thirty, my son Wm with him, and thay [*emigrants -* JLC] continued to overtake us untel we had 75 wag-ons. but by 2 or 3 of our party fawling in, we only had 12 hands to open the road X but we had got started in, we could not do better than to go on and git through the best we could X

now this was a seareous and difficult task for me, for this party was the rear of the emogrant trane and, of corse, with a very few excpetions, was the porest teams and the most slothfull and indilent men. we was often [*detained -* JLC] an hour or two by one man being slow and carless giting redy to start. it would not do hear to leave a lone famly mongst the hostile indians which was very neumers [numerous] hear and was watching us all the while and we seldom was a half mile from camp of a morning when we started until thay would be in it rumageing round to se what thay could pick up, but thay was wild and very fearfull of whites. by going along without enterfearing /55/ with them, and watching them closly a formadel [formidable] party could travel through thare country in safety. altho thay believe it all right to take the life of a white man, thay would as soon kill him for his shirt as a deer for its hide, and generly go in for extinction, slay men, wimmen, and children whareever opportunity offers.

we had to stick together and keep a good lookout for our stalk, altho we sildom seen one. not seing any indians made the indilent men more carless and backward about garding or looking after thare stalk. this made dissatisfaction in camp and traveling together so long seing a goodeal of difficulty thay became disgusted with each other and [*rarely* - JLC] any two agree on any subject. thay donat care for themselves or anybody else. speak just what thay think and often without thinking atall. this keeps a continued rangel [wrangle] in camp.

Takeing all together, a man that has any brains atall sees but little peace. I had traveled with emogrants be- /56/ fore, but circumstances made this the most difficult croud I ever got into. X

[Chapter 12]

now the first 3 or 4 hundred miles was an open country and compareatively level but rocky and banks and chasums. in going out we had not marked out a road for wagons but only took a view of the country soficient to satisfy us it could be done. now I had this to do ahead of the teams. thare was landmarks I could keep my corse by but these obstickels I had to look out for and wind round them the best I could. this kept me continuly going and comeing.

now many of them expeced me to furnish watter, gras, and a good road all the way through. this was imposable for thare was no road atall and in many places nithur gras nor watter but I got along without a grate deal of complaint when I gave the description of /57/ any difficulty or bad place we had to go through. I would invariable give it much worse than it rely was. when we would come to those places thay would feel agreeable disapointed and thare was no other person in the croud who knowed whare we was or how to git any place else so thay could not dispence with my assistance.

we came to one place in the evening whare thare was not a soficient suply of watter to camp overnight. it was 20 miles to the next water [this would have been Rabbit Hole Springs] over a level plane, a plain land mark [*Black Rock* - JLC] to stear to. we started acros this plane at sunset. we started to the landmark untel it got too dark, then took stars to go by. we got through about daylight the next morning but through carlessness thay let thare stalk squander. some came through and some thay never got /58/ Some of the teams did not git through tel 10 oclock. we lay by heare two days recruiting and looking after missing stalk. X

Now we had 20 miles to the next water over a sandy sage plane, heare we had 5 or 6 miles of hills to cross, then came to what is called high rock caneon. this is a perpendickaler ledg of rock on both sides of a level flat from one to two hundred feet wide, the rock about the same higth, a small stream runing through heare in the wet season only, standing in holes in the fall, but some good springs 4 or -5 miles through this.

then a broken and dry country only ocational spring for three days travel. hear a woman died [*Mr. Burch's wife in 1847* - JLC] layed by one day to bury hur, then crost a level marsha plane one day, then came to foot of saranevady [Sierra Nevada, but actually Warner] mountain, traveled northerly along the foot of it one day [*camped at Plum Creek* - JLC], then crosed this mountain. it was only a single ridg 4 miles across it, then one day to goos lake, then two days to gofs Spring.

heare we lay be two days. /59/ this was a very rocky regin allmost everywhare a pavement of rock for 4 or 5 miles, then came to clear lake vally, then 12 miles and we came to a level north of tooly lake, about 20 miles across this to fall river [not the Fall River, nor the Sacramento River which Scott reported in his waybill, attributed to Jesse Applegate, and Pringle recorded in his diary, but the Lost River.]. this is a small stream runing in to toolly lake.

we crosed this, a rock bridge, a flat rock about 20 feet up and down the stream, a fall of 8 feet 2 rods above it. heare the indians stole 4 head of cattle.

the next camp was clammoth lake. X

[Chapter 13]

The next morning, at the time to leave camp, thare was a man, Tanner, reported mising. I perposed to go back with two or three others, serch for him, and let the teams go on. we went to whare he was last seen. we found his track after going a mile. we could see by the tracks he had been runing. on examining, we found an indian track on each side of the road, a piece furthur we found the man in the road had fell to his knees, we seen the prints of his knees and hands in the sand, a littel further he had fell again and the indians track closed in on him. he had scuffeled round /60/ considerble heare and we found blood on the ground. we serched some time before finding any furthur trace of him.

at length, we found whare thay had carried and draged him about forty steps from the road into a thick bunch of sage brush, bent the brush down over him. thay had striped every stich of his clothing and his boots off of him. had shot a number of arrows into him. we had naughthing but butcher knives to dig a grave with but it was loose sand and with our knives and hands we dug a grave, raped him up in the best blanket we had with us, and buried him the best we could. This man or [illegible word] in the he had fell in with a man to drive team or stalk for his board acros the plains to oregon but was sick now, not able to do anything, and the man he was with refused to let him ride in the wagon and he had to go on foot, said naughthing about his being mising untel the next morning.

after we had buried him, we went on and overtook the trane. the next day we got to clammoth river, then went down the river 8 miles.

now we had come to timber. the party who had sent ahead to open and mark out the road all we had to depend on. the next 30 miles it was partly level. we found the rout blazed but porely opened. we freakquently had to stop the trane and work on the road, being no loose hands to send ahead.

now murmer began in earnist tho thay said directly to me apelgate had went ahead to open this road and was personly known to some and by caracter to the most of the croud, it was him thay put all thare reliance on. he was known to head the party that viewed this road and was not presant. thay say what thay pleased; this road being so porly opened we did not reach water, had to camp in the timber, do without super, and herd and gard thare stalk.

the next morning we was off early, traveled 4 miles, came to a small stream of water [*Beaver Creek* - JLC]. some of the chearful began to smile a little, others didant git over it for a week.

2 days from heare we got on the siskau mountain. the next day we got into rogue river vally. now we /61/ had watter and grass plenty from this on to willammette vally but some very ruff road and steep hills.

now we went on making our fifth camp on rogue river from hear about fifty miles. thare had a band of sheep stolen. thay was mising when the stalk was gatherd to start. soposed the indians had drove them of, and started without them, got 2 or 3 hundred yards from camp, thare was a cow mising, went to look for hur and the indians was butchering the cow close by the camp. the indians run off, thay saw no more of them.

we went on down the river about forty miles and crosed it. the 2nd day from heare we came to a place we couldant pass without stoping to work.

I looked out the rout and we went to work. we got through. this was on lous creek.

from hear 2 or 3 days to jump off jo creek. heare we had to work two or three hours. the road party had done naughthing hear atall.

this creek took its name from a man who was always called Jo runing from a party of indians, to make his escape jumped off a bank 15 or 20 feet high down into a patch of thick brush.

now we traveled three days and came to a hed of tributery of grave creek. we fowllowed this down to its junction through thick timber and brush. the road being porly opened the train was frequently stoped to remove obstickles found left in the road.

at one of these, one of the teamsters noticed a dog he had with him rase his bra-sels [bristles] and snuff as to he cented something unusual. he looked and saw an indian squated behind a large log about 15 steps from the road, his gun laid across the log, presented twards him. X

he run to wagon to git his gun and hist the dogs. three dogs broke for the indian at his biding. the indian broke and run soon out of sight, but the dogs caught or treed him, for we could hear quite a hubbub with them about a hundred yards off. a few minutes then the dogs came back, one of them wounded with an arrow but not mortaly.

now before we got through this brush a yung woman [*Leland Crowley* - JLC] /62/ which had been sick for some time, died and we camped til next morning, then drove on to grave creek. lay by that day and buried the corps. this circum-stance grave creek took its name from.

now this train drove thare wagons all closed up in circle forming a corell to collect and yoak up thare teams in, dug the grave in the middle of it, buried the corps, filling it, packing the earth titely, covering so as to give it as much the appearance of the natural ground around is as posabel. after corelling the teams and giting redy to leave, drove thare wagons, one after another in a line over the grave, but after all the indians found the grave, opened it, left it standing open, and I sopose, acording to habits thay was on the hills watching us all the time we stoped thare.

the evening we came, two men comeing into camp in the dusk of the evening, had several arrows shot at them not more than two hundred yards from camp. The indians was conceald in a clump of brush and could not be seen. we put out a strong guard to watch the stalk and train and told them to fire several guns into the brush whare those arrows came from and fire off a gun every fifteen minutes all night. when thay commenced fireing, thay was anserd by the fireing of guns on the mountain.

From heare we was three days giting to cow creek, about 25 miles; then went about 8 miles the next day.

the next morning when we was about redy to start, two men, Jack Jones and [*Tom Smith of Oregon City* - per JLC] from the oregon settlements came to our camp. of corse our party was ancious to hear from whare thay was going, all hands commenced asking questions of these men.

Tom Smith was very much apposed to a suthern emagrant road, and he told them thay could only go 6 miles further til thay must stop. thay could not git through the umcaw caneon with wagons or stalk. This was a damper on the whole croud and thay stud in amasement.

it was now early in the morning and was three oclock in afternoon before I could git them to move from this camp, then only moved about two miles and camped. the next day we only moved 3 or 4 miles and camped again. /63/ now we went a short distance and came to the dredid caneon.

heare I spent two days trying to git a party to go with me through this caneon but all in vane. no one would go. I caled the attention and told them I was going through the next morning. if some of them would go with me, we would see what had to be done on the road before wagons could pass through. if we found work had to be done, would come back, rais all the help we could and go and do it and git the trane through if it was posable. if none would go with me, I would go home.

[I said,] "I will not stay heare and see you all perish because you wont try to help yourselves. you know naughthing can be done without trying. now you can do as you please. I mean just what I say." X

this was the worst ten miles of a road I ever saw traveled. foure men was redy to go with me the next morning. we went through and concluded with a few days work the trane could pass through. X

went back next day. all that could be spared from camp went to work and worked foure days, then thought we could git through, but thare was one difficulty we could not remada [remedy] or avoid. thare was a creek runing this caneon very swift in places, very rockey, perpendicular rock banks, smooth sideling or pitching bed rock, short bends and large bolders in the channel. the channel of this in many places was the road from fifty to two hundred yards in a place. in low water very little in it, but only few hours rain would make it swimming. now the winter raines had set in which generly almost continuous from november until march and the creek was deep in places.

now thay started in. a grate part of the road was so narrow when a wageon stopetd, all behind was stoped. thay got along best they could, but only too wagons got through the first day being no feed until thay got through. several brought thare teames out, returned next day.

[The next story in Scott's original manuscript was about a man named Barker with a barrel of pork. It was moved to the story of 1847 by Collins.]

after the wagons all got out but one wagon which belonged to a man, small famly with plenty of provisheons. he, Barker, had a barrel of pork. several who was out had tried to buy meat from him before he got into the caneon but he /64/ refused to let them have any, said he might need it after he got through. his wagon was broke down. it would take a couple of days to repare it. he got his famly wagon through. circumstances alters cares.

he went to some of those who called on him for meat, told them if thay would wait for him, he would let them have all the meat thay wanted, but thay told him no, he would not let them have any to save thare lives, now we will not take any to save yours. it was said the barrel of pork set rite on the wheel of his wagon that broke down, he got no one to wate for him but his father-in-law. he only staid for his wifes sake. [End of Barker and barrel of pork story.]

now thare was another train came through this place after us that sufered much worse than we did X thay abandoned thare wagons and lost most of thare teams and starved very near to death themselves.

[Chapter 14]

some of them was going to shute apelgate on sight, but when thay got to whare he was, thay didant shoot any more.

now when we left heare, we went 6 miles to south umquaw. camped and look out a road acros a hil 5 or 6 miles. next day got to south umcaw again. we kept on down this stream til we crosed deer creek. heare we left it and steard for north umcaw.

heare a man with a small family campted. after he had stoped a short time an indian came, appeared friendly, and ask for his gun, said he would kill a deer and bring it in for him. he gave him the gun. the indian took and a while came back about dusk without any game. came to the mouth of the tent whare the man was laying down in side and shot him, then made his escape with the gun. [Scott's version of the story of the killing of Newton varies considerably from that told by other travelers with the Newtons. Collins modified it to conform to the other versions.]

when got to north umpcaw, it was up so we cold [could] not ford it and no other means of crosing. I had crosed it 3 or 4 miles below. we then went down to that place. heare it was very deep and rocky but by giting a canoe from an indian to cros the famlys and bagage in, we got acros with the teams and wagons at the ford.

now it was open from heare to foot of calapoua mountain, 15 miles. the 2nd day
we reached that point. now heare was a hevy /65/ timbered mountain, 15 miles
acros it without a stick cut to open it or a blaze to mark it out. a trane of exosted
emagrants out of provishon who had traveled over two thousand miles through
the hot sun and dust with ox teams, and a hundred and fifty miles from whare
thay could obtain anything to subsist on and a raining more or less almost every
day. X

I knew the corse we had to [go] but knowing naughthing of the ground we had
to go over, but I ralied a small force of hands. I would blaze on apiece then come
back and help cut up. a party was sent to the settlement for provishons and assistance but I believe that Enoch Garrison was the only one man worked any on
the road except emogrants and myself.

at length we got through. by this [time] some wagons met us with provishons.

heare my task ended. wagons had come from the settlement but the watters had
got up so the difficulty was not over yet. theare was one man, Herman Buckingham, whos team had failed, bilt a raft [*at the mouth of the Coast Fork* - JLC] and
put his goods and family on it and started down the willammette river, run into
a snag, tore his raft to pieces, bearly saved himself and famly, everything else he
had aboard was lost.

I went on with the foremost teames. we had to dig out a canoe to cros Long Tom
creek. this stream got its name by a tall man who was caled tom comeing near
giting drounded in it and is a long slugish stream.

heare the party I was with began to drop off and locate, all scatering and setteling
in the suthern settlements and vecinity except one man who stopted in umpcaw
vally and wintered. In the spring fowllowing came into willammette vally and
settled.

I wintered in frontear settlement.

now this exploreation of forty-six was intirely, we got naughthing, only the curses
and abuse from the emogration and a few of the old settlers in the northern
settlements.

in the fall of 45, a party of emogrants atemted cross the cascade mountain with
wageons [*on the Barlow route* - JLC] only got well started in til thay had to
abandon thare wagons and git to the settlements the best way thay [could]. thay
suffered sevearly before thay through and many of them thaught the wagons
never could be brought /66/ through.

this led to the suthern exploration and view of a road in 46. but during the
spring and summer, with the help of the settlers, thay got thare wagons through
and a temporary road scetch out. [This is a clear reference to the experience of

the Barlow and Rector parties on Mount Hood and the opening of the Barlow Road.]

now two roads for emogrants to come into the settlements on. the two [1 or 2 illegible words] which was two hundred and fifty miles apart into the most deserable portion of the country.

at that time the only market or speculation in this country was off of the emogration. like all new countrys, a portion of the first settlers is of the most unscrouples. thay will take the last cent a man has for the least favor thay do.

[Sidney Moss story—meanest man in Oregon, refer back to Chapter 8]

I had a proof of this. when I came to oregon, I inquired, in talking to a man I met one day, I [asked] if he knew whare I could git a job of work. "No," he said, but I will enquire and let you know if I find any." a few days after this [I] met him again. he told me whare I could git a job. I went to the man who he said wanted the work and got a job. after this a short time, I done a job of work for the man I first inquired of. when we settled, he had a bill against me of three dollars for contracting. I thought this prity ruff, but it was in his own hands and he kept it. [end of Sidney Moss story.]

now in 47 I was Employed by some of the settlers to meet the emogration and convey them through on the suthern road. I got a very [*small* - JLC] salury [*one hundred bushels of wheat, gotten up by subscription, Felix Scott got up the subscription and gave 20 or 30 bushels himself. He was killed by the Indians near Goose Lake, he had gone back to States, and was coming with stock. No information of his party except what the Indians told. One of his finest stallions was afterwards found and recognized at Salt Lake City.* - JLC] but went out with a party which was going to the states. I made some cutoffs on the road and bettered in places. I met the first emogrants on [*Ham's Fork the day I left* - JLC] bear river. heare I had been stoping with some old mountainears which was camped on the road. I stayed heare ten days. I then fell in with the emogrants. thare was a grate deal of inquire made by them concerning the different roads. I told them I had come out on the suthern road and was going back the same way with all who wished to go that road, but did not come to solicet or advise anyone else to go one or the other of the roads but all that went to the road I did, I would assist and help all I could. when we got to the forks of the road, the most that I was with took the suthern road with me.

with exceptions of some deprodations by indians, smothly all the way through. The misshap by indians, a good looking young indian fell in with us, appeard very formelier [familiar] and tried to help drive stalk and make himself as /67/ usefull as posable in every way he could. some of the boys took a likeing to him and thaught thay would take him to oregon with them and have an indian of thare own. he redily ageed to go with them. thay dressed him with pants, shirt, and vest, a good pare of shoes, and hat, made quite a good looking man of him. about the third or fourth night, he took three blankets and some clothing and left in the morning. when thay got up, thay was mineous an indian.

[Between pages 58 and 59, as originally numbered by Scott, and actually pages 66 and 67 by counting, Collins inserted a lengthy handwritten note. Begin Note 58a.]

There was a party of about 30 men, some going back to the States, some of whom expected to meet friends coming to Oregon, in which case they would return, I believe B.F. Burch was the only one who returned. They elected me captain. I refused unless they all consent to obey my directions. on a small branch of Bear Creek, in Rogue River valley, near Phoenix, we were attacked by the Indians. During the day, we could see Indians on the hills, and hear them hallow. That night almost 60 yards from brush camped for fear of an attack. Sometime in the night the horses being picketed close to camp, guard noticed alarm among the horses. On examination he found a mule shot. Some several arrows were shot into the camp, several arrows striking the tent, one near a man's head. We fired into the brush. Then, Little Osborn, got on a horse and galloped around the camp to see if there were any Indians in the tall grass, to scare them out if there were, found none. The next morning we found a mule had been shot in the hip, and a horse in the muscle of his hind leg, mule not injured—the horse was lame, The arrow had broken off. We caught him and got the piece out. We then started on, and went about a ¼ of a mile 5 men concluded to go back to camp, supposing Indians would come to camp. They rode over the hill fast as they could and saw several Indians in camp—one on horseback. They charged on the Indians and fired on them. Those on foot ran into the brush. The Indian on horse back ran to the brook, but /page two of JLC note 58a/ could not get across with his horse, so he jumped off, and left his horse. The horse proved to be one belonging to one Miller of our party which had been stolen from him, in Rogue River valley the year before. This Miller had been one of the Road workers of 1846.

In going around Klamath Lake we found a loose horse dragging a rope which we supposed to be another stolen by the Indians from the emigrants. We took the horse on with us. I do not remember who took him.

When we got through High Rock Canyon, I wished to make a cut off. We started and went across a spur of Black Rock mountain about 12 or 14 miles, in the East side, we found a small lake and camped. In the edge of a sage plain from 10 to 20 miles across, that looked level, in the direction of Humbolt [sic]. Company became discouraged, Black Harris opposed it, we concluded to steer more southerly, and struck Humboldt some distance above where the original trail left it. We camped one night before we got to Humbolt on a little spring branch three or four miles from the river, which was so high we could not cross it. We traveled upon it a day and camped on a small branch of Humbolt. The next day went up till we could cross after which we struck the trail of 1846. Went on to Fort Hall—Steggs story— Went on to Smith river where we found old mountaineer Pegleg Smith, and two others—with their Indian familes. I stopped with them about 2 weeks—I stopped with Anderson—quite intelligent. Pegleg's wife had a son about 5 months old—he though[t] a great deal of child. She let the child roll off her lap—he jerked out pistol and fired, clipping a lock of hair out of her head, she gathered up the child and submitted. Smith's wife was a Flathead, Anderson's a Ute and the Frenchman had a family of 3 children.

[End of Note 58a.]

[Chapter 15]

[The next story, about Barker with the barrel of pork, was moved to the story of 1847 by Collins. It was originally at pages 55-56 by Scott's enumeration and pages 63-64 by counting pages.]

after the wagons all got out but one wagon which belonged to a man, small famly with plenty of provisheons. he, Barker, had a barrel of pork. several who was out had tried to buy meat from him before he got into the caneon but he /64/ refused to let them have any, said he might need it after he got through. his wagon was broke down. it would take a couple of days to repare it. he got his famly wagon through. circumstances alters cares.

he went to some of those who called on him for meat, told them if thay would wait for him, he would let them have all the meat thay wanted, but thay told him no, he would not let them have any to save thare lives, now we will not take any to save yours. it was said the barrel of pork set rite on the wheel of his wagon that broke down, he got no one to wate for him but his father-in-law. he only staid for his wifes sake.

[End of story of Barker and barrel of pork.]

we went on without any more truble til we got ways down humbolt river. then the indians run off six head of oxen, we found trale of them and fifteen of us got our horses and followed them. when we got within a mile of whare thay had drove to, we saw an indian [coming] rite from whare the cattl was. some of the boys took after him and caught him, brought to whare we was trailing the cattle. he [pled] inocence biterly, but he showed rite whare the cattel was and wanted us to let him go, but we took him to whare the cattle was. we [found] everything just as he described. he told us other indians had done it, showed which way thay went, and he would help track them, but it was useless to fowllow them. he knowd very well we could do naughthing with them, but he would do or say anything to make out his inocence, but we believed him guilty. two of the cattle was butchered, the meat cut redy for drying. two was about in the act of dying and two slitely wounded X these we took to camp X

we was now in quandary what to do with this indian. two men was ancioius to shoot him, had thare guns cocked and pointed it [at] him. others beging for him. I had not said anything. someone perposed leave it [to] me, which thay all agreed to. the indian was standing by the meat which had been cut up. I said, "Shoot him on the meat, it a caution to others."

expecting to hear the guns fire, I turned round to walk off, but thay didant shoot. no one would shoot him. I told them I wouldant shoot him but we would take him to camp and give him up to the owners of the cattle that had been drove off.

we had 15 miles to go and [it was] now near sundown, level open ground. the indian was afraid, run from us as we drove him a long with the cattle til dusk, then tied him /68/ we tied one end of a long rope round him above the hips and tied his hands behind him, then we could drive or lead him.

I took charge of him and thaught I would drive him ahead of me, but [he] would blunder, turne one way and then the other, making all the trouble he posable could. I put him behind to lead him. he would not lead no better than drive. then I thaught I would break to lead anyway, so I rapt the rope round the horn of my sadel. the [next] blunder he made I spured my horse, jurked him down, and dragd him apiece, let him up but had to serve him the same trick over, then started my horse in a trot and kept that gate rite a long. the indian troting behind me had no more trouble tel we got to camp. kept him tied tel morning.

the owners of the cattle said, "Let him go, he might be inocent." but I said then we would linch him anyhow. I ast a man who had said but little about the matter if he would wip [whip] him. he said yes, he would [be] glad to do so and he got five or six bent willow sprouts he could find. we turned him loose, 6 or 8 men standing round with guns in hand, detarmed to shoot him if he run. commenced on him about as good a linching as he could stand, then shoed him to leave. he started slowly, looking back, the further he got away, the faster he run, as far as we could see him he didant slacken his gate.

from heare we had no more trouble untel we reached the settlement. the most of these emogrants settled in the uper willammette vally. now I staid in the border settlement.

three others and my[self] went to oregon city on foot the first ten miles, git a small boat and go from heare by watter. another party had went down on the boat but was expected back soon. we stoped heare two days and no boat came.

it was commen heare for every person when traveling to cary his beding, we had our blankets but no provisheon. thare was a french man living heare. one of our party by the name of Smith who was acquainted with this frenchman went to him [to get] something to eat. he had an indian wife and not mutch better than indian fare. when was ast, he says, "I got no bread and got no meat very good, all de same monseur smith, I got plenty provishen. /69/ you eat wiv me. fe [if] I got nun [none], by god you cant have sum. I bleve it best for you go on my garden, dig some small potates, make fire." up rose, we got some potatoes, thay was small for he had a very pore crop, but when roasted we relished them very well after being without eating all day.

we staied heare two days then went on afoot 6 miles to willammette river. heare another lived with a squaw wife and number of half breed children. we went in heare to git something to eat. thay had poles laid overhead in thare house making an open flore, and that coverd with salmon smokeing and drying it. this made an awfull smoke and much worse smel in the house, so we went on without asking for anything to eat.

went to shampoig [Champoeg]. heare an american lived who we was acquainted with. we went to his house. he was not at home. he had a squaw wife. we ast hur for dinner. "No, no," she says, speaking very short and crusty.

Thare was a french man living near by who kept pubalick house and squaw wife and half breed daughter, a young woman. we went to the tavern thinking to git an extra meal, caled for dinner. thay went to cooking amediately. the old lady made a fire, put on a kittle of watter for tea, set down flat on one side of the hearth, didant seem to want anything but hur but end to set on. the yung [woman] commenced making batter in a large pan she picked up at the dore, then picked up a frying [pan] from the corner of the fireplace, set it on the fire with some kind of grese in it, then set her pan of batter on the hearth with a fork in one hand and spoon in the other, she sat down flat on the hearth just as the lady had done.

two or three dogs laying round the fire watching this cookery as close as we was. every now and then a dog would make a grab at a flitter [fritter?], but always stopted by a blow on the head with the spoon or the fork stuck in his nose.

now we was seted in the back part of the room, impationly waiting for our much needed meal. at length, it was set on a bench and the lady looked towards us and pointed to the bench,saying, "chahco mucamuc," that is to say, "come to dinner" or "come and eat."

so /70/ we picked up our three legd stools we was seting on and moved up to the bench but was quite alarmed by a busel with the dogs to see which could git the first lick at the pan the yung lady had set down in the flore.

we had a tin cup of surup on the bench and nife and fork each, a tin plate. these plates had to take on our laps. the old lady set on bench a tin full of tea. we went to work and demolished the grater part of what was set before us.

that afternoon a boat passing bound for oregon citty. we got a pasage on her and were on to oregon citty. we X staid heare over night, got a pasage on a boat and returned back home [*to Salt Creek* - JLC].

stoped heare untel the whitman masacre took place. vollinteers was sent out aganst the indians. thare was not a soficient number of white men in the country to subgu the indians.

Provisional Governor George Abernethy's Advice to Emigrants of 1847[1]

Gentlemen:—It being made my duty, as Superintendent of Indian affairs, by an act passed by the legislature of Oregon, 'to give such instructions to Emigrants to this Territory, in regard to their conduct towards the natives by the observance of which, they will be most likely to maintain and promote peace and friendship between them and the Indian tribes through which they may pass,' allow me to say in the first place, that the Indians on the road to this country, are friendly to the whites. They should be treated with kindness on all occasions. As Indians are inclined to steal, keep them out of your camps. If one or two are admitted, watch them closely. Notwithstanding the Indians are friendly, it is best to keep in good sized companies while passing through their country. Small parties of two or three are sometimes stripped of their property while on their way to this Territory, perhaps because a preceding party promised to pay the Indians for something had of them and failed to fulfil [sic] their promise. This will show you the necessity of keeping your word with them in all cases.

There is another subject upon which I would say a few words. A number of the emigrants of 1845 took a cut off, as it [was] called, to shorten the route, leaving the old road; the consequence was, they were later getting in, lost their property, and many lost their lives—Some of those who reached the settlements, were so broken down by sickness, that it was some months before they recovered sufficient strength to labor.

A portion of the emigrants of 1846 took a new route, called the Southern route. This proved very disastrous to all those who took it. Some of the emigrants that kept on the old road reached this place as early as the 13th of September, with their wagons, and all got in, in good season, with their wagons and property, I believe, except a few of the last party. While those that took the Southern route, were very late in reaching the settlements—they all lost more or less of their property—many of them losing all they had and barely getting in with their lives; a few families were obliged to winter in the Umpqua mountains, not being able to reach the settlements.

---

1   George Abernethy, "Circular: To The Oregon Emigrants," *Oregon Spectator,* Jan. 20, 1848, 2, col. 4.

I would therefore recommend you to keep the old road. A better way may be found, but it is not best for men with wagons and families to try the experiment.

My remarks are brief, but I hope may prove beneficial to you.

Dated at Oregon City, this 22d of April, 1847.

George Abernethy
Governor of Oregon Territory and Superintendent of Indian Affairs.

APPENDIX 3

Scott's Letter to the *Oregon Spectator,* October 25, 1847[1]

When the Oregon Provisional Legislature authorized Scott to improve the new route so he could charge tolls, they also recommended that he explore a direct connection to Greenwood's Cutoff.[2] Jesse Applegate had already proposed such a route in his "Road to Oregon No. 4" letter,[3] but Aubrey L. Haines credited Scott's letter as first noting the potential of combining the 1844 Greenwood cutoff (known after 1849 as "Sublette's" cutoff), a fifty-mile desert crossing that eliminated the detour to Fort Bridger and saved some fifty miles, and the 1849 Hudspeth cutoff from Soda Springs to the Raft River. Both cutoffs lacked water and grass, and consequently wore down draft animals.[4] Scott's proposed route from today's Cokeville, Wyoming ("the termination of Greenwood's cut-off, on Bear river") would actually run south of the Oregon Trail, Soda Springs, and the Hudspeth trail. Scott never again traveled there. Thanks to Will Bagley for clarifying the geography.

Mr. Editor—Since it has become known to the people, that the immigrants by the northern route are suffering great losses, and misfortunes, and those who travelled under my guidance the southern road arrived here with their property in safety, some are inclined to censure me for not inducing a greater number to travel that road, and others assert that I selected a company of choice teams and pushed them through, in order to establish a favorable character for the southern route.

As a statement of facts will fully exonerate me from all blame in the case, I hope you will indulge me, so far as to give this letter a place in your paper.

The unfortunate issue of the southern route last season, to those who look only to results without examining causes, has created even in the minds of those not personally interested in the location of the road strong prejudices against it.

---

1   *Oregon Spectator*, Nov. 11, 1847, 3, col. 1-2. Jesse Applegate may have providced assistance with drafting this letter.

2   "AN ACT to improve the Southern Route to Oregon [Dec. 23, 1847]," *Oregon Spectator,* January 6, 1848.

3   *Oregon Spectator,* April 15, 1847.

4   Haines, *Historic Sites Along The Oregon Trail,* 302.

Though misfortunes of equal magnitude have been of yearly occurrence since the year 1842, yet persons interrested [sic] in the arrival of immigrants by the old route have greatly enlarged upon the disasters suffered by the southern immigrants, and have labored to impress upon their minds that their losses are attributable wholly to the route they traveled, hence a majority of those who traveled the southern route last year have reported unfavorably of it to their coming friends; besides these, hundreds of letters written by persons interrested in the old route, were sent to meet the immigrants, not only cautioning them not to travel the south route, but advising them, to starve, whip, and even murder any person who advised them to do so, and this sanguinary counsel was particularly given in reference to myself. And lastly Mr. Abernethy in his official capacity of Superintendent of Indian affairs and Governor of Oregon, issued to them a circular giving all the weight of his high official station to an exagerated [sic] account of the losses and calamities suffered by immigrants on the new route, and strongly recommending the old road without informing them that it was subject to like disasters to an even greater extent.[5]

It is not reasonable to suppose that I a private individual (had I been disposed to make so mad an attempt) could have withstood so high a functionary—such 'a cloud of witnesses' and such a torrent of invective.

When at the solicitations of my friends I consented to return upon and make amendments to the southern route, I promised to conduct such immigrants as voluntarily chose to follow me; in this as well as making considerable improvement upon the road I have been successful.

In giving my opinion to the immigrants of the southern road, I was careful neither to overrate its advantages nor underrate the difficulties to be encountered in traveling it, and if any friend of the southern route wish it painted in stronger colors, or for the immigrants to be flattered into the belief that by taking it their troubles are over, they must employ some other messenger, more eloquent and less scrupulous.

How much better it would have been for the immigrants if the friends of the old road had dealt with them in the same candid manner; had they been correctly informed in regard to both roads, I have no doubt a majority of them would have taken the south road and would now in all probability be in this valley with their property in safety. Under these circumstances it is not surprising that only a small party (25 wagons) under my guidance took the southern route, and I take this opportunity of expressing the respect and high opinion I entertain for the gentlemen composing it. In the advantages taken of the ground, and in straightening the road, (which I think much improved, and about 40 miles shorter than the route traveled last year,) they had about 70 miles of new road

---

5   See Appendix 2.

to make, besides several days' labor in improving the pass of the Umpqua and Calapooia mountains, which they performed in a manly and cheerful manner.

As the party for the United States, with which I traveled last spring, were unwilling to leave the road, or delay time for the purpose of examining the country, I was unable to make examinations which, I am satisfied, from information on which I can place the fullest confidence, that a road may be made from the termination of Greenwood's cut-off, on Bear river, to the head of the Cajeux or Raft river, which, without passing over worse ground than the old road, will be well supplied with grass and water, and will cut off 100 miles of travel.[6] But these improvements cannot well be made but by a party sent expressly for that purpose prepared to open as well as explore them. Experience has fully proven that the delay and the increased labor upon the teams of immigrants in making new roads, however advantageous to those who follow, generally injure the first travelers.

In conclusion, I would recommend not only to the friends of the southern route, but to every friend to Oregon, and his fellow-men, that these improvements be made, and I will venture to say that half the value of the property lost by the immigrants in reaching the valley the present year, would be amply sufficient to apply a permanent preventive to such misfortunes in [the] future; and I would ask those who yearly extend charities to the suffering and bereft immigrants, if their means would not be better expended in enabling these sufferers to arrive among us with their property, as independent citizens, rather than objects of pity and the prey of famine?

Very respectfully, yours, /s/ Levi Scott.

---

6   As noted in the introduction to this appendix, there were two well-known cutoffs that some felt might be combined: "Greenwood's," which became known as "Sublette's" cutoff, first used in 1844, was a dry route; it saved about fifty miles by cutting out the loop south to Fort Bridger. The second cutoff, known as Hudspeth's, led emigrants on a similarly dry haul across the hills of southeast Idaho from Soda Springs to the Raft River, thereby avoiding a loop to the north by Fort Hall. Both cutoffs saved little time for the effort due to the necessity to rest and recover the draft animals because, despite Scott's belief, there was no water and little grass on either route. The Hudspeth route was first traveled by the Bidwell-Bartleson party in 1841 but ignored after that until the 1849 Gold Rush. Jesse Applegate had, of course, proposed that there might be such a route in his letter titled "Road to Oregon No. 4" in the *Oregon Spectator*, April 15, 1847. Bagley, *With Golden Visions*, 190.

"From Oregon," by John Luce

The following letter by John Luce was printed in the Defiance Democrat *(Ohio), November 25, 1847. Luce's name was spelled various ways ("Long" and "Lose" and "Loose"), but this is the spelling on the patent for his Donation Land Act claim. Born in Pennsylvania in 1800, he arrived in Oregon as a single man with the 1846 emigration. No other emigrants mentioned him. He settled in the vicinity of Alpine and Monroe, Benton County, Oregon. He married Margaret Wright, a widow with five children, in 1849. They had another child together. He died in 1865 in Coos County, Oregon. His letter tells the story of his journey from Fort Hall to the Willamette Valley.*

WALLAMET VALLEY, Polk co.,
Oregon Territory.

I take this opportunity to address you from Wallamet Valley, my long desired place, at which I have at length arrived. I feel thankful for the good health I enjoy. Tho' there are many mountains, rivers and dales that separate us, yet my mind is often with you, yet I have no desire to be there in person. I found the country better than I anticipated; and will now inform you of the incidents that occurred in our migration from Fort Hall, where I wrote last to you. There were some men who met us near Fort Hall and through their persuasion we took the new route, an off cut as it was called; or properly the California road, leaving Snake river on the north, we travelled on the Cassia and Goose rivers. The roads were very bad, pasture indifferent, having heavy beds of sand without wood, water or grass, for 45 or 50 miles, to travel through; the dust was intense, the sand appears to be mixed with lime and salt, and both man and beast had to cough and sneeze, the cattle would frequently bawl from suffering. The Indians were friendly but would be [?]. We at length arrived at Mago [Mary's, now known as Humboldt] river and travelled down it three or four hundred miles, (this river is in California) and here we were among what is called the 'Root Diggers'—Indians who are homely, deformed, and destitute of clothing; and among these creatures depredations commenced; they stole our horses and cattle, and shot their arrows into them during the day to disable them to be sure of them at night. They also killed some of our men, and we in return killed them, for our feelings were not friendly towards each other.

At a place called Rush Bottom [Lassen Meadows, Nevada], a good camping ground, a party of these Indians collected, from 100 to 400. I presume, there was a good band of them. We stopped for the night within three miles of that place. 3 wagons passed by us from a company in the rear and went on to this camp ground; a few Indians came to them in the evening and appeared to be friendly; the men used them well by feeding them, they left at night, and the small company felt themselves secure; but in the morning they went to look for their cattle in the rushes, which are 7 or 8 feet high, and as thick as hemp, to their astonishment their cattle were all shot and taken by these savages; and secreted in the rushes, they gave the war whoop and were ready to fight. By this time it was 9 o'clock in the morning, when we arrived with our small company of 19 wagons; and Capt. West's company of 21 wagons came up 2 o'clock, when we held a council to determine what to do, and 14 of our number went out to fight, well armed, on horseback. As we advanced they made their appearance at the edge of the rushes, while they kept up a continual whooping and jumping as we rode up, fearless in appearance but not in feelings in meeting such an unequal force, though their braves gave back, and our men charged on them, for fight they would but could not see an Indian, as they soon secreted themselves in the rushes patiently waiting our approach. Three of our men got right amongst them, their arrows flew like *streaks*, they had full view of us being on horse back and we had some difficulty in making our retreat; we had to dodge the arrows though three of our men were wounded. —The Indians still remained in the rushes and kept up their fierce shrieking to frighten us I suppose.

McNeley,[1] Lippincut[2] and myself went to the west end of the rush bottom to set it on fire; the rushes were fine and dry, and took fire well. The chief with about forty of his warriors stood on an eminence, and gave an alarm (as we supposed) commanded the Indians to desert their hiding place; a small band of them issued forth, and made toward the corell (our camp;) upon this band we fired and killed three, while the others made an effort to escape to their fortification but we headed them and drove them back, and whenever any of them made their appearance we sent the black pill after them until they all made their escape on the other side of the bottom and reached their fortification in that way, (their fortification is rocks piled up on the top of a hill or mountain: we kept up our shooting at them until 2 o'clock, when we returned to our camp, and learned that Capt. West's commpany [sic] had arrived.

We then left it to vote whether we should again renew the attack upon them. Nineteen volunteered to give them another brush and we kept them uneasy with our guns until sun set. We had two more of our men wounded. One, an Englishman by bursting his rifle; Mr. Lippincut was shot through the knee, the

1   *See* oregonpioneers.com: John McNeil, age 26. Without more information, this is only a possible identification.

2   *See* oregonpioneers.com: a Mr. "Lippingcott" was identified as a member of the Henry Smith company. He was wounded in a battle and continued on to California rather than Oregon. *See* note 3, below.

arrow went through the wound and the feather cleansed it of the poison and it healed up very soon.[3]

On the next morning we visited the battle ground; and found that the horses that had been killed had been eaten, and the bodies of the Indians carried away.

One of our men died of his wounds,[4] after which the Indians received no quarters; until after we crossed the Cascade mountains, after having travelled near 700 miles through these hardships,[5] and about 100 of our company died on the road.

The route through which we travelled is about 1200 miles from Ft. Hall to Oregon City, and through the old route it is but 750.[6]

The emigrants are not all in yet. We passed over mountains where it took 12 to 16 oxen to pull a wagon—going down we had to lock all the wheels. We frequently left our wagons and goods to the mercy of the Indians; took our packs, and when we got through some had four, and some but one, and others threw nearly all they had away.

Our provisions gave out e're we got within 200 miles of this place.[7] We killed our cattle, which were very poor, and eat them. Flour was not to be had, and in this situation my mind was strongly impressed with the place where I had enjoyed plenty, at least to eat.

We passed through some places where the water was like ley [alkali], and no doubt it is exposed to fire, for some of the springs were so warm that the water would scald your hand if thrust into it; and strong enough to drive three pair of mill burrs, and so deep and clear that you can see it bubbling to the depth of 30 or 40 feet. It looked rather scaly to me when we got through the Rangan [Rogue?]. I concluded to take what things I could on my back, it being a poor place there to starve. I found a secret place and lifted my heart in devotion to Him who controls the destinies of man, and asked that I might be conducted safely through the savages by which I was surrounded until I landed with civilized men.

---

3   This battle was also described by Edwin Bryant who heard the story from Lippincott. Capt. West's party had a battle with Indians in the vicinity of the turnoff to Oregon near Lassen's Meadows. *What I Saw in California*, 249, 339. A man named Sallee was killed in the battle and his death was frequently commented upon. For additional comments on the battle and death of Sallee, *see* Morgan, *Overland in 1846*, 774-76.

4   Sallee.

5   When Luce entered the Rogue River drainage near Ashland, he had traveled about 800 miles from Fort Hall.

6   The actual distance by "the old route" and the Barlow Road from Fort Hall to Oregon City was close to 715 miles. The actual distance by the Southern Route from Fort Hall to Oregon City was nearly 1,100 miles.

7   Assuming his distance was accurate, he was out of provisions at about the same place and time as he reached Canyon Creek Canyon.

I started with what I thought I could carry, and left the rest with my companions, if they save their own, they will save mine, too. A little Englishman[8] went with me (though it rained all the time in the valley, it snowed on the mountain) we travelled three days and I was completely exhausted, and almost starved, when we passed three wagons of emigrants, one of which agreed to carry my pack; we pushed on that day and met a Wallamet Indian, who showed us the way to his lodge, or house, and told us he had plenty to eat; — he went to hunt. We found his house as he said, well furnished with meat of different kinds. I told him I was hungry, and his squaw, and daughter who were well dressed, soon fried us some venison in Elk's tallow and baked some very good bread, as I tho't, made good soup, and we were well furnished with a sumptuous meal. He invited us to stay all night, said they had plenty to eat. — In the morning he desired us not to travel that day, it being Sunday, and we remained until Monday morning. When I asked him what was to pay, he said:

"Why, you pay nothing, you was hungry, and I had plenty to eat."

After leaving his hospitable domicil we had to travel three days without any thing to eat, when we arrived at the place where I now am; and a place I long to be.[9]

Our miseries were almost inconceivable, in consequence of going the lower route. — Those who went the old route fared well, and arrived in September; but we did not arrive until January.

---

8   Oregonpioneers.com does not identify anyone as English or from England who might have been Luce's companion.

9   While the location is unclear from this cryptic comment, his dateline indicated "Polk County," which at the time included what became Benton County where he later filed his land claim. He would have passed close by this place in 1846 and seen that there were already settlers in the area. The reference in the next sentence to his arrival suggests that he originally traveled to Oregon City, where he would have arrived in January and could make the comparison with those who traveled "the old route." Then he returned to the beautiful country he had earlier noticed, the place he longed for.

Acknowledgments

I WAS DRAWN INTO EDITING THIS MANUSCRIPT by Arlie Holt. He and I met by coincidence and he happened to have the manuscript reminiscence of one of Oregon's 1844 pioneers who also had a role in the opening of the Southern Route of the Oregon Trail in 1846. From Arlie I learned the name of the otherwise unnamed "excellent man" of the family history who kept a ten-year-old girl and her family alive long enough for her to become my great-great-grandmother. That man was Levi Scott. Arlie trusted me with the manuscripts of Levi Scott's reminiscence and other documents which illuminate the stories of early Oregon settlement by Americans. Our friend W. Mike Barber also shared his research and transcriptions of Scott's manuscripts. The librarians, especially Normandy Helmer and Linda Long, at the Knight Library, Special Collections, University of Oregon granted me access to the Collins Collection and have otherwise encouraged the work.

The Oregon Historical Society Davies Family Research Library and its staff, especially Geoff Wexler, Scott Daniels, Shawna Gandy, and Steve Hallberg gave unflagging assistance and thoughtful suggestions as I pestered them with arcane requests. The *Oregon Historical Quarterly*, editor Eliza Canty-Jones and assistant Erin Brasell, published two articles I wrote relating to the stories of Levi Scott and the emigrants of 1846. The society is lucky to have such a dedicated, professional, and friendly staff to assist its patrons in the library and at the *Quarterly*.

My friends in Trails West, especially Richard Silva, Rod Latimer, Don Buck, and Bob Black, shared their research and time in the field with me. Our days and nights searching for and documenting authentic traces of the Southern Route to Oregon and its California Trail variants are some of my best memories.

Three friends have been generous with their research and time for years: Stephenie Flora, proprietor of the oregonpioneeers.com website; Will Bagley, author and editor of multiple histories of the west, especially those relating to the story of Levi Scott: *South Pass, So Rugged and Mountainous,* and *With Golden Visions Bright Before Them* from the Overland

West series; and Kristin Johnson, author, editor, librarian, historian, and proprietor of the website "New Light on The Donner Party," utahcrossroads.org/DonnerParty. And I have a new friend to thank, Dr. MacKenzie Moore, who pointed out unlikely but incredibly useful sources which I had overlooked and then shared her dissertation on the Americanization of Oregon Country.

The folks at Washington State University Press have been a joy to work with for this first-time author.

Bibliography

Abernethy, George. "Circular: To The Oregon Emigration [April 1847]." *Oregon Spectator*, January 20, 1848, 3.

Applegate, Jesse [Z, pseud.]. "Road to Oregon, No. 3." *Oregon Spectator*, March 18, 1847, 1-2.

_____. "Road to Oregon No. 4." *Oregon Spectator*, April 15, 1847, 1, col. 1-3.

Applegate, Jesse, attributed to; written by Levi Scott. "Waybill, From Fort Hall to Willamette Valley." *Oregon Spectator*, April 6, 1848, 1-2.

Applegate, Jesse. "Immigrants arriving via the Southern Route." *Oregon Spectator*, October 14, 1847, 2.

_____. Letter to George Abernethy, March 20, 1848; Oregon Historical Society Research Library, Mss 929.

_____. Letter to Samuel A. Clarke, June 23, 1878, Oregon Historical Society Research Library, Mss 1156.

_____. "Umpqua Agriculture, 1851." *Oregon Historical Quarterly* 32, no. 2 (June 1931): 137.

_____. "Views of Oregon History," Bancroft Library Mss P-A 2.

Applegate, Jesse A. "A Scrap of Early History." *Oregon Statesman*, May 7, 1886, 8.

_____. "Wearing Buckskin in the Forties." *Polk County Observer*, March 13, 1903, 1.

Applegate, Lindsay. "Notes and Reminiscences of Laying Out and Establishing the Old Emigrant Road into Southern Oregon in the Year 1846." *Quarterly of the Oregon Historical Society* 22, no. 1 (March 1921): 44.

Applegate, Shannon. *Skookum*. New York, William Morrow & Co., 1988.

Bagley, Will. *So Rugged and Mountainous*. Norman: University of Oklahoma Press, 2010.

_____. *South Pass: Gateway to a Continent*. Norman: University of Oklahoma Press, 2014.

_____. *With Golden Visions Bright Before Them*. Norman: University of Oklahoma Press, 2012.

Bancroft, Hubert Howe. *History of Oregon, Vol.1: 1834-1848*. San Francisco: History Company, 1886. Vol. 29 of *Works of Hubert Howe Bancroft*. San Francisco, A.L. Bancroft & Co., 1882-90.

Barlow, William. "Reminiscences of Seventy Years." *Quarterly of the Oregon Historical Society* 13, no. 3 (September 1912): 240-81.

Bassett, Karen, Jim Renner, and Joyce White. *Oregon Historic Trails Report*. Salem, OR: Oregon Trails Coordinating Council, 1998.

Beckham, Stephen Dow. *Land of the Umpqua: A History of Douglas County, Oregon.* Roseburg, OR: Douglas County Commissioners, 1986.

Booth, R. A. "History of Umpqua Academy." *Oregon Historical Quarterly* 19, no. 1 (March 1918): 1-48.

Boyd, Robert, ed. *Indians, Fire, and the Land.* Corvallis: Oregon State University Press, 1999.

Bright, Verne. "Black Harris, Mountain Man, Teller of Tales." *Oregon Historical Quarterly* 52, no. 1 (March 1951): 1-20.

Brock, Richard K., ed. *A Guide to the Applegate Trail, The South Road to Oregon, Second Edition.* Reno: Trails West, 2005.

Brock, Richard K., and Donald E. Buck, eds. *A Guide to the Applegate Trail from Lassen Meadows to Goose Lake, Third Edition.* Reno, NV: Trails West, 2010.

Brown, J. Henry, "Settlement of the Willamette Valley," Mss P-A 8, Bancroft Library.

Brown, Tabitha. "A Brimfield Heroine." in *Covered Wagon Women, Diaries and Letters from the Western Trails, 1840-1849*, ed. and comp. Kenneth L. Holmes, 11 vols. Glendale, CA: Arthur H. Clark Co., 1983.

Bryant, Edwin. *What I Saw in California.* New York: D. Appleton & Co., 1848; reprint, Lincoln: University of Nebraska Press, 1985.

Burke, Joseph. Volume LXIII North American Letters 1839-1850, folio 142, Library and Archives, Royal Botanic Gardens, Kew, Richmond, Surrey, England, author's collection; excerpted in McKelvey, Susan Delano, *Botanical Exploration of the Trans-Mississippi West 1790-1850.* Jamaica Plains, MA: The Arnold Arboretum of Harvard University, 1955, 813-15; reprint with a new introduction by Stephen Dow Beckham. Corvallis: Oregon State University Press, 1991; excerpted in Morgan, *Overland in 1846.* Citations to the excerpt published in Morgan.

Burnett, Peter. *Recollections and Opinions of an Old Pioneer.* New York: D. Appleton & Co., 1880; reprinted serially in *The Quarterly of the Oregon Historical Society* 5, no. 1 (March 1904) to no. 4 (December 1904).

Canse, John M. "The Diary of Henry Bridgeman Brewer." *Oregon Historical Quarterly* 29, no. 2 (June 1928): 189-90.

Carey, Charles Henry, ed. "Diary of Rev. George Gary." *Oregon Historical Quarterly* 24, no. 3 (September 1923): 328.

_____, ed. *The Oregon Constitution and Proceedings and Debates of the Constitutional Convention of 1857.* Salem, OR: State Printing Department, 1926; reprint, Portland, OR: Press of the Oregon Historical Society, 1984.

Carter, Tolbert. "Pioneer Days." *Transactions of the Thirty-Fourth Annual Reunion of the Oregon Pioneer Association* (1906). Portland, OR: Peaslee Bros. & Chausse, Printers, 1907, 65-103.

Clark, Malcolm, Jr. "The Bigot Disclosed: 90 Years of Nativism." *Oregon Historical Quarterly* 75, no. 2 (June 1974): 112-18.

Clark, Keith, and Lowell Tiller. *Terrible Trail: The Meek Cutoff, 1845*. Caldwell, ID: The Caxton Printers, 1967.

Clark, Robert Carlton. "The Military History of Oregon 1849-59." *Oregon Historical Quarterly* 36, no. 1 (March 1935), 14-59.

Clarke, S. A. "Overland to California in 1851." *The West Shore* 5, no. 8 (August 1879): 226-27.

Clarke, Samuel A. "Pioneer Days, Article XXIII [Joseph Watt]." *Sunday Oregonian*, September 27, 1885, 2.

_____. "Pioneer Days, No. VIII [Indian fires]." *Sunday Oregonian*, June 7, 1885, 2.

_____. *Pioneer Days of Oregon History*. Portland, OR: J.K. Gill Co., 1905.

Collins, James Layton. In Dean Collins Papers, Special Collections and University Archives, University of Oregon Libraries.

Colvig, William. "Annual Address." *Transactions of the Forty-Fourth Annual Reunion of the Oregon Pioneer Association* (1916), Portland, OR: Chausse-Prudhomme Co., Printers, 1919.

Corning, Howard McKinley. *Dictionary of Oregon History*. Portland, OR: Binford & Mort Publishing, 1965.

_____. *Willamette Landings: Ghost Towns of the River*. Portland, OR: Binford & Mort Publishing, 1947.

Crawford, Medorem. "Gov. George Abernethy [and J. Quinn Thornton]." *Transactions of the Fourteenth Annual Reunion of the Oregon Pioneer Association* (1886). Portland, OR: Press of Geo. H. Himes, 1887.

Cross, Col. Osborne. *March of the Regiment of the Mounted Riflemen in 1849*. Washington, D.C.: C. Alexander, Printer, 1851; reprint, Raymond W. Settle, ed. *The March of the Mounted Riflemen*. Glendale, CA: The Arthur H. Clark Co., 1940; reprint *March of the Regiment of Mounted Riflemen to Oregon in 1849*. Fairfield., WA: Ye Galleon Press, 1967.

Cummins, Sarah J. "Autobiography and Reminiscences of Sarah J. Cummins," Oregon Historical Society Research Library, Mss 1508; reprint, Fairfield, WA: Ye Galleon Press, 1999.

Daughters of the American Revolution, Sarah Childress Polk Chapter No. 6, compiled by. *Polk County Pioneer Sketches*. 2 vols. Dallas, OR: The Polk County Itemizer-Observer, 1927, 1929; reprint, Monmouth, OR: Polk County Historical Society, 1977.

Davidson, Alfred. Alfred Franklin Davidson Papers, Oregon Historical Society Research Library, Mss 386.

Davis, Charles George. *The Oskaloosa Company: Last Wagon Train to Skinner's in 1847*. Portland, OR: Frontier Publishing, 1996.

_____. *Scott-Applegate Trail: 1846-1847 Atlas and Gazetteer*. Memorial ed. North Plains, OR: Soap Creek Ent., 1995.

_____. *The South Road and the Route Across Southern Oregon: Short Studies in the History of the Oregon Country, Including Strategies in the Cold War Over the Far West Frontier*. North Plains, OR: EmigrantsWest.com, 2000.

Deady, Matthew. "Southern Oregon Names." *Oregonian*, December 5, 1883, 1, col. 7.

Delano, Alonzo. *Life on the Plains and Among the Diggings*. Auburn, NY: Miller, Orton & Mulligan, 1854.

Douglas. "Deer Creek, Douglas Co." *Oregon Statesman*, June 23, 1857, 2.

Drury, Clifford M. *Marcus and Narcissa Whitman, and the Opening of Old Oregon*. Glendale, CA: Arthur H. Clark Co., 1973.

Earl, Robert. Robert Earl Papers, Oregon Historical Society Research Library, Mss 793.

Edwards, Cecil L. *Chronological List of Oregon's Legislatures*. Salem, OR: Legislative Administration Committee, 1993.

Elliott, T. C. "'Doctor' Robert Newell: Pioneer." *Quarterly of the Oregon Historical Society* 9, no. 2 (June 1908): 103-26.

Emigrant of '46, [Truman Powers]. "A Pioneer's Reminiscence." *Oregonian*, March 12, 1879, 1, col. 2.

Engeman, Richard H. *The Oregon Companion*. Portland, OR: Timber Press, 2009.

Evans, Elwood, Col. L. F. Mosher, et al. *History of the Pacific Northwest: Oregon and Washington*. Portland, OR: North Pacific History Company, 1889.

Fullerton, Charles P. "Miss Crowley's Grave." *Oregonian*, November 23, 1883, 2, col. 2.

Garrison, Abraham Henry. "Reminiscences of A. H. Garrison, His Early Life, and Across the Plains and of Oregon from 1846 to 1903." Oregon Historical Society Research Library, Mss 874.

Garrison, Rev. Abraham Elison. "Forty-Two Years in Oregon, Life & Labour of Rev A E Garrison, seven months on the plains." Oregon Historical Society Research Library, Mss 1009.

Gibbs, George *Dictionary of Chinook*. Washington, D.C.: Smithsonian Institution, 1863.

Gilliam, Washington Smith. "Reminiscences of Washington Smith Gilliam." *Transactions of the Thirty-First Annual Reunion of the Oregon Pioneer Association* (1903). Portland, OR: Peaslee Bros., 1904, 202-220.

Glen, Julia Veazie. "John Lyle and Lyle Farm." *Oregon Historical Quarterly* 26, no. 2 (June 1925).

Goeres-Gardner, Diane L. *Necktie Parties: Legal Executions in Oregon, 1851-1905*. Caldwell, ID: Caxton Press, 2005.

Goff, David [James W. Nesmith]. "For the Oregon Spectator." *Oregon Spectator*, April 29, 1847, 4.

Good, Daniel H. Letters, Princeton University Library, Princeton, New Jersey; transcription, Oregon Historical Society Research Library, Mss 173.

Gowans, Fred R. *Rocky Mountain Rendezvous*. Provo, UT: Brigham Young University Press, 1976. Reprint, Layton, UT: Peregrine Smith Books, 1985.

Gudde, Erwin G. *Bigler's Chronicle of the West*. Berkeley: University of California Press, 1962.

Haines, Aubrey L. *Historic Sites Along The Oregon Trail*. 4th ed. Tucson, AZ: The Patrice Press, 1994.

Hambleton, James H., and Theona J. Hambleton. *Wood, Water & Grass: Meek Cutoff of 1845*. Caldwell, ID: Caxton Press, 2014.

Harris, Moses. "For the Oregon Spectator." *Oregon Spectator*, November 26, 1846, 3.

Hasselstrom, Linda M., ed. *Journal of a Mountain Man, James Clyman*. Boise, ID: Tamarack Books, 1998.

Hastings, Lansford W. *The Emigrant's Guide to Oregon and California*. Cincinnati: George Conclin, 1845; facsimile reprint, Bedford, MA: Applewood Books, 2010.

Hazelett, Stafford. "Letter." *Oregon Historical Quarterly* 110, no. 2 (Summer 2009): 317-18.

———. "'Let us honor those to whom honor is due': The Discovery of the Final Link in Southern Route to Oregon." *Oregon Historical Quarterly* 111, no. 2 (June 2010): 220-48, www.jstor.org/stable/10.5403/oregonhistq.111.2.220.

———. "'To The World!!' The Story Behind the Vitriol." *Oregon Historical Quarterly* 116, no. 2 (Summer 2015): 196-219, www.jstor.org/stable/10.5403/oregonhistq.116.2.0196.

Heitman, Francis B. *Historical Register and Dictionary of the United States Army*. Urbana: University of Illinois Press, 1965.

Helfrich, Devere. "The Applegate Trail." *Klamath Echoes* 9, Klamath County Historical Society, 1971; reprint, *Journal of the Shaw Historical Library*. Vol. 10. Klamath Falls, OR, 1996.

———. "The Applegate Trail Part II: West of the Cascades." *Klamath Echoes* 14. Klamath County Historical Society, 1976; reprint, *Journal of the Shaw Historical Library*. Vol. 10. Klamath Falls, OR, 1996.

———. "Stagecoach to Linkville." *Klamath Echoes* 11, Klamath County Historical Society, 1973.

Hileman, Levida. *In Tar and Paint and Stone*. Glendo, WY: High Plains Press, 2001.

Himes, George H. "History of the Press of Oregon, 1839-1850." *Quarterly of the Oregon Historical Society* 3, no. 4 (December 1902).

Hines, Rev. H.K. *An Illustrated History of the State of Oregon.* Chicago: The Lewis Pub. Co., 1893, 131–32.

Holman, Frederick V. "A Brief History of the Oregon Provisional Government and What Caused Its Formation." *Quarterly of the Oregon Historical Society* 13, no. 2 (June 1912), 89-139.

Holmes, Kenneth L. *Covered Wagon Women: 1840-1849.* Vol. 1 of *Covered Wagon Women: Diaries and Letters from the Western Trails, 1840-1890.* 11 vols. Glendale, CA, and Spokane, WA: Arthur H. Clark, 1983-93.

Holt, Thomas. "Diary of Thomas Holt." *Oregon Spectator,* March 4, 1847, 4, reprint in Morgan, *Overland in 1846,* 191-98. Citations to Morgan.

Howell, John E. "Diary of John E. Howell." *Washington Historical Quarterly* 1, no. 3 (April 1907).

Hulin, Lester, "Day-Book or Journal of Lester Hulin," monograph. Lane County Pioneer-Historical Society, 1959; reproduction copy at Oregon Historical Society Research Library, Call Number 917.91 L24H, 1959.

Illinois Adjutant General's Office. *Record of the Services of Illinois Soldiers in the Black Hawk War, 1831-32, etc.* Springfield, IL: Journal Company, 1902.

Jackson, Donald, and Mary Lee Spence, eds. *The Expeditions of John Charles Frémont.* Urbana: University of Illinois Press, 1970.

Johnston, Robert B. "Two Jesses and the Modoc War." *The Journal of the Shaw Historical Library* 5, nos. 1 and 2 (1991): 1-43.

Jung, Patrick J. *The Black Hawk War of 1832.* Norman: University of Oklahoma Press, 2007.

Kendall, Dr. Reese P. *Pacific Trail Camp-Fires.* Chicago: Scroll Publishing Company, 1901.

LaLande, Jeff. *First Over the Siskiyous.* Portland, OR: Oregon Historical Society Press, 1987.

Lang, Herbert O. *History of the Willamette Valley.* Portland: G. H. Himes, 1885.

Lansing, Ronald. *Nimrod.* Pullman: Washington State University Press, 2005.

Lockley, Fred. "Impressions and Observations of the Journal Man [Barlow Road stories]." *Oregon Journal,* Aug. 28, 1928, 10.

———. "Impressions and Observations of the Journal Man [Lucy Henderson Deady]." *Oregon Journal,* Jan. 24, 1923, 6; Jan. 25, 1923, 8; Jan. 26, 1923, 8, col. 6.

———. "Impressions and Observations of the Journal Man [Mrs. R. E. Dersham, daughter of William J. J. Scott]." *Oregon Journal,* Nov. 25, 1926, 10, col. 6-7.

———. "Impressions and Observations of the Journal Man [Absolom F. Hedges], *Oregon Journal,* Jan. 4, 1938, 10.

———. "Impressions and Observations of the Journal Man [W. W. Scott, son of Wm. J. J. Scott]." *Oregon Journal,* Nov. 26, 1926, 14, col 6-7.

———. "In Earlier Days [David Guthrie]." *Oregon Journal,* Jan. 23, 1914, 6.

_____. "Reminiscences of Mrs. Frank Collins, Nee Martha Elizabeth Gilliam." *Quarterly of the Oregon Historical Society* 17, no. 4 (December 1916), 358-72.

Looney, Jesse. Jesse Looney Papers, Oregon Historical Society Research Library, Mss 2263.

Lovejoy, Asa, and Henry E. Reed. "Lovejoy's Pioneer Narrative, 1842-48." *Oregon Historical Quarterly* 31, no. 3 (September 1930).

M, Letter, *Oregon Statesman*, September 25, 1852, 2.

Macy, William M., et al. "The New Emigrant Road," *Oregon Statesman*, March 19, 1853, 2, col. 1-2.

McArthur, Harriet K. (Nesmith). "Biographical Sketch of Hon. J. W. Nesmith." *Transactions of the Fourteenth Annual Reunion of the Oregon Pioneer Association* (1886). Portland: Press of Geo. H. Himes, 1887.

McArthur, Lewis A. and Lewis L. McArthur. *Oregon Geographic Names.* 7th ed. Portland, OR: Oregon Historical Society Press, 2003.

McBride, John R. "Annual Address." *Transactions of the Twentieth-Fifth Annual Reunion of the Oregon Pioneer Association* (1897), Portland, OR: Geo. H. Himes & Co. Printers, 1898, 31-55.

McLaughlin, Mark. *The Donner Party: Weathering the Storm,* 3rd ed. Carnelian Bay, CA: MicMac Publishing, 2008.

McNary, Lawrence A. "Oregon's First Reported Murder Case." *Oregon Historical Quarterly*, 36, no. 4 (December 1935): 359-64.

Menefee, Leah Collins, and Lowell Tiller. "Cutoff Fever, I-VI." *Oregon Historical Quarterly* 77, no. 4 (December 1976) to 79, no. 1 (Spring 1978).

Minter, Harold Avery. *Umpqua County, Oregon, and Its Pioneers.* Portland, OR: Binfords & Mort, 1967.

Minto, John. "The Occasional Address." *Transactions of the Fourth Annual Reunion of the Oregon Pioneer Association* (1876). Salem, OR: E. M. Waite, 1877.

_____. Papers, "Capt Levi Scotts Company in the Cayuse War," Oregon Historical Society Research Library, Mss 752.

_____. "Pioneer History, A Struggle On Snowshoes in Southern Oregon 50 Years Ago." *Oregonian*, December 30, 1894, 11.

Moore, MacKenzie K. L. "Making Place and Nation: Geographic Meaning and the Americanization of Oregon: 1834-1859." University of California (Berkeley), Fall 2012.

Morgan, Dale, ed. *Overland in 1846: Diaries and Letters of the California-Oregon Trail.* 2 vols. Georgetown, CA: Talisman Press, 1963; reprint, Lincoln: University of Nebraska Press, 1993.

Morrison, Dorothy. *Outpost: John McLoughlin and the Far Northwest.* Portland, OR: Oregon Historical Society Press, 1999.

Neiderheiser, Leta Lovelace. *Jesse Applegate: A Dialogue with Destiny.* Mustang, OK: Tate Pub. & Ent., 2010.

Nesmith, James W. "Diary of the Emigration of 1843." *Quarterly of the Oregon Historical Society* 7, No. 4 (Dec. 1906): 329-359.

_____. "Southern Oregon History." *Oregonian,* November 23, 1883, 2, col. 2.

One of the Road Hunters. "For the Oregon Spectator." *Oregon Spectator.* April 15, 1847, 2-3.

Oregon Spectator. "AN ACT to improve the Southern Route to Oregon [Dec. 23, 1847]," January 6, 1848, 4.

_____. "Married [Newton-Powers]," Sept. 2, 1847, 3.

_____. "Public Meeting," June 25, 1846, 2.

_____. "Resolution and formation of militia in response to Whitman Incident," Dec. 10, 1847, p. 2.

Oregon Statesman. "Trial of William Kendall for the Murder of William Hamilton, in Marion County Circuit Court, at March Special Term, 1851," April 18, 1851, 1.

_____. "Trial of William Kendall, etc.," April 25, 1851, 1.

_____. October 20, 1-3, and October 27, 1855, 1-2.

The Oregon Weekly Times. "Indian Hostilities South." October 13, 1855, 2.

Oregonian [anon.]. "New Roads to Oregon, No. 2." *Oregon Spectator,* March 18, 1847, 2-3.

Oregonian. "Amusements," December 12, 1870, 3.

_____. "The Late Captain A. F. Hedges," March 8, 1890, 6-7.

_____. "The Rogue River Massacre, Story of the Killing of Nineteen Persons on October 9, 1855." December 20, 1885, 3, col. 4-6.

Palmer, Joel. *Journal of Travels Over the Rocky Mountains.* Cincinnati: J.A. & U.P. James, 1847; reprinted Ye Galleon Press, Fairfield, WA, 1966.

Peltier, Jerome. *Black Harris.* Spokane, WA: Ye Galleon Press, 1986.

Portrait and Biographical Record of Western Oregon. Chicago: Chapman Publishing Co., 1904. 485.

Powers, Truman, *see* Emigrant of '46.

Pringle, Virgil. "Diary," Pacific University Archives, Forest Grove, OR; Oregon Historical Society Research Library, Mss Microfilm 1194; Dean Collins Papers, Special Collections and University Archives, University of Oregon Libraries; "Diary of Virgil K. Pringle, 1846." *Transactions of the Forty-Eighth Annual Reunion of the Oregon Pioneer Association* (1920). Portland, OR: Chausse-Prudhomme Co., 1923, 281-300; *OPAT* reprint, in Morgan, *Overland in 1846,* 163-88. Citations to Morgan.

Read, Georgia Willis, and Ruth Gaines, eds. *Gold Rush: The Journals, Drawings, and Other Papers of J. Goldsborough Bruff, Captain, Washington City and*

California Mining Association, April 2, 1849–July 20, 1851, 2 vols. New York: Columbia University Press, 1944.

Rieck, Richard L. "Geography of the Oregon Trail West of Fort Hall: A Plethora of Options." *Overland Journal* 17, no. 2 (Summer 1999): 9-23.

Robertson, James R., and Alanson Hinman. "Reminiscences of Alanson Hinman." *Quarterly of the Oregon Historical Society* 2, no. 3 (1901).

Rucker, Maude A. *The Oregon Trail and Some of its Blazers.* New York: Walter Neale, 1930.

Rumer, Thomas A. *The Wagon Trains of '44.* Spokane, WA: The Arthur H. Clark Co., 1990.

Sargent, Alice Applegate. "A Sketch of the Rogue River Valley and Southern Oregon History." *Quarterly of the Oregon Historical Society* 21, no. 1 (March 1921).

Sawyer, R. W. "Abbott Railroad Surveys, 1855." *Oregon Historical Quarterly* 33, no. 2 (June 1932).

Scott, Leslie M. "Beginnings of East Portland." *Oregon Historical Quarterly* 31, no. 4 (December 1930).

Scott, Levi. Letter, *Oregon Spectator,* November 11, 1847, p. 3.

_____. "To His Excellency, George Abernethy, Governor of Oregon." *Oregon Spectator,* March 9, 1848, 2, col. 5-6.

_____. "To His Excellency, George Abernethy." *Oregon Spectator,* March 23, 1848, 2, col. 6.

Scott, William J. J. Oregon, "1846 August 14," Andre De Coppet Collection, Manuscripts Division, Department of Rare Books and Special Collections, Princeton University Library, Princeton, New Jersey; in Morgan, *Overland in 1846,* 2:638-40. Citations to Morgan.

Settle, Raymond W., ed. *The March of the Mounted Riflemen.* Glendale, CA: The Arthur H. Clark Co., 1940; reprinted as *March of the Regiment of Mounted Riflemen to Oregon in 1849.* Fairfield, WA: Ye Galleon Press, 1967.

Shaver, F. A., compiler, in collaboration with Arthur P. Rose, R. F. Steele, and A. F. Adams. *An Illustrated History of Central Oregon.* Spokane, WA: Western Historical Publishing Co., 1905.

Silva, Richard. "Emigrant Trail Through Photography." *Overland Journal* 18, no. 2 (Summer 2000): 7.

Smith, Ross A. "The Southern Route Revisited." *Oregon Historical Quarterly* 105, no. 2 (Summer 2004): 292-307.

Steeves, Sarah Hunt, ed. *Book of Remembrance of Marion County, Oregon, Pioneers 1840-1860.* Portland, OR: The Berncliff Press, 1927.

Stern, Theodore. *Chiefs & Change in the Oregon Country.* Corvallis: Oregon State University Press, 1996.

Sunday Oregonian. "First Student Says Loan Saved Oregon University," October 24, 1926, 10.

Tetherow, Solomon. "For the Oregon Spectator." *Oregon Spectator*, March 18, 1847, 3.

Thompson, Erwin N. *Shallow Grave at Waiilatpu.* 2nd ed. Portland, OR: Oregon Historical Society Press, 1985.

Thornton, J. Quinn. "The Emigrants—Southern Route." *Oregon Spectator*, December 10, 1847, 1.

_____. "The Occasional Address." *Transactions of the Sixth Annual Reunion of the Oregon Pioneer Association* (1878). Portlabd, OR: E.M. Waite, 1879, 29-71.

_____. *Oregon and California in 1848.* 2 vols. New York: Harper & Bros., 1849; reprint, New York: Arno Press, 1973.

Unruh, John D., Jr. *The Plains Across: The Overland Emigrants and the Trans-Mississippi West, 1840-60.* Urbana: University of Illinois Press, 1979.

Victor, Frances Fuller. *The Early Indian Wars of Oregon.* Salem, OR: F. C. Baker, State Printer, 1894: 504-20.

_____. *The River of the West.* 2 vols. Hartford, CT: R. W. Bliss & Co., 1870; reprint, Oakland, CA: Brooks-Sterling Co., 1974. Citations to Brooks-Sterling edition.

Walker, Claiborne, and William B. Walker. "Letter Home." *Northwest Trails: Newsletter of the Northwest Chapter of the Oregon-California Trails Association* 20, no. 8 (Nov/Dec 2005): 3.

Walling, A.G. *History of Southern Oregon.* Portland, OR: A.G. Walling, 1884, 424.

Walling, Albert G. *Illustrated History of Lane County, Oregon.* Portland, OR: Printing House of A. G. Walling, 1884, between pp. 196 and 197.

White, Elijah. Compiled by A. J. Allen. *Ten Years in Oregon.* Ithaca, NY: Press of Andrus, Gauntlett, & Co., 1850.

White, Richard. *Remembering Ahanagran: A History of Stories.* Seattle: University of Washington Press, 2003.

Williams, Mentor L. "A Columbia Lancaster Letter about Oregon in 1847." *Oregon Historical Quarterly* 50, no. 1 (March 1949): 41-44.

Winterbotham, Jerry. *Umpqua: The Lost County of Oregon.* Brownsville, OR: Jerry Winterbotham, 1994.

Index

Italicized numbers refer to illustrations

Abbott, Lt. Henry L., 154n176. *See also* Army, U.S.

Abernethy, George, 61, 138n144, 165n195, 177, 178, 181, 182, 227-28, 230. *See also* Oregon, provisional government of

American Falls (Idaho), 39, 41, 199

American Fur Company, 21, 54

American Rifle Regiment, 183

antelope, 13-14, 102-03, 211

Antelope Spring (Nev.), 101n97, 102-03, 119, 211

Applegate, Charles, 59, 68n55

Applegate, Jesse, 56, 59, 64n51, 67-88, 93-101, 105-06, 111-114, 122, 124, 125n128, 126n132, 135-36, 143, 151n168, 154n176, 157-58, 171n200, 173, 181-82, 186, 203, 205, 207-08, 210-12, 214-15, 218, 229, 233; 1848 mission to California, 56, 181; newspaper articles by, 113n114, 138n144, 151n168, 171n200, 182, 229; personal letters by, 136n142 (re Thornton), 138n144 (re Scott's waybill), 146n162 (re weather); Southern Route exploring party leadership, 67-68, 70-71, 74, 78-81, 86-88, 95-101, 105-06, 113, 205-08, 210-12, 233; Southern Route road-clearing party leadership, 105-06, 111-114, 122, 124, 126n132, 135-36, 138-40, 142-49, 153-55, 212-13, 215-19, 233; threats or complaints against, 112, 135-36, 157-58, 215, 218-19. *See also* waybill for emigrants

Applegate, Jesse A., 8n7, 73n63

Applegate, Lindsay, 59, 67, 70n59, 73n63, 74, 88, 126n132, 203; reminiscences of the exploration, 59, 67, 70n59, 73n63, 74, 88, 96n87, 97n89, 101n96, 104n101, 126n132, 146n161, 182n4, 203

Applegate Trail. *See* Southern Route to Oregon

Army, U.S., 25n21, 39n28, 56n38, 154n176, 183-85

Ash Hollow, *18*, 21

Astoria, Oreg., 54, 203

Avery, Joseph C., 156-57

Bagley, Will, 229

baking soda. *See* salaratus

Barlow Road, 7, 106n106, 126n132, 159, 164n193, 219-20, 235n6

Barlow, Samuel, 7n5, 159n187, 220

Barlow, William, 7, 159

Barnett, Joseph, 27n24. *See also* Grammaticher

Bear Creek (Oreg.), 73, 138, 160, 221

Beaver Creek (Oreg.), 73, 137, 215

bees, 11, 147

Bennett, Charles, 6, 10, 14, 21, 27, 182, 191

Bennett, Mrs. (Mary Ann Shannon), 6, 10, 13, 27, 191, 194

berries, 37-38, 198-99

Berry, T. W., 53

Beulah, Oreg., 5n1, 187, 189

Big Tableland (Oreg.), 128–130

Black Rock Point, 85-86, 95-96, 98, 100-02, 119-20, 161-62, 183, 208, 210-11, 213, 221

Black Rock Desert, 85-88, 95, 101-02, 119-20, 162, 183, 208, 210, 213-14, 221

Black Rock Spring, *85*, 102, 119-20, 161, 162n192, 183, 208

Blue Mountains, 45, 122n124, 184, 201

Bogus, John (aka Henry Boygus, Henry Boggs), 68, 88, 97, 98, 99, 100n94, 211

Boon, "Texas," 133

Bounds, Mrs. John B, 153

Bridger–Fraeb trading post, 25n22

Brewer, Henry B (missionary), 47-49, 201-02

Brown, Orus, 106n106, 126n132, 155n179

Brown, Tabitha, 106n106, 107n107, 141, 142n152, 157n184

Bruff, J. Goldsborough, 95n86, 183n6

Buckingham, Herman, 156, 219

buffalo, 14-17, 19-20, 194-95

Bull Spring (Calif.), 79n69

Bunton, Elijah, 51, 202

Burch, Benjamin F., 62, 67, 70, 88, 122, 160, 208, 221

Burch, Wesley and family, 170, 214

burials, 27, 120, 140-42, 144, 147, 153, 170, 183n7, 188, 196, 214-16

Burns, Hugh, 54n36

Burton, Richard F, 25n21

Butcherknife Creek. *See* Louse Creek

Fort Bridger, 24n20, 25n22, 26-27, 36n27, 42, 162, 164n193, 195, 229, 231n6

Fort Hall, 6n2, 8n7, 35-41, 44-45, 99-100, 101n95, 103-105, 106n106, 114, 162, 164n193, 183-84, 199, 211, 222, 231n6, 233, 235n5; trading at, 36-38, 40-42, 100, 199-200, 211. *See also* Grant, Captain Richard; Hudson's Bay Company

Fort Laramie, 21, 195

Fort Vancouver, 178, 184. *See also* Hudson's Bay Company

Free Emigrant Road, 158n186, 186n11

Frémont, Captain John C., 25n21, 39n28. *See also* Army, U.S.

Fullerton, Charles, 142n152

Garrison, Mr. (teamster 1849), 183

Garrison, Rev. Abraham E., 62n47, 112n111, 114n116, 132-33, 135n141, 143n154, 145n159, 154-55n177, 157n183

Garrison, Abraham H., 56n39

Garrison, Enoch, 145n159, 154-55n177, 219

Garrison, Jeptha and Joseph, 145n159, 154-55n177

Germans (companions in 1844), 7, 9, 10, 14, 26-29, 32-35, 38-43, 55, 191-92, 197-98. *See also* Grammaticher, Heck, Hovias, and Zummordie

Gilliam, Cornelius, 10, 27n24, 43, 59, 62-63, 65-66, 179, 204

Gilliam, Robert, 125

Goff, David, 8n7, 60n44, 62, 67, 81-82, 88, 101n95-96, 104nn101-02, 108n108, 112nn111-12, 113nn113-14, 151n168, 207

Goff, Pauline, 60

Goff's Spring, 81, *82*, 113, 125, 207

gold and gold rush, 6n3, 132n138, 146n161, 172n204, 173n208, 182-85, 187, 231n6

Goodhue, Samuel, 62, 68, 88

Goose Creek, 104, 212, 233

Goose Lake, *80*, 83, 124-25, 160, 220

Grammaticher, 26-27, 195. *See also* Barnett, Joseph; Germans

Grande Ronde River and valley, 45, 187, 201

Grant, Captain Richard, 36-38, 40-42, 44, 101n101, 199-201. *See also* Fort Hall, Hudson's Bay Company

Grants Pass, Oreg., 72n62, 139n146, 139n148, 140n149

Grave Creek (Oreg.), 71, 139-42, 216

graves, *82*, 134, 141-42, 156, 170, 189, 215-16

Graves, Charles B., 133

greasewood, 22, 24, 91-92

Guthrie, David M., 133-34, 141n151

Haines, Aubrey, 229

Hall family, 156n180

Harris, Moses "Black," 8-9, 12, 20 62, 66, 68, 70n59, 88, 101nn95-96, 104, 108n108, 112n111, 113n114, 151n168, 162, 192, 204, 212, 221

Hawkins, Lt. George W., 183. *See also* Army, U.S.

Heck, Mr., 21, 55, 58, 203. *See also* Germans

Hedges, Absalom F., 6-7, 10, 12, 20, 48, 60, 191, 194, 202

Helfrich, Devere, 166n196

Helms, Charles, 133

Henderson, Robert, and family, *119*, 120. *See also* Deady, Lucy Henderson

Hess, Mr., 69

High Rock Canyon, 83-84, 120, 161, 169, 183, 207, 214, 221

Holt, Arlie, *189*

Holt, Thomas, 151n169, 155n179, 156n180

Hood River (Dog River), 49-50

horse incidents, 16-17, 19-20, 30-32, 36-37, 40-42, 47-50, 55-56, 64, 66, 92-93, 98, 114-18, 160-61, 195, 197, 199-202, 209, 211, 221

Hovias, William, 14, 55, 57, 203. *See also* Germans

Howell, John, 164n193, 165n195

Hudson, W. P., 132-33

Hudson's Bay Company (HBC), 36, 38, 42, 44, 52, 54, 61, 63n50, 68, 71, 73n63, *80*, 86n78, 177, 199, 205, 207. *See also* Fort Hall; Fort Vancouver; Grant, Captain Richard; Ogden, Peter Skene

HBC Trappers Trail, 68-73, 203-05, 207. *See also* California Trail (Oregon to California)

Hulin, Lester, 164n193, 170-71n199

Humboldt River, 8n7, *80*, 86, *87*, 93, 96-97, 99-104, 114-19, 122, 124, 161-62, 166-70, 183n6, 184, 188, 210-11, 221-22, 233

Humboldt Sink, 93, 100n93

Hunt, Wilson Price, 173n208

Illinois, 51, 202

Illinois River (Oreg.), 185n10

Independence, Mo., 7-9, 154n175, 191-92

Independence Rock, 22-23

Indian wars, Oregon and Washington, 6-7, 68n55, 72, 138, 176-79, 225; Klamath and Modoc, 77, 225; Seminole, 10